THE SIKHS AND AFGHANS,

IN CONNEXION WITH INDIA AND PERSIA,

IMMEDIATELY BEFORE AND AFTER THE DEATH

OF

RANJEET SINGH:

FROM THE

JOURNAL OF AN EXPEDITION TO KABUL, THROUGH THE PANJAB AND THE KHAIBAR PASS

By

SHAHAMAT ALI

GYAN

ISBN : 978-81-212-1638-8(HB)

First Published, 1847

Published, 2018

Published by

Gyan Publishing House
5, Ansari Road
Daryaganj, New Delhi-110002
Phone: 011-47034999, 9811692060
www.gyanbooks.com
E-mail: books@gyanbooks.com

Printed at: G. Print Process, Delhi.

PREFACE.

Being a stranger to the English people, and their language one foreign to my own, it may be expected that I should give some account of myself, the source to which I am indebted for the little knowledge I possess, and the motives which have encouraged me to publish my Journal.

I owe my education to the benevolence of the British Government in restoring, for the benefit of Indian youths in Delhi and the neighbouring provinces, the College founded in the time of the Mogul emperors, which had shared the fate of other public establishments in that city on the decline of their empire.

On the 20th of October, 1832, Mr. J. H. Taylor, the secretary to the Committee which superintended the affairs of the college, sent for me, and said that an application had been received from Captain, now Sir C. M. Wade, and then political agent at Lodiana, for one of the students who understood both English and Persian; and that in consultation with Mr. C. E. Trevelyan, who was then secretary to the Resident at Delhi, and one of the greatest friends and patrons of the Institution,* I had been selected as a candidate for employment. As I was desirous, however, of prosecuting my English studies, I hesitated to accept the offer: but being assured by Mr. Taylor, who like a kind friend was deeply interested in our welfare, that the situation I was to fill would be highly beneficial to my worldly interests; and at the same time, that if I were resolved to continue the study of English still further, I should find time to do so, and improve my mind by reading the most approved authors; I willingly agreed, and have often gratefully remembered the advice of my respected patrons and the paternal kindness with which I was treated by them. I accordingly left the school on the 30th of the same month, to join the

* Appointed on his return to England, in 1839, Joint Secretary to the Treasury.

Captain at Lodiana, who was then preparing to proceed on a mission to the courts of Lahore and Bhawlpore to form treaties with those states for opening the navigation of the Satledge and Indus, in pursuance of the Mission of Lieutenant-Colonel, now Sir Henry Pottinger, to Sindh, who had shortly before visited the Amirs for the same purpose.

Before leaving school, I will briefly state the cause of its restoration and its progress since it became an English institution.

The British government, which had long been anxious to extend the benefits of education to its subjects, resolved in 1823 to restore the Mahomedan College in its original form, which continued till the arrival of Mr. Trevelyan, in 1827, who established in it an English class, which my friend Mohan Lal and myself were the first to join. Some months after his plan was enlarged, and towards the end of Earl Amherst's Government (the first Governor-General who visited the Imperial City and saw the state of the college), on the recommendation of the Committee, it was formed into a separate institution, now known as "The Delhi English College." The Committee was composed at that time of Mr., now Sir Thomas, Metcalfe, Dr. Rankin, and Mr. Trevelyan. Instruction in English was then confined to the schools in Calcutta and its vicinity. Assisted by the late Mr. Andrew Stirling, then Persian Secretary to Government, it is to these gentlemen that we owe the facilities of learning their language and the important privileges which it has conferred on our country.

A selection of such of the Persian scholars as were desirous of learning English was then made from the Persian class: some boys from the city also applied and were admitted. Mr. Rennell, an East Indian, was appointed as teacher in the infancy of the school. No sooner had it commenced than the *Molvies*, or Mahomedan professors in the Persian and Arabic college, either from jealousy or from the excess of their prejudice, declared that, by beginning to receive an English education, we had lost our creed; and all the Mussulmans regarded us as infidels, and abstained from eating and drinking with us. The consequence was, that the Mahomedan boys, with the exception of a youth named Hadi Hussein, myself, and one or two others, left the English and returned to the Persian school, and were immediately readmitted into their caste, while we continued for some time to be considered in the light of *Kafirs*. At length, one day Mr. Trevelyan asked the *Molvies* the reason of the Mahomedan scholars having been excluded from their faith. They could give no good cause for it, and confessed that the study of English was not prohibited by the Mahomedan religion; on which Mr. Trevelyan suggested that we should be readmitted, to which they agreed without any objection, and we were again made Mussulmans in the superstitious and self-founded opinion of the *Molvies*. This was the only obstacle the school met with. Afterwards the number of students was much increased, and instruction in English diffused on a more extensive scale than before. Mr. F. Taylor, the son of Mr. J. H. Taylor, a person of superior talents and learning, was appointed the head teacher, while the scholars of the first class acted as assistant teachers to instruct the junior classes, being then only ten in number altogether. There were six lads in the first class, and they stood in gradation as follows :—

1st. Ram Kishan, a very clever and intelligent scholar.

2nd. Myself.

3rd. Sheoparshad.

4th. Mohan Lal.

5th. Jawahir Lal.

6th. Hadi Hussein.

In the year 1831 my friend Mohan Lal was taken away from the school by Lieutenant, the late Sir Alexander Burnes, to accompany him on his journey to Afghanistan, Bokhara, and Persia. He had left the school ten months before I quitted it in the manner I have mentioned. Our schoolfellows, seeing us depart to seek our fortunes in the world, were ambitious of following us; and the kind patrons whom I have named soon found opportunities of providing for them.

Before I left the school I had—besides the rudimental books in ancient history, viz. the Histories of Greece and Rome, and the History of England, by Goldsmith—gone through four books of Euclid, an Abridgment of Arithmetic, Keith's Use of the Globes, and Guy's Geography. The above formed the whole stock of my instruction in the English language, and with it I departed from the school, with little confidence that I could be of much use in that branch of my duty to the officer who was about to employ me. On my arrival at Lodiana, I found Sir Claude Wade had already started, and I therefore hastened through the Panjab to join him at Pind Daden Khan, near the Salt Mines on the river Jehlam, where he was encamped with Ranjeet Singh. The first thing he ordered me to do was to keep a regular diary of every place we visited, and to note down events of importance. Thus I not only improved myself in English, but acquired a habit of writing a journal, and continued the practice in the various Missions on which that officer was employed.

In 1837-8 I was deputed on a special duty to Lahore, to convey some presents, and explain the settlement of some local cases in dispute between the two governments, on which occasion I had the honour of receiving the approbation of the Right Honourable the Governor-General, Lord Auckland, for the reports I submitted of my communications with the Maharaja, and their satisfactory result.

. Shortly afterwards I accompanied my master in the military expedition on which he was sent to conduct Shah Zada Taimur, the eldest son of Shah Shuja-ul-Mulk, with the Sikh auxiliary force, by the Khaibar Pass to Kabul. On that occasion I also kept a journal, which I have been allowed to correct by comparing it with that of Lieutenant (now Captain) J. D. Cunningham, of the Bengal Engineers, who kindly lent me his for that purpose, and took much interest in encouraging me in my studies. It is necessary to remind the reader that the following pages having been mostly written before the death of Ranjeet Singh, the description of his court and its officers is no longer applicable; but the mode in which he conducted his administration, and the increasing importance of passing events in that quarter, have suggested their publication. It is the misfortune of India, the conquest of which has been termed "the brightest jewel in the English crown," that it should be so little known by the distant nation which governs its millions of fellow-subjects. I hope, for the sake of my country, that their interests may hereafter be better understood, and more truly estimated. After giving these personal details, I can only express a hope that my imperfections will be pardoned; and that, having long wished to visit England, I may venture to offer the humble tribute of my pen as a passport to the indulgence of the English, should I ever be permitted to visit their great country; and as a token of gratitude to those who have enabled me to write in their language, and assisted me through life by their countenance and favour.

CONTENTS.

CHAPTER I.

CHAPTER II.

CHAPTER III.

CHAPTER IV.

CHAPTER V.

CHAPTER VI.

CHAPTER VII.

CHAPTER VIII.

CHAPTER IX.

CHAPTER X.

CHAPTER XI.

CHAPTER XII.

CHAPTER XIII.

CHAPTER XIV.

CHAPTER XV.

CHAPTER XVI.

CHAPTER XVII.

CHAPTER XVIII.

CHAPTER XIX.

CHAPTER XX.

CHAPTER XXI.

JOURNAL

OF

SHAHAMAT ALI.

Chapter I.

The Satledge—The Governor-General visits Ranjeet Singh at Lahore—Makes a treaty with him—Reviews—Various festivities—The Shah Zada takes leave of Lord Auckland—Preparations for departure—The Mission takes leave—Ill-health of the Maharaja—His avarice—The Shah Zada is joined by some Afghan *Khawanin* from the service of Sultan Mahomed Khan.

The Governor-General of India (the Earl of Auckland), after meeting Maharaja Ranjeet Singh at Firozpore, where the army of the Indus had been assembled preparatory to its departure for Afghanistan, was specially invited by his Highness to accompany him on a visit to Lahore *via* Amritsir. His Lordship and suite, attended by a large escort,* accord-

* Consisting of a European troop of horse artillery, one regiment of native cavalry, and two battalions of native infantry.

ingly crossed the river below Firozpore, by a bridge of boats on the 16th of December, 1838. Before, however, I proceed with his Lordship on his tour to Amritsir and Lahore, a brief account of the ferries and the nature of the river Satledge will be desirable.

The river Satledge is nowhere safely fordable between its confluence with the Bias and Firozpore; but last year a ford was found below Mamdot; it was used, however, with extreme difficulty and danger, on account of its quaggy bed. About forty-seven years ago it is related that a party of Kasoor troops, on an urgent occasion, forded the river near the village of Nalcha, six kos below Firozpore. It is a common opinion among the natives that the Satledge is never fordable; but I learn from authentic sources that it is very erroneous, and that the river can be crossed by fords every year in many places above Harikee; but it is difficult to ascertain them with accuracy, as their discovery would materially affect the interests of the boatmen, who, being the only persons having a knowledge of them, try their best to conceal the fact. I have been told by a native of Harikee that the Satledge becomes fordable at a place a little distance below that ferry; but, as the river is liable to very great changes in its course, it is not probable that the ford can be always found in the same spot.

The ferries between Harikee and Firozpore are as follows :—

Harikee,	Nagarka,
Bhao,	Bara,
Asyake,	Bareke.
Pallee,	

Above the confluence of the two rivers, as far as Roper, there are numerous ferries, of which Talwend, Filore, and Tihara, are the principal. The boats are of a peculiar construction, very flat and shallow, rising to a point at the stern, and quite square at the other end (forming in shape an acute angle), but they are well calculated for the use to which they are applied; they are moved across the river by poles, and are not suited to any other kind of navigation.

In his progress to Lahore, as well as during

the Governor-General's presence at that place, the Maharaja showed him every attention due to the dignity of his exalted station. Lord Auckland was the first of the British Indian Governors who had stepped as a friend in the Panjab. After visiting Amritsir, where he was entertained in a style by the Maharaja worthy of the magnificence of the Sikh court, and amused by the sight of their holy temple, which was illuminated for the occasion, and saw the famous fortress of Govindgarh where his treasures are kept, his Lordship, accompanied by his host, went to Lahore. On encamping near the celebrated gardens of Shalamar he was again entertained by Ranjeet Singh, and conducted thither by his son Kour Kharak Singh about an hour before dusk. The gardens were illuminated in a grand style, and the fountains playing freely, and fireworks let off, which produced a very interesting scene, and highly gratified the party.

The following morning, the 21st of December, the camp moved to Lahore and pitched to the west of the city between the river and the fort, on a fine green plain across a branch of the Ravi, on one side of which are some hunting preserves, and on the other a succession of gardens belonging to the Maharaja or his courtiers, where he inspects his troops and passes much of his time when staying at Lahore. Accompanying each other, the Governor-General and his Highness, on their way to the camp, passed through the city; and while his Lordship remained at Lahore his time was employed as follows:—

On the evening of the 22nd of December was a review of the Sowars, composed of the Maharaja's own household, irregular cavalry, and the contingents of his relatives Sirdars Atr Singh and Ajit Singh, Sindhanwalia. In the course of the interview a reference was made to Sultan Mahomed Khan, who had been introduced to Lord Auckland the night before, regarding the force of his brother Dost Mahomed Khan and the other members of the Barakzai family at Candahar. Ranjeet Singh then spoke of the anxiety of his people to have the conditions relative to the return of the army through the Panjab settled, that nothing might remain to be discussed or explained when the time came. These conditions were, First, not to permit the slaughter of kine. Second, not to allow the present to be a precedent for the future passage of the British troops through the Sikh country. Third, that the usual marks of respect and consideration to his government should be observed on the part of the British army.

23rd.—The Governor-General, in company with the Honourable the Misses Eden, in the afternoon, went to see the tombs of Jahangir and the famous Noor Mahal, across the Ravi. He was attended by Kour Sher Singh. During the absence of his Lordship the gentlemen of his suite paid a visit of ceremony to Kour Kharak Singh.

24th.—About 9 A.M. the contingents of Raja Hira Singh, Raja Golab Singh, and Raja Seocheit Singh, were paraded for inspection, and appeared a fine body of feudal cavalry. In the evening a review of Sultan Mahomed Khan's contingent took place, which, consisting of Afghans, formed a novel sight when contrasted with the showy dresses and martial air of the others. Though he has dispossessed him of authority in Peshawr, the Maharaja has found it prudent to keep Sultan Mahomed Khan and his brothers in that territory, by conferring large jaghirs on them in lieu of military service. After these reviews Lord Auckland and his host conferred privately together.

25*th.*—Christmas day, passed in camp. In the evening visited some of the gardens adjoining the palace.

26*th.*—Visit of his Lordship to the fort, and an entertainment in the evening, when it was brilliantly illuminated. The Maharaja took that opportunity of showing his palace and displaying his costly jewels to his guests. The ladies were invited to the party, and were delighted with the exhibition.

27*th.*—A hunting party was arranged in one of the preserves near camp, but the game was scarce, and disappointed the sportsmen.

28*th.*—In the morning the British troops

were shown by his Lordship to Kour Kharak Singh and Naonihal Singh. Ranjeet Singh, owing to symptoms of a recurrence of his old illness,* not being able to attend in person, hearing of which the common people began to believe that his English guests had wrought some spell upon him. In the evening the parting interview took place, on which occasion his Lordship introduced to the Maharaja, Shah Zada Taimur, the eldest son of Shah Shuja-ul-Mulk, who was to proceed with Lieutenant-Colonel, now Sir Claude Martine, Wade, through the Khaibar Pass to Kábul. The plan of operations was explained, and the Governor-General expressed his assurance of the cordial support and co-operation of that part of them which had devolved by treaty on the Sikh government, to which his Highness willingly assented, after which the usual presents were produced, and Lord Auckland took leave, accompanied by Kour Sher Singh, who is a polite and courteous person. He had been acting as Mehmandar to his Lordship during

* Paralysis.

his visit, and was directed to attend him on his return to the left bank of the Satledge.

In the evening of the same day the Shah Zada visited his Lordship to take leave. He was received with the honour due to his rank, and after receiving some words of good advice for his future guidance, the prince was dismissed with suitable presents He is a well disposed young man, and seems entirely attached to the English.*

From the 1st to the 12th of January, 1839, the time was employed in collecting the personal escort intended (agreeably to the treaty between the British Government, Shah Shuja-ul-Mulk, and Ranjeet Singh) to accompany the Shah Zada from the Sikh government, and in providing him with his marching equipage and other necessary establishments for his approaching journey. In the meantime the camp was removed to the ghat or ferry on the Ravi, and pitched in the order in which it was hereafter to encamp.

* As has been proved by his conduct during the disasters in Afghanistan. Vide the despatches of the late Sir W. Nott and Major Rawlinson from Candahar.

Notwithstanding the sickness of the Maharaja, minute attention was paid by him to every requisition. But the dilatory manner in which his orders were executed caused some delay. At length every preparation was completed, owing to the strict and constant endeavours of the Lieut.-Colonel, to whose care and guidance the whole of the expedition on the Peshawr frontier was entrusted by the British Government.

On the morning of the 12th inst., Sir Claude Wade, accompanied by the other officers attached to his Mission,* proceeded to the

* "Lieut.-Colonel Wade, political agent and chief of the Mission; Lieut. Cunningham, 1st assistant to ditto; P. B. Lord, Esq., Bombay Medical Service, an assistant in the political department to Mr. MacNaghten (doing duty); Lieut. Maule, artillery, assistant in the political department; Lieut. Dowson, 5th regt. Native infantry, ditto; Lieut. Barr, H. A., ditto, and commanding detachment of horse artillery; Lieut. Hillersdon, 53rd N. I., assistant in the political department; A. Reid, Esq., Bengal Medical Service, in medical charge of the Mission; Capt. Farmer, 21st N. I., commanding British troops; Lieut. Corfield, ditto; Capt. Ferris, 20th N. I.; Lieut. Rattray, ditto, adjutant to British troops."—*Barr's Journal from Delhi to Peshawr to join Sir Claude Wade*, published in 1844, pp. 219, 220.

palace to take leave of his Highness. His health was now very declining; he had almost entirely lost the faculty of speech, and could hardly stammer a few words. One of his oldest and best officers, named Bhäe Mahu Singh, was appointed to attend us to Peshawr, and see our wants readily supplied. The Maharaja stated that he had ordered his army to assemble, and that it would follow after the *Holi* festival; before which, with reference to the advance of the Shah with the British troops *viâ* Shikarpore to Candahar, and the necessity of a simultaneous co-operation between the two armies, the presence of his army was not required. He also expressed his wish of proceeding with it himself, in which Sir Claude earnestly joined. As, from his feeble state, his Highness could not endure the fatigue of sitting with convenience any longer, the usual presents were brought and delivered to each officer of the party; including myself. I was astonished on this occasion to find that the pair of shawls which formed a part of my *khilat*, or dress of honour, was kept back, in lieu of a pair which the Maharaja was pleased to confer on me a few days before, when I waited on him with a message from Sir Claude Wade. Although on former visits he usually granted me some present or other, yet he never made any deduction from the *khilat* which is formally given on the day of dismissal. It shows that his avarice increases with his age and the disappointments of his life; for it is only of late that his Highness has shown such a covetous disposition. The Maharaja lastly requested that Sir Claude would constantly write and report to him our progress; and then the Mission took leave of his Highness and his officers, and returned to the camp.

It is worthy of remark that, soon after our arrival at Lahore, several Afghan *Khawanin*, or men of noble descent, in the service of Sultan Mahomed, being disaffected to their master, wished to desert him and join the Shah Zada. They made overtures on the subject; but Sultan Mahomed Khan being one of the feudatory Barakzai chiefs of the

Sikh government, it was thought that to encourage them would have been considered unbecoming the friendly relations of the three states; but as, on the other hand, it would discourage other Afghans from joining the Shah Zada, the treated was treated with indifference, and they were allowed to follow their own inclinations. After a time, they almost every one of them joined the Shah Zada, and continued to serve him. Among others, Khan Mahomed Khan, the son of Yar Mahomed Khan, Popalzai, was the first who joined the Shah Zada. His father is at Herat, to which he and his son retired after the flight of the Shah from Candahar. They joined the Shah on his last expedition at Shikarpore. The son appeared at Lahore with twenty Sowars, accompanying Sultan Mahomed Khan from Peshawr; but encamped separately from him when they joined the Shah Zada. Sultan Mahomed Khan sent him many messages to come to his camp, but he declined the offer.

Chapter II.

The Government of Lahore—Mode of conducting business—The Governors—Habits of the Maharaja—The Darbar—Disposition of the various officers of the Maharaja's court—Governors of provinces—Revenue of the Maharaja's dominions—Strength, organization, and expense of his army.*

The government of Lahore is a pure despotism, and the entire direction of its affairs, foreign or domestic, is, according to the Oriental saying, on the tongue of his Highness. Although some of the courtiers are men of wisdom and intelligence, and the Maharaja has a share of that consideration and respect which every ruler must have for the prejudices and opinions of his countrymen, yet, possessed of a vigorous mind himself, and having a great reliance on his own penetration and judgment, he is generally guided by his own opinions, though he may ask that of his courtiers.

* Since this journal was written great changes have taken place in the court of Lahore; almost all the principal persons mentioned have died of violent or natural deaths, and the army been destroyed.

In affairs of importance he consults the *Grunth,* the religious book of the Sikhs, and often acts as he is guided by that oracle. His correspondence with foreign states, as well as with his own functionaries, is solely dictated by himself; and, though illiterate, he exercises a minute criticism in correcting the diction of his secretaries. An habitual reserve in matters of business forms a striking feature of his character. It is an invariable rule with him never to mention his object to any one until the time for execution has arrived.

During the early part of his reign, he and the other Sikh chiefs had no system of official records ; business was conducted by verbal orders, and continued so with Ranjeet Singh until Diwan Bhowani Das, a clever native of Peshawr, was employed. When he came into his service he divided the transaction of the affairs of state into different offices or departments, keeping the accounts, farming of districts, and preserving every record of importance, commenced only from that period. At present there are twelve *Daftars* or offices where the civil and military business of the government is arranged.

Diwan Dinanath is at the head of them. Formerly, neither were there any forms for the *Deodhee*;* they were introduced about the same time. Bhae Ram Singh, and Bhae Govind Ram, and Faqir Azizuddin, assist his Highness in civil affairs; the Faqir also acts the part of chief secretary for foreign affairs. The letters to functionaries are also frequently written by him. Misser Beli Ram, a respectable Brahmin, is in charge of the regalia and the treasury. A separate account of these functionaries will be given, and no observations need therefore be made on their merits or character here.

The affairs of the country are conducted by means of Governors or *Kardars*, who are appointed to each district. They manage the whole business connected with the administration of the territory entrusted to them, and seldom report any case to the court unless it be of high importance, when his Highness's orders are communicated by issuing *Parwanas*.† The

* Corresponding with the Lord Chamberlain's office, literally the entrance to the court.

† Official orders.

settlement of the revenue, the audit of accounts, and their adjustment, both in the military and civil department, are done entirely by the Maharaja; but in the last two or three years, owing to his bad state of health, he has sometimes delegated that duty to Raja Dhian Singh. He has news-writers in every quarter of his dominions, and the news of foreign courts is always read to his Highness in the morning.

His Highness disposes of his time in the following manner:—In the morning and evening he always goes out either on horseback or in a litter to take the air; when in ill health he seldom denies himself that exercise, or even in rainy or stormy weather. After his ride in the morning he takes a hasty breakfast, and then holds his *Darbar*,* and sometimes on the plain under the shade of a tree or a camp, which continues till twelve o'clock. The whole business of the day is transacted by him with rapidity and despatch during that time. When the *Darbar* is over, the Maharaja takes a short repose of half an hour only, when he

* Court of audience.

resumes his seat, and hears the *Grunth* for about one hour and a half. After that ceremony he again takes the air. In these exercises he generally employs himself in inspecting his troops, or other military exercises, or receiving the petitions of his people.

With the exception of the five functionaries already named, the annexed list contains the names of the other courtiers, chiefs, and military commanders who attend the Darbar. Nearly all the old Sikh Sirdars or chiefs are now extinct. Those only of them who survive are Sirdars Jawend Singh, Mowakil, Dhuna Singh, Malwai, and Sham Singh, Atariwala, but they possess very little influence in the court. The rest are either the descendants of old families or the creations of a few days, owing their rise to His Highness.

Sirdar Atar Singh, Sirdar Ajit Singh, and Sirdar Lehna Singh,	Sindhanwalia the relations of the Maharaja.
Sirdar Lehna Singh Majithia.	
Sirdar Sham Singh, the father-in-law of Kour Naonihal Singh, Naonihal Singh and Sirdars Jei Singh and Jagat Singh, Sher Singh and Karam Singh,	Atariwala.

Sirdar Dhuna Singh, Malwai.

Sirdar Jawend Singh, Mowakil.

Pertab Singh, the son of the late Jawala Singh, Bherania.

EUROPEAN MILITARY OFFICERS OF THE REGULAR ARMY:—

General Allard, lately dead.

General Ventura.

M. Avitabile.

M. Court, besides several others, viz.: Messrs. Foulkes, Steinbach, &c., with inferior commands.*

NATIVE OFFICERS OF RANK:

General Teij Singh.

General Ram Singh, the son of Jemadar Khoshal Singh.

General Misser Sukhraj, to each of whom the Maharaja has given separate divisions of his army.

All the other officers and functionaries at the time of *Darbar* wait in the outer yard next to the palace: when any one is required he is sent for to the presence.

Besides the above Sirdars, Sirdar Cheit Singh and Sirdar Mangul Singh, who are called the ministers of Kour Kharak Singh and Diwan Hakim Rae and Sirdar Fateh Singh, those of Kour Naonihal Singh, attend the court in the company of their masters.

* MM. Avitabile and Court are also styled generals by courtesy.

The Sirdars and officers of the Maharaja's court are for the most part well disposed towards Kour Kharak Singh and Naonihal Singh, and have respect for their authority, but they are not so well affected towards Kour Sher Singh. A bad feeling also prevails between the latter and Kour Kharak Singh and his son. The Jammoo family and Jemadar Khoshal Singh were not formerly on good terms; but at the last great fair of the Komb held at Hardwar, Raja Golab Singh and the Jemadar, who met there, exchanged turbans with each other standing in the water of the Ganges,* since which they have always remained intimately allied. All the other Sirdars are generally on good terms with the Jammoo family, either from inclination or necessity. Sirdar Ajit Singh of the Sindhanwalia family has lately exchanged turbans with Raja Hera Singh, but Jemadar Khoshal Singh on the one hand and the Sindhanwalias, four Bhaes, and the Missers on the other, are not on good terms, and try to injure each

* A solemn mode of reconciliation.

other. The Missers and the Rajas have also had a difference, which is scarcely healed It took place between Raja Dhian Singh and Misser Ram Kishan, the brother of Beli Ram, on account of the latter having been stopped on his entrance at the *Deodhee* when he proceeded as usual to the "Darbar," and high words were exchanged on either side, which went so far that the Raja proposed to resign, but the officers of the court interposed, and brought about a partial reconciliation.

The following is the list of the chief functionaries or Governors appointed to the several provinces within the Maharaja's dominions, showing their names and the amount of revenue derived from each province ;—

	Amount in Rupees.	
Diwan Sawan Mal, the governor of Multan . . .	38,98,550	0
Misser Roop Lal, the governor of Doaba of Jalandar	18,72,902	0
Raja Gholab Singh, in charge of the country lying between the Chinab and the Jehlum	25,45,000	0
Raja Socheit Singh, of the district of Vazirabad .	10,55,726	4

	Amount in Rupees.	
Sardar Lehna Singh Majithia of Manjha, and the territories in the hills between the Satledge and Ravi . . .	14,87,475	0
Mian Singh, the governor of Kashmir	36,75,000	0
M. Avitabile, the governor of Peshawr . . .	18,34,738	0

Besides the above, there are other officers and *Kardars*, such as the sons and nephews of the Faqirs and the Missers, &c. who govern small districts. The remittances made by these officers are mostly by means of Hundwis on Amritsir. No sum is received from Peshawr. The revenue of that province is consumed there, and large remittances made from court to pay the force employed in that quarter. The capture of Peshawr has been an expensive conquest to the Maharaja.

The whole revenue derived from the country within the rule of his Highness is said to amount to three crores twenty-seven thousand seven hundred and sixty-two rupees, which is derived from the following sources:—

	Rupees.
Khalsa	1,96,57,172
Jaghirs given to different people	87,54,590
Khirajdars	12,66,000
Transit duties between Akora and the Satledge . . .	5,50,000
Total of Rupees .	3,00,27,762

I shall now briefly touch on the strength, organization, and expenses of the Maharaja's army.

Maharaja Ranjeet Singh has a large and well-disciplined army. It is better regulated than that of any native chief in India. He himself, being passionately fond of the military profession, has chiefly devoted his attention to the organization of his army.

It consists of 31 regiments of infantry, 9 regiments of cavalry, and 288 pieces of artillery of various calibre, of which 143 pieces are drawn by horses, 147 by bullocks, and 8 howitzers, besides 11,800 irregular Sowars. Nearly one-half of his regular army is commanded by the French and other European officers, and the rest by his native officers.

Besides these troops the following are furnished by the Jaghirdars.

Irregular Sowars, 6460.
Regular infantry, 9 regiments.
Ditto cavalry, 5 regiments.
Horse and bullock artillery, 87 pieces.

Of these regular troops three regiments of infantry and two regiments of cavalry are furnished by Kours Kharak Singh and Naonihal Singh, and four regiments of infantry and one regiment of cavalry by the Jammoo family, while two regiments of infantry are provided by Sirdar Lehna Singh, Majithia and Jemadar Khoshal Singh, and the two other regiments of cavalry by the Sindhanwalia family and Sirdar Lehna Singh.

The troops forming his garrisons in different forts, and the establishments maintained for police and other purposes, are not included in the above enumeration. The annexed is the statement of the annual expense incurred by the Maharaja in the payment of his regular army:—

	Rupees.
Infantry, 31 regiments . .	28,09,200
Cavalry, 9 regiments . . .	24,53,656
Horse artillery, 288 pieces . .	3,24,864
Irregular Sowars, 11,800 . .	72,08,562
Total rupees .	1,27,96,482

A great many deductions are made from the pay of the troops, which reduce the actual expenditure considerably. They are armed and clothed by the state, and, with the exception of two or three battalions commanded by the English officers, are organised according to the French system. The men composing the army are almost entirely Sikhs, with whom the regular service of the Maharaja is popular. In enduring fatigue, absence from the prejudices of caste, and patience of discipline, the Sikh is not easily surpassed. He only requires the skill of European officers and instructors to make him an excellent soldier.*

* They have established their military fame by their gallant conduct in the late war.

CHAPTER III.

The Ministers and other Officers of State—Raja Dhian Singh—Jemadar Khoshal Singh—Bhaes Rham Singh, Govind Singh, and Gormukh Singh—Faqir Azizuddin —Nuruddin—Misser Beli Ram—Diwan Dinanath.

RAJA DHIAN SINGH.

RAJA Dhian Singh, besides having charge of the *Deodhee*, may be called the prime minister of his Highness, if that title be not misapplied to a ruler who governs chiefly by himself. The Raja is the channel of conveying the petitions and representations of the people, and carrying the Maharaja's orders regarding them into effect. At night, when he returns from the court, he is in the habit of holding a *Darbar* in his own house, which the officers of the army and some of the Sirdars also attend, to facilitate the transaction of their business with his Highness. The reports of such of the troops as may be present at court are likewise received at the same time, and the necessary orders issued regarding them without consulting the Maharaja, excepting in cases of an important nature. The recruits entertained are now also passed by Raja Dhian Singh, but the orders connected with the movement and despatch of troops, and with regard to their pay, clothing, and promotion, originate solely from his Highness himself.

The Maharaja places great confidence in the Raja's good sense and fidelity, and considers him one of his sincerest friends. He entrusts him with the investigation and settlement of affairs of importance both in the financial and judicial departments of the state; and the mildness and propriety of conduct with which he transacts his business is not among the least of his good qualities and claims to approbation, since he has held his present high office at the court of Lahore. The power which the two elder Jammoo Rajas have of late years been acquiring is chiefly owing to the great influence which the constant presence of Raja Dhian Singh at court enables him to exercise in the affairs of their family.

JEMADAR KHOSHAL SINGH.

THE *Deodhee* was formerly in charge of Jemadar Khoshal Singh; but on account of the arbitrary use he made of his power, he disgusted both the people and the officers of the state, and it was taken from him, and given to Raja Dhian Singh. At present no distinct duty is assigned to him, but he regularly attends the Maharaja as a matter of ceremony. When his Highness inspects the troops, the Jemadar is generally employed in the execution of his orders, and in regulating their movements. He may be termed the aide-de-camp of the Maharaja.

From the severity and badness of his temper he is not liked by the courtiers in general; neither does Ranjeet Singh himself entertain a good opinion of him. The crimes and offences of which he and his family have been guilty would have long caused his disgrace; but it is said that when the Maharaja gave him the *Pahol,** and made him a convert to his religion,

* The ceremony of initiating a Sikh in his faith is so called.

the Jemadar exacted a promise from his Highness that he would never degrade him from his situation; he has, in consequence, hitherto escaped punishment and the resentment of his master on many occasions.

BHAES RAM SINGH, GOVIND SINGH, AND GORMUKH SINGH.

THESE persons were admitted to the councils of the Maharaja in the year 1827; and in imitation of the system of the British Indian Government they were appointed his councillors. Bhae Ram Singh and Bhae Govind Ram are the sons of Bhae Bastee Ram, a man formerly possessed of some religious celebrity in the city of Lahore, and much respected by the people. The Maharaja himself used occasionally to visit him to invoke his holy blessings. His sons are also respected by his Highness, but he has no great confidence in their integrity. They serve him more in their spiritual than in their temporal capacity, and may be seen in daily attendance at the "*Darbar*," and from their holy character sit on chairs beside the Maharaja; but it has been an established rule with them never to enter the court until a man has been sent by his Highness to conduct them.

Besides being Sanscrit scholars, they have a knowledge of Persian as well as of the medical art; but their sagacity is not equal to their learning. They sometimes act as interpreters to his Highness, and are closely connected with the Kours Kharak Singh and Naonihal Singh. The two Bhaes enjoy a Jaghir of forty thousand rupees, besides fees and benefits which they derive from their office of priests, and the patronage which their situation at court gives them the opportunity of exercising for their friends.

Gormukh Singh is the other Bhae who attends the court; but his attendance is not regular, nor has he so much influence as the others. He is also allowed a seat, but is intriguing, and not often consulted in the affairs of state. He is the son of the late Sant Singh, *ghiani* or chanter of the *Grunth* in the temple of Amritsir, of which city he is a native, where his father's name is still highly respected. The bias of his son seems to be in favour of Kour Sher Singh and Jemadar Khoshal Singh, but he is not on good terms with the other two Bhaes; indeed they are always at variance with each other. The former is perhaps of opinion that the only way he has of maintaining his influence is by siding with a different party from them. In quickness of apprehension, as well as in his address and manner, he is superior to the other two, but is deficient in their prudence and knowledge of the world.

FAQIR AZIZUDDIN.

Faqir Azizuddin is the chief secretary of the Maharaja for foreign affairs, and also serves him as physician. In the latter capacity he first entered his service, when the Maharaja took Lahore. Being a man of great abilities, and possessing a good judgment, he was soon admitted to a participation in the affairs of state. At the time of Sir Charles Metcalfe's mission, in 1809, the Faqir was employed as the means of communication between him and the government, and having acquitted himself in the discharge of that duty to the satisfaction of the Maharaja, was put in charge of his correspondence with foreign states. His Highness generally employs him also as his interpreter, and places great confidence in him. The Faqir has a general knowledge of the sciences taught in the schools of Asia, and may therefore be regarded as a philosopher as well as a statesman and physician. In his conversation he tries to please his auditors with great success, and is fond of quotations and proverbs to illustrate his remarks. He and his whole family maintain great humility in their dress and manners, avoiding that ostentation which might be expected from men of their rank and station; but it accords with their interest at court, where, being Mahomedans, their influence is an object of jealousy to others.

He has two brothers, one named Nuruddin, the youngest, who has the charge of the city of Lahore, and the Golab khana or dispensary of the Maharaja; and the other, named Imamuddin, that of Govindgarh and the treasure there deposited. Faqir Azizuddin has two sons, named Shahdin and Cheraghuddin: the former is occasionally employed on business from the court. At present he is at Ferozpore, forwarding the wants of the British army assembled for service in Afghanistan. In their manners they all imitate Azizuddin. Their discretion has enabled them to remain on good terms with every one; and from their prudent and cautious conduct, they have maintained their position in a court where they have felt the necessity of acting with vigilance to conciliate all parties.

They have a jaghir of about fifty thousand rupees, besides fees and grants assigned to them by different chiefs and others about the court to facilitate the transaction of their business.

MISSER BELI RAM.

The next functionary is Misser Beli Ram. He is in charge of the regalia, treasury, robes, and other valuable articles. Documents of importance, such as treaties with foreign states, are also kept by him in the regalia. The Maharaja places great confidence in him.

He is a native of a village named Kahan, near Kitas. His uncle Bastee Ram was the treasurer of Maha Singh, the father of Ranjeet Singh. On the conquest of Amritsir and Lahore the Maharaja entrusted Bastee Ram with the charge of Amritsir, and desired him to appoint some one of his family to that of the Treasury. He recommended Beli Ram, his nephew, who was then about eleven years old. Since that time to the present period he has continued with his Highness. No one keeps any account of the *Tosheh khana* but the Misser and his family; and such is the trust reposed in him that he has never been called to render an account of his charge.

Beli Ram has three other brothers, Misser Roop Lal, Misser Ram Kishan, and Sukhraj. The former is governor of Jalendar, and Ram Kishan constantly remains in attendance at court, while the third is the commander of a division of infantry.

Besides farming many districts yielding about two lakhs of rupees annually, they have jaghirs of sixty or seventy thousand rupees assigned to them.

Of all his brothers Beli Ram is considered the most sensible. He is an intelligent and amiable man; but from the high favour he enjoys, he is much envied about the court, and has many little differences with the Sirdars, who try to injure him; but as the Maharaja is aware of his worth and devotion to his interests, their enmity is harmless.*

DIWAN DINANATH.

DINANATH is the head person in charge of the civil and military accounts. He is a shrewd, sensible man, and possesses great statistical and financial information regarding every part of the Panjab. The whole business in that line

* On the death of Ranjeet Singh and the conspiracy formed by Raja Dhian Singh to take the life of Cheit Singh, the favourite of Kharak Singh, Misser Beli Ram and his brothers were seized and tortured, and some of them cruelly put to death.

is conducted through him, and the Maharaja places great reliance in his abilities as a good accountant. He is the nephew of the late Diwan Ganga Ram of Delhi, who arrived in the Panjab about twenty-five years ago, and entered the service of his Highness. At that time Dinanath acted under him as a *Mutsuddee* or writer, but after his death, the latter having made himself master of the business conducted by his uncle, he was appointed his successor, while the son of the late Diwan, named Ajuddhianath, was promoted to the office of Diwan, or treasurer, with the troops commanded by Generals Allard and Ventura. Though Dinanath has been employed in the *Daftar* since the death of his uncle, it is only lately that he has received the title of Diwan. His family came originally from Kashmir and settled at Delhi, but they have now emigrated to Lahore. In every corps and district Dinanath has some of his own men employed, and through them he acquires every information necessary to the discharge of his important office. He receives twenty rupees a-day, besides a jaghir of six thousand rupees, and enjoys assignments on Kashmir, Multan, &c., besides many other fees and emoluments which he readily derives from his official station. His brother is still employed in the French legion.

Chapter IV.

The rise of Khoshal Singh—His humble position in early Life—He enters the Army—Embraces the Sikh Faith—Supplants Bastee Ram in the charge of the *Deodhee*—Quarrels with Misser Diwand Chand—His nephew, Teij Singh—His son, Ram Singh—Residences of the family—Places held by Khoshal Singh.

Khoshal Singh is the son of a Brahmin, and a native of the village of Ikree, in the district of Sirdhana, near Meerut. At the age of eighteen, being in poor circumstances, and in want of a livelihood, he left his home and arrived at Lahore, where he was soon employed as a menial servant, at four rupees per month, by a person of the name of Ganga Singh, a sepoy in the body guard of the Maharaja.

On the death of Ganga Singh, which occurred shortly afterwards, Khoshal Singh was thrown out of employment, and reduced to such extremity that he mortgaged his shield and sword to a Khatri named Motee, a shopkeeper in the Hamam Street. The money obtained by the mortgage was also soon expended. He next applied for assistance to Misser Ganta, residing in the same street with himself, to whom he also pawned some things. The Misser, in consideration of his caste (Brahmin), offered to support him with bread and clothes if he liked to remain with him, stating that his occupation would be to assist him in performing his Brahminical offices. The Misser himself was the Parohit or priest to several families in the city of Lahore. It is customary among the Hindus, before they take their meals, to put some aside for their Parohits, which they collect every morning. Their subsistence depends chiefly on the food thus collected. Khoshal Singh was engaged in that duty, and continued so employed for six or seven months, looking out at the same time for some other employment. After a time Misser Ganta recommended him to a person named Lala Sajan Rae, who had him enlisted in the battalion commanded by Dhokal Singh.

Khoshal Singh was smart in learning his exercise. He soon acquired a perfect knowledge of it, and was promoted to the rank of Jemadar in the party of infantry forming the escort to his Highness, who was pleased with his activity, and ordered him to remain always in attendance at court. Soon afterwards Ranjeet Singh gave him the *Pahol*, and converted him to the Sikh religion; since which he has been called Khoshal Singh.

At that period Bastee Ram was the chamberlain in charge of the *Deodhee*. He absented himself one night from his duty, when the Maharaja sent for him; on which occasion Khoshal Singh, who was actuated by some ill will towards Bastee Ram, reported that he was always absent at night. His Highness directed the Jemadar to be immediately seized and confined, and transferred the charge of his office to Khoshal Singh. Bastee Ram remained in confinement for some days; he was then released, and restored to employment on paying a fine of 2000 rupees. Khoshal Singh farmed out the *Deodhee* for 40,000 rupees, which sum was soon raised to 60,000 rupees. Afterwards, Devi Das, the Keeper of the Seals, and the Accountant-General, fixed the fees of the *Deodhee* on each district in proportion to its revenue. He settled that they should be collected by the *Kardars* as a part of the revenue, and paid to Government through Jemadar Khoshal Singh. Likewise a sum of one lakh and sixty thousand rupees was fixed as *Moharana*, or the fees of the Privy Seal, which are levied from every Sowar at the rate of two rupees a head. The *Deodhee* continued for twelve years in charge of the newly appointed Jemadar.

One day, as Misser Diwan Chand was proceeding to the court, he was stopped at the *Deodhee* by the Jemadar, which offended the Diwan, who was a man of high spirit, and he reviled him by saying, that if the Jemadar were not a Brahmin, he would have him discharged; while he lost no opportunity of abusing Khoshal Singh before the Maharaja.

About the same time Raja Dhian Singh, who was then called Mian Dhian Singh, was rising into favour with his Highness, and at the recommendation of Diwan Chand he was vested with the charge of the *Deodhee*, when the Jemadar was removed, and refused admittance to the court.

Having patiently submitted to the sentence of the Maharajah, Khoshal Singh was soon retaken into favour, and ordered to attend the court as usual, like the other Sirdars. He is now considered next in consequence to Raja Dhian Singh at the court of Lahore, and holds a Jaghir, yielding a revenue of four lakhs two thousand six hundred and sixty-seven rupees. Parts of his Jaghir lie on the left bank of the Satledge, and the other portions are scattered throughout the country on the right bank of that river.

His relatives also hold high offices in the state. One of them is Teij Singh, his nephew, who is styled a Sirdar, and the general of a division, composed of four regiments of infantry, one regiment of cavalry, and ten pieces of artillery.

Three regiments of infantry, two regiments of cavalry, and ten pieces of artillery, are likewise commanded by Ram Singh, the son of Jemadar Khoshal Singh, on whom the Maharaja, about two years ago, conferred the rank of a brigadier-general. A year and a half ago, when the Jemadar was absent on duty at Peshawr, his son murdered a fine young man named Bishan Singh, a favourite of his Highness, from a feeling of shame and personal resentment originating in a crime which Ram Singh wished to conceal. The murderer was at first forbid the presence of his Highness, but was soon afterwards readmitted without any notice being taken of the infamy of his conduct.

The Jemadar himself, who is an active officer, but cruel and depraved, also commands 2000 Sowars, called the corps of orderlies. He has erected lofty and spacious houses both at Lahore and Amritsir. That at the former is close to the eastern gate of the palace, and the latter near the great temple of the Sikhs. These edifices are strongly built, and their sites have been well chosen to give their proprietor a commanding position in the event of any demise or revolution of the government. To each are attached extensive ranges for the accommodation of his immediate retainers, and that part of the fortifications which is opposite to his house at Lahore, has been included by Khoshal Singh within his own precincts, while a bazar has been established in the *Rownee** for the exclusive use of his own people; so that they may be said to form an independent quarter of the city. The lines of the troops commanded by the nephew and son of the Jemadar are so situated as to command the principal roads leading to Lahore on the land side. It is only within the last year that they have thought of forming permanent cantonments. That of the son is in the plain of Mian Mir, on the road to Kasur. The other is on the road to Harikee; but having been commenced without consulting the Maharaja, its progress has been stopped.

* *Fausse braie.*

LIST OF PLACES HELD IN JAGHIR BY JEMADAR KOSHAL SINGH, SHOWING THE AMOUNT OF THE REVENUE OF EACH.

Names of Places.	Amount of Revenue.	Remarks.
Kalra	15,600	Taken from Sirdar Diwan Singh and given to Jemadar Khoshal Singh in 1817.
Bhopalwala and Sahnwala	26,455	Taken from Sirdar Diwan Singh, Dodia.
Villages near Amritsir .	26,740	
Kangde and Lakoa .	11,225	Taken from Mai Sadakour in 1821, and given to Jemadar Khoshal Singh.
17 villages near Sealkot .	8,890	Ditto from Baba Saheb Singh Bedi in 1834, and given to the Jemadar.
25 ditto Kortal Gujra, &c.	38,320	Ditto from Jodh Singh, Vazirabadia in 1814, and given to the Jemadar.
10 villages Khosalgarh near Dhopalwala.	13,285	Ditto from Nidhan Singh in 1810.
2 villages Bal, &c. .	3,100	Ditto from Sadha Singh Dodia in 1806, and given to the Jamadar.
Handogiwala, near Nanor	5,400	Ditto from Gujar Singh and Lehna Singh, and given to the Jemadar in 1810.
3 villages near Lahore .	13,400	
14 villages Ratya, &c. .	22,942	Ditto ditto to Maha Singh, the father of the Maharaja.
14 villages Jassiwali, in 11 kos distant from Kajrus	7,500	
Jastarwal . . .	5,295	
5 villages, Fatehpur, &c.	5,350	
4 ditto Nanoke, near Siri Hargobindpur.	6,175	Taken from Sirdar Jodh Singh in 1811.
7 villages, Komooke, &c.	8,331	Ditto from Golab Singh in 1811.
7 ditto Phansian, &c. .	8,630	Ditto ditto ditto.
22 ditto Bajwat, &c. .	52,121	Ditto from Saheb Singh Gujratia.
25 ditto Adamke, &c. .	33,946	Ditto from Dal Singh in 1818.
8 ditto Fatehgarh, &c. .	16,300	Ditto from Dharm Singh in 1812.
Dharankot . . .	1,045	
17 villages, Chalia and Kaleke, &c. &c.	65,400	
Harigah . . .	775	Ditto from Sadha Singh and Lehna Singh, in 1826.
4 villages near Miam, &c.	4,350	Ditto from Lehna Singh in 1834.
14 ditto Gangrava, &c.	36,440	
Total Rs. . .	437,315	

Chapter V.

Passage of the Ravi—Nangal—Difficulties encountered by the Mission—Nanake—Gujranwala—Hari Singh—He is defeated and killed at Jamrud by Mahomed Akbar Khan—Ranjeet Singh resumes the whole of his Jaghir—Nath—General Avitabile—His improvements at Vazirabad—Distant view of the Himmalaya.

12th January, 1839.—Leaving Lahore with Shah Zada Taimur, we crossed the river Ravi, which is the smallest and the narrowest river of the Panjab. We passed it by a ford as well as the ferry; the baggage being brought over by the latter, while the camels and horses went by the former. The river is, however, not always fordable. We encamped on a level and extensive plain, between Shahdera and a water palace of the Maharaja, situated immediately on the right bank of the river, and called from the moistness of its situation *Targarh*.

Our party consists at present of five hundred

Ghorcheras, one battalion of *Najibs*, and two pieces of artillery of the Sikh service; the first commanded by Pir Dowlat Khan, one of the Afghans of the respectable family of Kasoor; the second commanded by a son of the late George Thomas, escorting Shah Zada Taimur; besides one hundred Sowars, and a company of infantry, forming his personal guard; as well as two companies of the British Native infantry, attending his Royal Highness as a guard of honour from that Government. Two companies of regular infantry, and fifty troopers of Ranjeet Singh, form an escort to Sir Claude Wade; besides forty-three irregular Sowars, and fifty-three matchlockmen entertained by him for the same purpose on the part of the Indian Government.

Some boats on the Ravi having been engaged to carry supplies of grain, which the Lieut.-Colonel had procured for the consumption of the army of the Indus, to Shikarpore, and there being consequently but few boats left at the ferry, the whole of the baggage was not brought over till next day; on which we were obliged to halt, and took advantage of it to bring to a conclusion every affair requiring to be arranged with the court of Lahore. We noticed the improved shape of the boats on the Ravi, from the mere rafts used on the Satledge. They do not carry so much, but are much better suited both for sailing and rowing.

14*th.*—Started at sunrise, and encamped at a village named Nangal, surrounded by an extensive low jungle, distant twelve kos, held in jaghir by Faqir Nuruddin, the brother of Azizuddin, his Persian secretary. It was a cloudy day, and before we arrived it began to drizzle. No tráce of cultivation was seen on either side of the road. The soil is generally barren, and of a saline nature. Several sites of towns and villages were observed scattered here and there, which bespoke the prosperous state of the country in former days. There are several fine preserves for hunting in the vicinity, near one of which the Maharaja has built a *Baradari*, or pavilion. Raja Dhian Singh's fondness for the sports of the field is so eager, that he often passes whole nights in these preserves in an ambush to shoot hogs and tigers.

The village of Nangal is small, and the ground about it becomes almost a swamp after heavy rains, and, in consequence, there is no good encamping ground near. No supplies procurable here, unless previously collected. Water good; and road tolerable, but only a cart-track. We crossed a *Nala*, or small stream, called Baghbacha, fordable, a famous haunt for tigers.

On reaching the camp, we had a heavy shower of rain, which collected round our tents and formed islands of them. We had great trouble and confusion; and the tents being soaked through, we were obliged to halt there the following day to let them dry. Three of our camels sunk under their loads and died, and some of them were seriously injured. To add to our discomforts, we were compelled to send for our supplies to a considerable distance, which determined Sir Claude to rely no longer on the Maharaja's officers, but to form a commissariat of his own. He found also that our progress was much impeded by some *hackeries* belonging to our party, which he ordered to be exchanged for camels, and the baggage of every one to be limited to the smallest possible quantity.*

16*th.*—Marched at sunrise, and stopped at a village named Nanake, the jaghir of Jemadar Khoshal Singh, distant nine kos. The morning was foggy and gloomy. The road lay over a low swampy tract of country, but better peopled and cultivated than that of the preceding day. The snowy range beyond Jammoo in sight. Encamping ground very broken, and soil sandy. Water good, but supplies scanty.

On our arrival in camp, it was reported that the Shah Zada's tents in the rear could not be brought on from want of carriage, and three of the Sowaree, or riding elephants, were therefore sent back to bring them.

17*th.*—Started at the usual time, and halted at Gujranwala, north of the town, on an open

* The baggage of an Indian army is a great encumbrance.

and level spot close to the fort. The distance traversed was ten kos. The morning very chilly and clear. The thermometer at sunrise ranged at 45°. The view of the snowy mountains became more distinct. The road continues the same as yesterday. Soil improves, and agriculture was observed in a better state than in the course of the two last stages.

Gujranwala is the native place of Ranjeet Singh, and the seat of his ancestors. Their possessions did not extend beyond its limits. It was formerly a village, with some lands attached, but it was not a place of any fame. Since the charge of it was conferred by the Maharaja on his faithful servant the late Sirdar Hari Singh, it has been greatly improved. The Sirdar built a high mud wall round the town; also a fort to the north of it, surrounded by a ditch. Inside the fort there is a fine *Baradari*,* and a house after the Eng-

* "It consists of three stories, each containing a room about fifteen feet square, the lower ones being enclosed by broad verandahs; and below ground there is an apartment to retreat to from the hot winds. A range of fountains extends close to the entrance front, and at the corners of

lish fashion, where the Sirdar used to live. The town is now very populous, and contains

the 'chabootra,' on which the dwelling is erected, are circular ornamented seats, which, when used, are covered with silk carpets or Kashmir shawls. At the top of the second and third stories similar conveniences are also constructed; those of the latter being made after the model of the lotus flower, and the exterior of the elevation is covered with the finest chunam, free from any of those tawdry embellishments natives are so apt to consider as ornamental to their abodes. We could only gain admittance to the lower apartments, as the individual who had charge of the keys had gone to the city; and the circumstance was to be regretted, as we were told the second story is very beautifully fitted up, whilst that we entered had nothing particularly attractive about it. The garden is laid out in rather a pretty manner, and, in addition to some very pretty cypress trees, can boast of two or three large vineries. We were shown the 'dota ka mukum,' or abode of the idol, which is situated at some distance from the house, and close to a reservoir by which the fountains are supplied with water. It is a small domed temple, built upon a chabootra (or terrace) in an enclosed area. A flight of three steps leads to it, and immediately on the right of the entrance is the image of a bull in a sitting posture, the hump of which our guide touched, and salaamed to with great reverence. On the door of the temple being thrown open, I could not help feeling disgusted at the idea of the glorious Deity being represented by nine oval stones, kept constantly moistened by means a good bazaar of about five hundred shops, where every thing may be had; but it has no manufactories of its own.

Some account of Hari Singh, who was one of Ranjeet Singh's most distinguished officers, will not be out of place here. Originally he was a common *khidmatgar*, or personal attendant. The Maharaja, always desirous of encouraging bravery and soldierlike conduct, observing Hari Singh to be a very bold and active man, and that on many occasions he had evinced an enterprising disposition, began to raise him in his favour, till at last he was appointed governor of Kashmir, where he remained for a few years, and established a new rupee of base coinage, which still bears his name. He was afterwards put in charge of the important fort of Attok. But as he was a very bigoted Sikh, and owed a hearty

of water dripping through an aperture in an earthen pot suspended above them, to which the sepoys who accompanied us commenced praying. When will men cease to worship the works of their own hands?"—*Barr's Journal*, pp. 134, 135.

grudge to the Mussalman race, in the year 1833, accompanied by Kour Naonihal Singh, he attacked Peshawr, and occupied it without any apparent resistance, while its chief, Sultan Mahomed Khan, retired to Kabul. Since that time Peshawr has remained in the possession of the Sikhs. It had frequently been invaded and plundered by them before, but restored to its former rulers.

In the year 1837, Hari Singh advanced towards Khaibar, and repaired and occupied the fort of Jamrud, situated close to the entrance of the pass; which alarmed the Khaibarees so much, that they invited Dost Mahomed Khan to join them in attacking Hari Singh, and expelling him from the fort. A great battle ensued between Mahomed Akbar and the Sirdar, in which the latter was killed, and the turned of victory turned in favour of the Afghans.

Hari Singh's loss was deeply deplored by Ranjeet Singh, who placed the greatest confidence in him. He was regretted also by his countrymen and those who knew him.

His sons did not inherit the bravery or ability of their father; and Ranjeet Singh, deeming them incapable of exercising so great a charge, resumed the whole of the Sirdar's jaghir, yielding about eight lakhs of rupees revenue annually, and divided it chiefly among the other Sirdars of his court, making but a small provision for the family of the deceased: they are now in very reduced circumstances. Hari Singh has left four sons, named Jowahir Singh and Goordat Singh, from his first wife, and Arjun Singh and Panjab Singh, from his second wife. The two latter now hold a jaghir of 40,000 rupees; in return for which they furnish his Highness with a party of sixty or seventy Sowars.

The district of Gujranwala is at present farmed for a little more than a lakh of rupees to Misser Ram Kishan, the younger brother of Misser Beli Ram. The country about Gujranwala is fertile and productive: there are some gardens also to be seen outside the place, in one of which, near the road from Lahore, rest the remains of Maha Singh, the father of Ranjeet Singh, and of his mother and grandfather, over whose ashes some fine tombs have been erected. On account of rainy and cloudy weather we halted here three days, receiving every attention from the local authorities. Numerous Kashmirians are settled here who were driven from that province in the late famine.

We renewed our march on the 21st inst., and encamped at Nath, a village nine kos distant: road good; supplies scarce; encamping ground, which is south of the village, low and swampy from rain; water good.

22*nd.*—Started early in the morning and proceeded to Vazirabad: two kos from it comes in view a large gateway leading into the town. In the year 1832, when on our way to the Maharaja at Pind Dadan Khan, we passed by this place: the gate was then being built by General Avitabile, who was the governor of the district, and has a fine residence here, in which we were hospitably entertained. It is a large town, and abounds with supplies of every description: the streets are well arranged, and cut each other in right angles, many buildings which stood in the way having been levelled to the ground. General Avitabile is an Italian officer in the service of Ranjeet Singh. He established a good system of police and revenue throughout the territory, and made a great many improvements in the town. It was formerly, like others in the Panjab, a dirty and irregularly peopled place. There is a large straight bazar through which you may see without interruption from one gate-way of the city to the other. It is intersected by another small bazar, and the regularity of both adds greatly to the appearance of the place. A mud wall surrounds the town, which is prettily situated on the left bank of the Chinab. The streets and buildings raised by the General afford a good idea of his architectural taste: at present that officer is the governor of Peshawr.

At the northern end of the town is a garden containing a fine house called Sheshmahl, where the Maharaja on his visits to Vazirabad resides. It is an old building, but has been repaired and beautified with mirrors by General Avitabile. The whole territory is now farmed to Raja Seocheit Singh, one of the Jammoo family, for twelve lakhs of rupees: Diwan Bheemsen, his servant, is also his deputy; and appears to be a sensible and clever man.

We encamped on the bed of the river Chinab, between the main stream and a *Nala* passing close by the town, a small and confined spot.

The population of Vazirabad consists of about forty thousand inhabitants, who are generally Khatris. There are other tribes, but the former predominate. Large quantities of coarse cloth are manufactured here and exported to the neighbouring places. Small tents and *Sholdaris* or marquees are also made here: though cheap, they are not very durable.

The salt range to the west, and the lofty Pir Panjal, one of the highest peaks of the Himmalaya on the south of Kashmir, were visible, and formed a magnificent spectacle. Faiztalab Khan, the son of Jahandad Khan, who in breach of his faith delivered over to the

Sikhs the fort of Attok, which he governed on the part of Shah Shuja-ul-Mulk, joined the Shah Zada here with twenty-four of his mounted retainers. He and his family have been living at Vazirabad on the bounty of Ranjeet Singh, for the great service which he had performed for him.

Chapter VI.

A Panjabee ferry—Gujrat—The adjacent country—Khawaspura—Kharian—Death of General Allard—Honours paid to his corpse by the troops attached to the Mission—His funeral—Delay of the Mission at Aurangabad—Order of march—Mr. Lord—Letters to Ranjeet Singh—Salt mines.

Halted three days at Vazirabad, and on the morning of the 26th, proceeded to Gujrat, distant six kos: rode over a bed of sand for three-quarters of a mile till we reached the main stream of the river Chinab: ferry across and road good from the right bank to the town, a distance of five kos. There is a ford, however, about thirty miles farther up, not a safe one, the river being full of quicksands, though it is said troops have passed over at a particular season of the year. The boats continue to improve in size and shape.

In crossing, as usual, a quarrel took place between a Sikh and an Afghan of the Shah Zada's party in attempting to take possession of a boat. The latter gave a sabre-cut on the head of the Sikh, who, to avenge the offence, was going to attack his antagonist, when some person standing by having interfered between them appeased the quarrel. On reaching the camp the circumstance was reported to Lieutenant-Colonel Wade, who, after inquiries, caused proper notice to be taken of the guilty, and made a regulation to prevent a repetition of such disputes in crossing the river: they are of common occurrence in the Sikh army, and are often attended with loss of life.*

* "At the Ravi we had a specimen of the manner in which a Panjabee ferry is conducted, and where anything but order and regularity was observed. As soon as the artillery had finished with the boats, a regular scuffle ensued for them, and, of course, strength and might won the day; those who had gained possession of them retaining it, by thrashing unmercifully any individual who attempted to enter the boat, except of their own party. One little fellow I observed making dexterous use of a short thick stick, with which he belaboured the heads and legs of those who, being no acquaintances of his, endeavoured to secure a seat; and the gentler sex, I am ashamed to say, were treated in no better manner; for those who got on board (and many did) had, after receiving their portion of thumps with the rest, to tumble in head foremost, or were dragged

We encamped to the north of the town about half a kos distant, near a *Baradari* and a garden formed by the Maharaja.

Gujrat is an old town containing about eight thousand houses. The inhabitants are generally Khatris and Gujars, who are notorious thieves. Its original ruler was Saheb Singh, but it was afterwards usurped by Ranjeet Singh. At present it is leased to Rajah Golab Singh, the elder brother of the Jammoo family.

The country round is open and flat, and the soil is exceedingly rich and productive. Gujrat

in by the feet or hands, whichever limb was nearest to their friends, who had previously obtained a footing. Children, too, were in danger of being crushed; and I understood it is not a rare occurrence for two parties to draw swords, and have a regular set to for the precedence; indeed, Foulkes mentioned that not long ago, a man deliberately levelled his matchlock and shot another who had disputed his right to a passage. As it was not our wish to enter into squabbles with the Panjabees, Ferris halted and sent a message to the Governor of Lahore to say he should remain where he was until the boats were cleared for our use. In about an hour, Nooroodeen, accompanied by General Tezie Singh, came down and directed that they should be immediately made over to us."—*Barr's Journal*, pp. 121, 122.

is noted for the manufacture of the common swords of the country, matchlocks, daggers, &c. Here is the tomb of Dowla Shah, a saint who is highly respected in the Panjab. It is superstitiously visited by barren women, who, if they afterwards bear children, bring their first-born to the shrine of the saint, who are called *chuhas*. I saw some of them thus presented. The principal road to Kashmir branches off from this place.

Halted three days also at Gujrat, and started on the 29th, and stopped at the Sarae of Khawaspura, distant ten kos: road fair but rather heavy when passing over the beds of two or three mountainous streams. No mark of cultivation was observed on either side of the road, but bushes and Dakh jungle were only to be seen. Numbers of cows and buffaloes were grazing about, from which it appears that there is abundance of pasturage for cattle. From this place there are three roads to Jehlam; one of these goes *via* Kharian over a low range of sand-hills which is impracticable for hackeries and guns, but might be made otherwise by a little labour. The other two lie along the sides of the ridge, one by Dheri on the right, and the other by Dinga on the left: the difference in these two routes and the other is ten miles.

The guns and wheel-carriages accompanying the mission separating here, started by Dinga, while the whole party passed on by Kharian.*

* "The direct road to Peshawr being impracticable for guns, on account of the steepness of some ghâts that cross a low range of mountains, extending through the country, almost parallel with, and not very far distant from, the river Jhelum; we were obliged to take a more circuitous route, which will eventually bring us to a lower ridge, where the hills are more undulating and less precipitous. Midway we came to a 'baoli,' or covered well—one of those constructions that do honour to the pious feelings of individuals who have been thus led to bestow their wealth for the general benefit of their fellow creatures: the weary find repose under its arches and refreshment in its waters. In a few minutes we resumed our journey, and after a march of twenty-three miles eventually reached the long-wished for town of Dinga.

"As we approached it, our attention was called to a small crowd, principally of women and children; and on riding up to see the cause of their assembling, perceived in the midst of them a man stretched on the ground at full length, who had, half an hour before, been deprived of both his hands, as a punishment for the crime of stealing. A few quiverings about the muscles of his legs were all that

Khawaspura is a small village inhabited within the Sarae, after which name it is called: the wall round it is *Pucka*, or of burnt bricks, but is now going to decay. The encamping ground was north-west, on a broken and confined spot; good shooting in a low and stunted jungle close by. There is only one well at the place: the water used was from a spring.

During the reign of Akbar these great Saraes were built at a distance of six or seven kos from each other between Agra and the Indus for the accommodation of travellers: Saraes were likewise erected at the same time on the road to Kashmir; they are now declining to ruin.

Started early on the 30th and encamped at Kharian, a small village. The road tolerable, encamping ground irregular. There are two large wells, and the deepest Baolee I

betokened he still existed; but he was insensible, and no wonder, as he had bled profusely, and he was thus being inhumanly left to perish, as no one dared to assist him. The block, a rude piece of wood, was lying by his side; but the hands had been carried off for the purpose of being exposed near the spot where he had committed the depredation."—*Barr's Journal*, pp. 148, 150, 151.

ever saw, the water of which is brackish. They are in good repair; one of them is descended by a flight of 114 steps: they appear of very old standing, and perhaps were sunk at the time when the Sarae of Kharian, of which no mark is to be traced at present, was built. Water was obtained from a dirty muddy pond at hand, but drunk in preference to that of the Baolee. Supplies were procured with difficulty.

31*st*.—Marched at the usual time. At about one and a-half kos we ascended the ridge to which I have alluded. The ascent was not difficult, the horses and camels easily passed over it; but the road is in some parts very narrow and rugged. The ridge extends four kos in breadth, and about fourteen kos in length. Midway there is a pool of water, where *kafilas** used to assemble and then to proceed together; otherwise travellers, especially the Sikhs, were plundered and killed by the neighbouring highway robbers: the road is now quite safe. On the bank of this pool there is a Hindu *Sheowala*, where such eatables as parched grain, &c., can

* Caravans.

be had. Proceeding four or five miles farther we encamped to-day at Aurangabad, a village surrounded by a high wall. No supplies procurable at the place itself, but being situated about two miles from Jehlam, they can always be obtained from thence. Water near, but though sweet to the taste, it is very unwholesome. It should be brought from the river Jehlam, though some distance off.

On the way to camp we heard the sad news of General Allard's death a few days ago at Peshawr, and that his body had been embalmed, and was to be conveyed for burial to Lahore. He is deeply regretted, particularly by the troops under his command, with whom he was very popular, and a favourite also with the Maharaja. His manners were mild and courteous, and gained on every one who associated with him. It is said that he died of an affection of the heart, and was seven days confined to his bed.

We halted eighteen days in this vicinity, ten at Aurangabad, and seven at the ferry. While at the former, the arrival of the late

General Allard's corpse having been announced, Sir Claude Wade directed a street to be formed by the troops in camp, along which the bier was conducted. It was received and saluted with great ceremony. On the coffin were placed the decorations of honour worn by the General. Every heart throbbed with sincere grief as his remains, escorted by a party of the French Legion, passed through our camp.*

Our delay here was owing to two reasons: one was that the grand army was delayed in Sindh, and no correct information was yet received of the settlement of affairs in that country: the other was, the vague reports

* "The salute we heard as we approached Lahore were minute guns firing in honour of General Allard, who lately died at Peshawr, and whose body had been brought to the capital for interment; it had this morning been removed from his house at Anarcolly to his country residence in the neighbourhood, where it will remain until a suitable grave can be prepared for its reception. On the occasion six regiments of the Maharaja's were paraded for the purpose of paying respect to the memory of the deceased, who was beloved both by Natives and Europeans, and whose death has cast a gloom over the city."—*Barr's Journal*, pp. 72, 73.

which were spread regarding the dangerous state of Ranjeet Singh's health, which was a subject of much anxiety to us, as on the exercise of his own exertions and authority the success of our part of the enterprise greatly depended.

Our time was employed in introducing order among the various parties in camp, that each might know its place in marching and halting, and we might maintain our credit for discipline. The different bands of Afghans on foot who had joined the Shah Zada being now about three hundred men, were divided by the Lieutenant-Colonel into two parties, under the command of Lieutenants (now Captains) Dowson and Hillersdon, two young British officers who were attached to the Mission, and ordered to proceed in advance to Peshawr, and complete their levies to eight Tomans or companies, from the Afghans who had joined Mr. Lord* at that place.

* Mr. Lord had been the medical officer with Sir Alexander Burnes in his mission to Kabul; and the following memoir, which appeared in the 'Athenæum' of the 10th

Shah Zada Yehya, one of the Saddozai family, who was settled at Kabul, having been

of April, 1844, gives an interesting account of his services and death :—

" ASIATIC SOCIETY.

"*March* 20.

" Professor WILSON in the Chair.

" The honorary Secretary read a Memoir of the late Dr. Lord, whose early death in the late Afghan struggle has been equally lamented by his friends, and regretted by the service to which he belonged, and where his talents were so beneficially exerted. The writer of the Memoir, Dr. Taylor, a member of the Society, who was an early and intimate friend of Dr. Lord, states that that gentleman, during his journeys in Central Asia, had made a regular series of valuable observations, which it was his intention to send to the Royal Asiatic Society for publication at the close of the war; and it is hoped that they may yet be recovered. The particulars of Dr. Lord's early life, and his connexion with the 'Athenæum,' were given in our hasty tribute to his memory (No. 689). In the latter part of the year 1836, Dr. Lord sailed for India as assistant surgeon in the service of the East India Company, and arrived at Bombay in June, 1837. He was soon after appointed to the Native cavalry in Gujrat; and, when there, was selected to proceed to a district beyond the British frontier, where the plague was raging, in order to report on the disease. He had actually departed on his mission when he was recalled, in order to go to Kabul, as surgeon to the embassy, which was about to set out under Sir Alexander Burnes. At Kabul he won the friendship turned out of that place by Dost Mahomed Khan, joined Shah Zada Taimur to-day with

of Dost Mahomed Khan, and other Afghan chiefs; and his fame reached the ears of the too well known Murad Beg, the dreaded Amir of Kunduz, who sent a mission to request his attendance on his brother, then threatened with blindness. Such an opportunity of gaining information respecting the political condition of the Uzbeks was not neglected; and Dr. Lord, about the end of November, 1837, penetrated into Tartary through the mountains of Hindu Kush. He found the case of Murad Beg's brother hopeless; and soon after prepared to return, but not before he had found time to make a number of valuable observations, which he embodied in a report to the Government. The report met with the highest approbation; and the writer was in consequence named Political Assistant to the Envoy sent to the king of Kabul; and was intrusted to raise all the well affected subjects of Shah Shuja, near Peshawr. He was there, as he says in a letter to his mother, 'busied in casting cannon, forging muskets, raising troops, horse and foot, talking, persuading, threatening, bullying, and bribing.' In the three days' fighting at the Khaibar Pass, Dr. Lord acted as aide-de-camp to Colonel Wade, and received the public thanks of the Governor-General for his conduct on the occasion. Soon after this Dr. Lord was sent to Bamian to superintend the negotiations with the states of Turkestan; his energy and prudence were crowned with success; and the result of the mission was, that he got in the whole family of the ex-chief of Kabul, and conciliated all the Uzbek states as far as the Oxus. The personal acquaintance of Dr. Lord his family. Other Afghans are also arriving daily, and joining the camp. The *Khawanin*, who had quitted Sultan Mahomed Khan and joined the Shah Zada's camp at Lahore, reported that the Sirdar, to retaliate on them, had seized their property, and put their families within his jurisdiction into confinement. As such a circumstance was likely to discourage other Afghans from joining the Shah Zada, and to defeat the object in view, prompt notice was taken of the subject by Sir Claude in an expostulatory letter to Ranjeet Singh,

with Dost Mahomed Khan led to his accompanying the military division which was sent to intercept that chief, as it was probable that his surrender might be facilitated through his agency; but it was, unhappily, the circumstance which led to his own death, which, with that of nearly all the officers of the troop, ensued upon the disgraceful flight of our cavalry. The subject has been already too often before the public to need repetition. Dr. Lord was spurring across the field to join a party which seemed to evince a better spirit, when he fell, pierced by more than a dozen balls. His death was instantaneous. The reading of the Memoir was followed by an extract of a letter from Sir Alexander Burnes, declaring the regret of the Indian Government at the loss of so zealous and able a servant; and expressing his own sorrow at the deprivation of so dear a friend."

suggesting the expediency of immediate redress being given to the complainants, and some security being taken for the future good and faithful conduct of his Barakzai feudatories towards the Shah in the present expedition.

In the meantime letters were addressed to all the Khaibar and other chiefs, intimating the approach of the Shah Zada, and inviting them to join him on his arrival at Peshawr.

A letter was also addressed to Ranjeet Singh, informing him of the receipt of intelligence that Dost Mahomed Khan was highly distracted on hearing the news of the armies of the two states being on their way against him in opposite directions, and that he was regretting the opportunity he had lost, of securing the friendship of the British Government through Sir Alexander Burnes. In the same letter his Highness was requested to furnish a copy of the Tripartite Treaty to his officers at Peshawr, that they might be aware of its terms, and co-operate with Sir Claude Wade accordingly. Another letter was written to the Maharaja on the 15th instant, requesting him to issue orders to his officers at Peshawr, to place a battalion of his regular infantry, with two pieces of artillery, at our disposal on the Shah Zada's arrival at Peshawr, as the escort now accompanying him would not be sufficient for the protection of the encampment in that advanced position near the enemy's frontier, and when it would be increased by many new followers.

Mr. Reid, our medical officer, started from camp to examine the salt mines which are visible from this place. I had seen them in our mission to his Highness in 1832. They are very curious, and yield a large revenue to Ranjeet Singh, which is managed by Raja Golab Singh.

CHAPTER VII.

The Jammoo family—Horrible treachery perpetrated by them—They found a town—They increase in wealth and power—Another dreadful tragedy—Various chiefs of this family—Rise of the Sikhs—Youth of Ranjeet Singh—Anarchy—Ranjeet annexes Jammoo to his dominions—Rapid rise of Golab Singh—Raja Sultan Khan—Conquest of Kashmir—Jaghirs.

THE tradition is that there were two brothers of the Surajbansi tribe of Rajputs. They having been actuated by a desire to travel and to lay the foundation of a town, and thus to raise their name in the world, left the Dekhan, their native country, in the disguise of *Kalanders*, a kind of monk; and having travelled throughout the country, acquired some knowledge of its affairs. When they reached the spot where the town of Jammoo now stands, they fixed their dwelling there. In the mean time a person of the Brahman caste also happened to be there, and inquired after the strangers. As a long experience of the world had matured their minds, they did not let him into their secret, but, on the contrary, asked him the reason of his coming. The Brahman simply stated that this spot (at that time called Chak), being very inaccessible, populous, and well fortified, had attracted the notice of an individual of the tribe of Mukta; that, having assembled his relatives and family, he occupied the place and enclosed their houses; that in a short time they grew rich and powerful by plundering the neighbouring people; that although they were bravely chased and pursued by large parties, yet, owing to the inaccessibility of their station, none of them could overcome them, and were put to flight or killed in the attempt; that in this manner the prosperity of these bandits had greatly arisen, and the Brahman continued to live among them.

One day the above two brothers observed that a lion, a wolf, and a goat were drinking water together at the same spot, from which circumstance they augured it to be an auspicious ground. In consequence they were resolved to build a town there, and with this view promoted their friendly relations with the Brahman. Night and day they used to sit together in company of each other. A rumour of their pious and religious character was spread among the people of every rank, low and high. Every one used to assemble at their place night and day to listen to their lectures and to receive their blessings. A long time elapsed in this way. The people placed great confidence in them, and none swerved from their command. One day the two brothers held a council with the nobles of the country, and asked them, as they had long remained under their protection, that they would accept their invitation to dine with them at night, which was accepted without objection; the two brothers prepared every kind of eatables and drinkables, and mixed poison in everything. At the appointed time the whole party assembled, and voraciously set to eat, while the hosts only attended to the wants of the party. No sooner had they done with their dinner than every one of them expired.

When the two Rajputs had established themselves on the spot, they set about building a town (the town of Jammoo), and adopted the predatory habits of the people. In a few days the fame of their bravery and courage was spread throughout the country. At length one of the brothers settled in the fort of Mahu and the other that of Jammoo. They had five sons, the elder one of whom was married in the family of Kirthu, the head Zamindar of Samba. The second was married at Jasrota, the third at Mankot, the fourth at Aknur, and the fifth at Shujanpore. As avarice generally follows on the heels of riches, no sooner, therefore, had they found themselves in affluent circumstances, than they aspired to deprive their neighbours of their property. With that view one day the brother who lived at Jasrota called on his brother settled at Samba. The wife of the latter brother, out of modesty, shrunk under the cot of her husband. As soon as the two brothers joined together, they concerted measures to exterminate the principal persons of the village of Samba. The wife having heard all that had transpired on the occasion, her husband, out of fear of the discovery of their plot, killed her on the spot by running a knife through her belly, and immediately transported the corpse of the deceased to Jammoo. One day they invited all the principal individuals of Samba to an entertainment, and with the usual treachery practised by their forefathers, destroyed them all the same day by means of poison, and took possession of everything they had. In the same manner every one of the five brothers, by means of gross intrigues, exterminated the chief persons of their respective villages and possessed their property. They continued to exercise similar tricks for a long time, and generation after generation, in order to raise their influence, till at last Raja Hari Das was born in their family. He was a very ambitious and enterprising individual. His first object was to extend the territory which he inherited from his forefathers, and he executed his design without any apparent resistance. He occupied the whole country belonging to his neighbours. As he became a man of consequence, he presented himself before the Mogul Emperor at Delhi, where he was treated with consideration and distinction. He assisted the Emperor in his expedition against the Dekhan, on which occasion he was killed by a sabre-cut.

Hari Das was succeeded by Raja Kaji Singh, his son. This Raja was famed for his justice and equity. No event worthy of mention in his life is on record. After his demise he was followed by Raja Dharabdeo, who soon added Jammoo and other places in its neighbourhood to his territory, and raised his name by making wars with distant and neighbouring chiefs. He is known for his attachment and obedience to the Mogul Emperor. He had four well qualified sons, named Ranjeet Deo, Ghansam Deo, Surat Singh, and Balwant Singh.

On his death he was succeeded by his elder son Ranjeet Deo. He was an ambitious and fortunate chief. He succeeded in 1730, and ruled for fifty-four years. He first directed his attention to the extension of his territory. Four great neighbouring chiefs were entirely reduced to subjection, and several others made tributary to his authority, viz., Amrit Pal of Basoli, Dia Pal of Bhadarwal, Azmet Deo of Mankot, Sayed ulla Singh and Karm-ulla Singh of Kishtwar.* The daily rising power of Ranjeet Deo alarmed the Mogul Emperor. In consequence, Khan Bahadar Khan, the Suba of Lahore, was ordered to proceed against him, and to seize and to remove him to the court. Accordingly Khan Bahadar Khan, with a considerable army, proceeded to Jammoo, and succeeded, without opposition, in apprehending the Raja, and transported him to Lahore, where he was confined for twelve years. Afterwards, on the payment of a ransom of two lakhs of rupees, he was released on the recommendation of Adina Beg Khan, the Governor of Jalendar, and was sent back to Jammoo, accompanied by Hakeem Khodabaksh Khan, the ancestor of Faqir Azizuddin. The

* The chiefs of Kishtwar and other petty states in that quarter were Hindus converted to Mahomedanism by Aurangzeb, and indiscriminately retain the names and titles of both sects.

Hakeem, after realizing one-half of the tribute settled on Ranjeet Deo, went to Lahore.

Soon after the release of Ranjeet Deo, Ahmed Shah Durrani invaded India, when the former, who had resisted the invader, fell into the hands of the Afghans, and was again sent to Lahore, and confined there. During his confinement, Ratan Deo, one of the Jammoo family, who had gone for service to the Dekhan, having given some offence to his employer, took flight, and availed himself of the absence of Ranjeet Deo to declare Ghana Deo, his younger brother, the nominal ruler of Jammoo, on the condition that he would not make use of his claim to govern the country. Shahwali Khan, the Prime Minister of Ahmed Shah, reported the affair to His Majesty, and recommended that, as the territory of Ranjeet Deo had been usurped, there was no use in keeping him any longer confined. The Shah ordered the prisoner not only to be set at liberty, but to be honoured with a *Khilat*, and to be restored to authority.

A large army was despatched to assist Ranjeet Deo in that object. When he appeared on the frontier of his country, he was attacked at night by the enemy at the head of a large party of Rajputs, whom Ratan Deo had collected from the neighbouring hills; but not being able to maintain a contest with the royal troops, he was repulsed with severe loss, and obliged to submit. Ranjeet Deo was reinstated in the chiefship of Jammoo, in return for which he paid a *Nazarana* of three lakhs of rupees to Shahwali Khan, who withdrew to Lahore.

On the return of Ahmed Shah to Kabul, revolts and insurrections broke out in nearly every part of the Panjab, and almost each town and district owned a separate and independent chief, who defied the power of the Durrani monarchy, and thought only of ruling for himself. Every one began to aspire to his neighbour's possessions: among others, Ranjeet Deo sent a large force, headed by Ratan Deo, to attack the territory of Raja Karm Chand, the grandfather of Rajah Sansar Chand Katoch. Many of the petty chiefs on the road by which the army advanced acknowledged his authority without offering any obstacle to the progress of the expedition. On its approach to Nadon it was bravely opposed by Raja Karm Chand, and a battle ensued between the two parties, in which the Katoch chief was defeated with great loss, and obliged to sue for peace. He agreed that his son, Mian Teij Singh, should remain a hostage with Ranjeet Deo, and that he would pay the latter an annual contribution of one lakh and ninety thousand rupees. Ranjeet Deo died after a long reign, and in addition to his original territory, acquired possession of the following places:—

Charal,

Shakargarh, formerly called Dialgarh,

Kabula,	Parwal,
Shahpore,	Chanda Majra,
Bura Dulla,	Andarwah,
Dousal,	Chakana,
Aknur,	Balwath,
Kot Bhalowal,	Jankawan.

It was during the lifetime of Ranjeet Deo that the Sikhs, particularly those of the Bhangi confederacy, were daily rising to importance, and became an object of alarm to their neighbours. Fearful of their power, the Jammoo chief sought the means of securing his territory from their constant inroads, and consented to pay them a *Nazarana*. The fate of Jammoo from that date has been dependent on the dominion of the Sikhs.

After effecting a settlement of their demands with Ranjeet Deo, the Bhangis directed their attention chiefly to the conquest of the country about Lahore; while Mahan Singh, the father of Maharaja Ranjeet Singh, whose possessions were contiguous to Jammoo, commenced making depredations on that territory, and compelled its chief to give him a contribution also.

In the year 1794 Ranjeet Deo died, and was succeeded by his son Birjraj Deo. He reigned twenty years, the greater part of which he spent in fighting with the Sikhs, and is represented to have been a brave and enterprising leader. In the beginning of his reign he was harassed and annoyed, not only by Maha Singh's incursions, but by Haqiqat Singh, who attacked him on the side of Zafarwal and Chapral, near Sialkot, and where Ranjeet Deo had built a fort called after his own name, Ranjeet Garh; but he soon secured the alliance of both parties, by paying a *Nazarana* of 60,000 rupees to one, and by exchanging turbans with the other. The above two chiefs again combined, however, to ravage the Jammoo territory, and Birjraj Deo adopted every means in his power to thwart their design. A battle was fought between them, in which the Jammoo chief was discomfited, and the city fell into the hands of the Sikhs. The victors occupied and abandoned it to the fury and rapacity of their followers; and the booty which was captured by the Sikhs on that occasion is said to have been immense.

The city of Amritsir had not then attained an equally flourishing condition with that of Jammoo; and its wealth, and a jealousy of its rising prosperity, had long been viewed with jealousy by the Sikhs, which induced them to remain there for some months, during which the place was completely plundered and ransacked.

Haqiqat Singh was obliged to hasten back from Jammoo immediately to the relief of Amr

Singh Bhaaga, who was besieged and reduced to the last extremity by his Sikh rivals, Jai Singh and Gorbakhsh Singh. He attacked the besiegers; and after compelling them to raise the siege and retire, and restoring order in the territory of Amr Singh, retraced his steps to Jammoo, where he soon afterwards died. The demise of Haqiqat Singh may be said to have left Maha Singh the sole master of Jammoo; but some time afterwards he restored it to Birjraj Deo, on the stipulation of an annual tribute.

Birjraj Deo left a son named Sapuran Singh, then very young, who was declared the successor of his father at Jasrota, where all the neighbouring chiefs assembled to acknowledge his title.

After the death of Maha Singh, a Sikh chief of note, named Dal Singh, who was in the service of the former, is said to have instigated the present ruler of the Panjab, then about the same age as Sapuran Singh, to take advantage of that youth's infancy and conquer his country. The Maharaja proceeded to execute the design; when Mian Mota, the regent or minister of Sapuran Singh, proceeded to meet Ranjeet Singh with his master, and readily submitted to his authority. The two youths, viz., Ranjeet Singh and Sapuran Singh, no sooner met than they began to play with each other. During the sport, Ranjeet Singh is said to have pulled off the cap of the other, who retaliated the treatment of his young host by taking his turban off his head also, which caused a quarrel between them: but the preceptors of each party interfered, and reconciled them to each other by an exchange of turbans; after which they retired to their respective homes.

Sapuran Singh had but a very short reign: he was attacked by the small-pox about two years after his accession, and died of that disease. Having left no direct descendants to succeed him, on his death a contest for power ensued, which continued for a long time to distract and ruin the affairs of the principality. The officers of which, seeing that the country could not be preserved in their hands, thought it advisable to declare Cheit Singh, the son of Dalel Singh, and the nephew of Ranjeet Deo, the successor. In the anarchy that had prevailed, many of the conquests made by Ranjeet Deo were lost.

The first act of Cheit Singh's government was to murder Teij Singh, who, during the reign of Birjraj Deo, had been incited by Mian Mota, the late regent of the family, to put to death Dalel Singh, the father of Cheit Singh, from a fear of whose vengeance the Mian himself took refuge in the Chakanah, a strong country near Jammoo, from which he was in the habit of making irruptions, and using every effort in his power to devastate that territory.

In these domestic dissensions and disputes, Ranjeet Singh saw an opportunity of taking entire possession of Jammoo and of adding it to his own territory. Accordingly in the year 1808, he sent a party of his troops and occupied the place, conferring a Jaghir, only adequate to his subsistence, on Cheit Singh, during his life.

The late Ranjeet Deo had two brothers named Surat Singh and Balwant Singh, the former of whom had four sons, namely, Zorawar Singh, Mian Ditta, Mian Mota, and Mian Bhopa. From Zorowar Singh descended Kishora Singh, and from him Golab Singh, Dhian Singh, and Seocheit Singh, the three brothers now in the service of Maharajah Ranjeet Singh.

On the death of Cheit Singh, he also left three sons, named Rakhar Deo, Devi Singh, and Bir Singh, who, when young, were taken by their mother to the left bank of the Satledge, on which side of the river they still reside near a place called Gangu̇wala, in the hills. One of them, Devi Singh, presented himself at one time before the Maharaja and entered his service; but one day, in the presence of his Highness, he said something offensive to the other members of the family, on which account, Raja Seocheit Singh treated him with such indignity, that, from a dread of losing his life, he recrossed the Satledge, and has never appeared at court since.

The rise of the present possessors of Jammoo

at the court of Lahore may he traced to the time of Mian Mota. During the lifetime of that chief, the Maharaja assigned in jaghir to Sirdar Hukma Singh Chimni the territory lying in the vicinity of Jammoo. Having possessed himself of it, the Sirdar aspired to add Jammoo also to his acquisitions. With that view he collected a large force, and proceeded against the place. Mian Mota, who had been allowed to retain the country by the ruler of Lahore, prepared to oppose the invasion. A great part of his troops consisted of the native Rajputs. Mian Golab Singh and Dhian Singh, together with their father, Kishora Singh, were also among the number. These men with a trusty band of their own followers were appointed to protect one of the gateways of the city named Goendwala. No sooner had Hukma Singh appeared before the place than he encountered a warm reception. Both parties fought desperately.. At length the assailants were defeated and obliged to take flight. In the course of this action, Golab Singh was distinguished for his energy and bravery, and soon afterwards, Mian Mota being summoned to the court, Golab Singh accompanied him there. One day, in speaking of the battle, the courage displayed by Golab Singh was the universal theme of admiration. The Maharaja immediately sent for Golab Singh to his presence; and being as young and active as he was brave, he entertained him in his service among the *Ghorcheras* on a salary of two rupees a day, in which situation he remained for three years.

In the meantime, a person named Sathru assassinated Mian Mota, the patron of Golab Singh. After the commission of the act, the assassin came to Lahore and entered the service of Kour Kharak Singh, which exasperated Golab Singh, who meeting with Sathru in one of his rides, resented the murder of his patron by shooting Sathru to death, and sought safety with Jemadar Khoshal Singh, who at that period stood very high in the favour of Ranjeet Singh. The case was reported to the Maharaja;, who, after inquiring into the facts, sent for Golab Singh and pardoned him, without remorse for the crime which he had perpetrated. About the same time, his Highness placed Golab Singh in charge of a party of sixty Sowars, and gave him the district Nihal in jaghir, yielding a revenue of 12,000 rupees, in lieu of which he was bound to furnish fifty additional Sowars. His influence was rising, and he met with rapid promotion. Dhian Singh, his younger brother, who was also engaged in the immediate service of the Maharaja, now began to attract the favour of his Highness. At the age of fifteen he was charged with the Deodhee, and in the same year Rajah Seocheit Singh, the youngest of the three brothers, who was then quite a boy, also attended the court, where his engaging qualities likewise met with particular favour from the Maharaja, who became so fond of him that he would never allow him to be absent from his presence. Dhian Singh received a jaghir of 2000 rupees before he had been a year at court.

At that period the three brothers were known by the title of Mians; but Golab Singh being constantly absent, either on duty with the troops of the Maharajah on their foreign expeditions or at his home, was little seen or known at court.

In the year 1816, Mian Kishora Singh, the father of Dhian Singh, was raised by the Sikh chieftain to the Raj of Jammoo when the administration of the place was conducted by Golab Singh, who, shortly after that event, reported to the Maharaja that he had attacked and killed Mian Didoo, one of the same family, who had for a long time past been leading a predatory and independent life, and exciting disturbances in the country near Jammoo. To mark his approbation of Golab Singh's conduct on that occasion, the Maharaja was pleased to confer on him another jaghir of 12,000 rupees, besides other honorary distinctions; but his attendance at court was merely confined to the festivals of the Bisakhi Maghi and the Desahira, when he received the usual *Khilats* and returned to Jammoo.

Mian Kishora Singh, who though not considered the rightful heir, was called by his subjects Raja, having died, Ranjeet Singh, at the request of his favourites, the sons of the deceased, proceeded towards Jammoo to perform the rites of condolence. On that occasion he invested them with *Khilats*, in return for which proof of his consideration his Highness demanded a Nazarana from them; and the three brothers exerted themselves to satisfy the demand.

While at Jammoo, Ranjeet Singh conferred the title of the Raja of Jammoo on Golab Singh, and that of Bhadarwal on Seocheit Singh, his brother.

In the year 1828, on the festival of the *Bisakhi*, Mian Dhian Singh, who now became a great favourite with the Maharaja, received the title of Raja of Bhimber, which place had been seized from Sultan Khan.

The ceremony was performed with great state; and to mark the estimation in which Ranjeet Singh held him, he added to it the title of Raja of Rajas, directed the officers of his court to present Nazars to him, and to regard the newly created Raja as his principal minister; while a proclamation was issued, that if any one in future called him Mian he should be fined 1000 rupees, and that if not a public servant, he should lose his nose and ears.

Raja Sultan Khan of Bhimber was a brave man and a good soldier. On the occasion when Ranjeet Singh occupied the territory of Saheb Singh, which consisted of Gujrat, &c., he summoned also the Bhimber chief to attend the court. As a close intimacy existed between him and the late ruler of Gujrat, he refused to comply with his Highness's order for fear of being taken prisoner; the Maharaja was offended at the refusal, and despatched two battalions under the command of Faqir Azizuddin, against Mangladour. Sultan Khan attacked them unawares, and cut down about six hundred men of the Faqir's party, the rest of whom sought safety in immediate retreat. This failure inflamed the fury of Ranjeet Singh: Diwan Mhokem Chand was then sent with a larger and fresh force: still Sultan Khan made preparations to give a warm reception to his enemies. The Diwan, foreseeing that he would not be able to compel the hill chief by the force of arms, spread the net of intrigues; and with this view made overtures of peace. The simple chief was deceived, and induced to accompany the Diwan to the court, where he was received at first with distinction. His Highness seated him on a chair, made him a *Sirwarna** of hundreds of rupees; besides which he granted him an elephant with a silver howda, and a horse with a golden saddle, and recalled the troops which were sent against his territory. When the safe return of his troops was reported, the Maharaja again called him to the *Darbar*; and, considering him a dangerous character, ordered him to be apprehended and confined, where he remained six years. Bhia Ram Singh, a native of India, commanding the troops of Kour Kharak Singh, was sent to introduce his Highness's authority in his territory. No sooner had he accomplished this object than the Bhia began to make irruptions into the Rajouree territory. At this time, Ata

* An offering of money to an honoured friend or relative to be distributed in alms.

Mahomed Khan being the ruler of Kashmir sent his troops to assist Agar Khan the Raja of Rajouree on one hand, while Vazir Rohilla Khan, the Raja of Ponch, with all his available troops, proceeded to aid him on the other. A battle ensued between the two parties, in which the son of Rohilla was killed; but victory remained undecided, and, in consequence, Ranjeet Singh's troops returned to Lahore without success. Afterwards Agar Khan, foreseeing that he would at last fail, sent an agent to his Highness's court to acknowledge his obedience. The next year Bhia Ram Singh again attacked Rajouree. Agar Khan was unprepared to defend himself, and took flight. The Bhia set his seraglio on fire, and plundered and ravaged the city. Agar Khan sent back the treaty which was concluded last year between himself and his Highness, to say, that, by the conduct of the Bhia, it was annulled; on which the Maharaja blamed his officer, and restored the chief to Rajouree, on condition that he would assist him to take Kashmir.

His Highness now made preparation to

conquer the valley of Kashmir; and with this view sent a large army against that place. It was at that time governed by Azim Khan, who, on the approach of the Sikhs, by the advice of Agar Khan and Rohilla Khan, spread a rumour that Ranjeet Singh's advanced troops were defeated. This report raised the peasantry, who harassed the Sikh army so much that the Maharaja was obliged to return to Lahore. In their retreat they were attacked and plundered by Agar Khan and Rohilla Khan, through whose territories they passed. This treacherous conduct enraged the Maharaja to a high degree, and from the same moment he was determined to exterminate these two chiefs. Soon after he released Sultan Khan with this view; and exacted a solemn engagement from him to assist the Maharaja in occupying Kashmir: and to remove the recollection of the distresses experienced by him during his confinement, he was now treated with the highest consideration and distinction. Ranjeet Singh then made preparations to renew his expedition against Kashmir. Misser Diwan

Chand, at the head of a large army, and in company of Sultan Khan, proceeded to his destination. During his progress towards Kashmir, the Diwan secured the alliance of all the hill chiefs, and among others that of Agar Khan, and held out to him assurances of pardon for his past conduct, and favour and consideration in future; but Agar Khan, being sensible of the offence which he had given to the Sikhs in their last expedition, made his escape. At the recommendation of Diwan Chand, the Maharaja exalted Rahmatulla Khan, his brother, to his *musnad*,* on condition of aiding the Sikhs to conquer Kashmir.

On the return of the army from the conquest of Kashmir, Sultan Khan was accordingly restored to a part of his territory; while Rahmatulla Khan, the chief of Rajouree, who had been very useful to the Maharaja on that occasion, was assured by his Highness that, as long as he had a beard (holding it with his hand), he should continue in possession of his country without molestation. Hitherto Ranjeet Singh

* Throne.

adheres to his promise, notwithstanding that the Jammoo family have often proposed to assume his territory.

Having failed in their object with the Maharaja, Raja Golab Singh tried to accomplish it by other means. When he returned from the expedition against Sayed Ahmed, he brought Sultan Khan and Rahmatulla Khan, who had accompanied him to Jammoo, and detained them two months. During their detention they were treated with outward marks of consideration, while Golab Singh was secretly engaged in the design of seizing and confining them. He invited them to his house; but Rahmatulla Khan, aware of the plot, went there without sitting down, and taking immediate leave of the Raja, returned to his camp, and escaped to Rajouree in safety. In the morning, when Golab Singh went towards the tents of Rahmatulla Khan, he was vexed and disappointed that he had been foiled in his intention of seizing the chief. Sultan Khan was taken afterwards to the fort of Rhiasi, where he died last year. His property, and the little territory which was left to him, were seized by the treacherous Raja, and his family removed to Jammoo.

It has been stated that the Bhimber Raj was conferred on Dhian Singh; and that the territory of Ponch is now in possession of Hira Singh. A jaghir of 2,000 rupees was afterwards settled on the late chief of that place, Sher Jung Khan, at the recommendation of Jemadar Khoshal Singh. But last year some of the servants of Raja Dhian Singh, on account of Sher Jung Khan running away with a woman of the district of Chapral, with whom he fell in lòve, having killed him, his jaghir was resumed by Dhian Singh. The murderer was also soon after killed by the servants of Sher Jung Khan. No individual of any influence has been now left in the hills who can dispute the authority of the Jammoo family. One of the illegitimate sons of Sultan Khan is in the service of Ranjeet Singh, and is in the receipt of ten rupees a-day. He is under the command of Sirdar Lehna Singh, Majithia.

LIST OF PLACES HELD IN JAGHIR BY RAJA GOLAB SINGH, SHOWING THE REVENUE OF EACH DISTRICT.

Names of Places.	Amount of Revenue.	Remarks.
Jummoo and fort of Kilas.	92,225	Taken from Rajah Cheit Singh in 1814.
Province . .	83,391	Ditto from Mian Anwer Singh, in 1814.
Purmandil . .	15,392	Ditto from Dewan Singh in 1814.
Bulwia Charia .	26,879	Ditto from Raja Cheit Singh, in 1814.
Pooma . . .	17,556	Ditto from Raja Soltan Khan, in 1823.
Anderwah . .	92,145	Ditto from Raja Cheit Singh, in 1823.
Yahdial . . .	8,116	Ditto from Raja Cheit Singh, in 1824.
Rihasi . . .	57,262	Ditto from Dal Singh, in 1814.
Hartal . . .	7,512	Ditto from Mian Dewan Singh, in 1814.
Seocheit Garh . .	5,675	Ditto by Golab Singh, from his brother, 1814.
Aknur . . .	29,719	Ditto from Mian Alam Singh, in 1822.
Kishtwar . .	120,595	Ditto from Raja Tegh Chand, in 1824.
Khera . . .	7,553	Ditto from Mian Badun Singh, in 1824.
Kermachi . .	12,930	Ditto from Mian Bahadur Chand, in 1824.
Badharwal . .	23,190	Ditto from Namdar Khan, in 1824.
Sad Garh . .	7,520	Ditto from Fateh Singh, in 1815.
Ram Garh . .	17,187	Ditto from Raja of Kishtwar, in 1824.
Ogarun . . .	37,625	Ditto from Deo Chand, in 1824.
Bahree . . .	10,302	Ditto from Dial Singh China, in 1824.
Bhimber . .	2,687	Ditto from Raja Cheit Singh, in 1824.
Dehra Baba Nanak .	637	Ditto from Baba Fateh Singh, in 1824.
Lala Chobarah .	27,019	Ditto from Bhag Hulo-Singh Holsuwalia, 1824.
Arz Garh . .	6,225	Ditto from Mian Dewan Singh, in 1824.
Deo Lasia . .	13,280	Ditto from Raten Deo, in 1824.
Chetor Garh . .	6,980	
Chini . . .	9,667	Ditto from Deal Singh Chiniwala, in 1840.
Total Rupees .	7,37,287	

List of Jaghirs held by RAJA DHIAN SINGH, showing the Amount of each District.

Names of Places.	Amount of Revenue.			Remarks.
Jhapal	10,972	0	0	Taken from Rajah Sultan Khan in 1824.
Kotli	3,980	0	0	Ditto ditto ditto.
Mangla Deo . .	28,681	14	0	Ditto ditto ditto.
Panadar . . .	16,881	0	0	Ditto ditto ditto.
Noshehrah . . .	15,304	7	9	Ditto ditto ditto.
Khoma	11,892	11	3	Ditto ditto ditto.
Walabal. . . .	15,652	0	0	Ditto ditto ditto.
Aman Garh . .	18,923	1	0	Ditto ditto ditto.
Jaghir Shahbaz .	9,965	1	0	Ditto ditto ditto.
Hawali	20,852	0	0	Taken from Rohilla Khan in 1824.
Mondi	28,281	15	0	Ditto ditto ditto.
Sobun	21,442	2	0	Ditto ditto ditto.
Bhairam Girda .	3,768	3	0	Ditto ditto ditto.
Tat Ders . . .	4,751	6	6	Ditto ditto ditto.
Poneh	7,642	8	0	Ditto ditto ditto.
Pargana . . .	69,729	0	0	Ditto ditto ditto.
Islambad . . .	4,181	12	0	Ditto ditto ditto.
Hira Garh . . .	11,511	0	0	Ditto ditto ditto.
Pattan	4,233	0	0	Ditto ditto ditto.
Mandahar . . .	22,853	10	0	Ditto ditto ditto.
Golab Garh . .	23,106	0	3	Ditto ditto ditto.
Beaupas . . .	8,825	0	0	Ditto ditto ditto.
Emnabad . . .	4,375	0	0	Taken from the wife of Bhag Singh in 1837.
Mindki	3,505	0	0	Ditto ditto ditto.
Euosuf Garh . .	3,[illegible]00	0	0	Ditto ditto ditto.
Ramesir . . .	13,100	0	0	Ditto ditto ditto.
Azizpore . . .	1,000	0	0	Ditto ditto ditto.
Narangpore. . .	600	0	0	Ditto ditto ditto.
Makanpore . . .	1,800	0	0	Ditto ditto ditto.
Total Rupees .	291,112	12	9	

RAJA SOCHEIT SINGH.

Names of Districts.	Amount of Revenue.	Remarks.
Bandralta	84,000	Taken from Raja Bhopdeo in 1823.
Janganu	11,050	Ditto from Raja Cheit Singh of Jammoo, and given to Seocheit Singh in 1830.
Mankot	22,100	Ditto from Raja Tori Singh, and given to Seocheit Singh in 1834.
Phidoo	12,215	Ditto from Raja Abhar Singh, and given to Seocheit Singh in 1831.
Adhar Sabar . . .	6,100	Ditto ditto ditto.
Khok	3,025	Ditto ditto ditto.
Darekdul Kala . .	3,035	Ditto ditto ditto.
Sandri Kot . . .	7,100	Ditto ditto ditto.
Samba	27,200	Taken from Ram Singh, and given to Seocheit Singh in 1832.
Samrath	12,250	Ditto from Raja of Jammoo, and given to Seocheit Singh in 1832.
Seocheit Garh . .	7,650	Ditto from Gormukh Singh, and given to Seocheit Singh in 1828.
Atal Garh . . .	16,050	Ditto ditto ditto.
Manajeke	11,100	Taken from Kalalwalia, and given to Seocheit Singh in 1836.
Dera Din Puneh . .	27,500	Ditto from Abdul Mahomed Khan in 1834.
Villages in the neighbourhood of Lahore.	6,900	
Nao Shehra . . .	6,140	Taken from Rajkouran, and given to Seocheit Singh, formerly belonged to Pind Dadan Khan in 1838.
Kotli Sarae . . .	9,100	
Villages in the neighbourhood of Amritsir.	5,050	
Kot Kana . . .	2,300	
Pholalwalah . . .	27,000	Taken from Saheb Singh Bhagee.
Total Rupees .	3,06,865	

RAJA HIRA SINGH.

Names of Districts.	Amount of Revenue.	Remarks.
Chapral	119,250	Taken from in 1834, given by Maharaja.
Zahura	6,877	Ditto ditto ditto.
Chittore	14,253	Ditto ditto ditto.
Hambur	16,992	Taken from Raja Sultan Khan in 1825.
Mirowal	8,760	Ditto from Sokha Singh Bhangee, and given to Hira Singh in 1834.
Kaleta	92,184	Ditto from ditto in 1820.
Villages in the neighbourhood of Lahore.	4,467	Ditto from Raja Sansar Chand in 1830.
Kala Khatae . . .	5,822	
Mosumba Mamla .	40,000	
Hagah Jasrota . .	153,510	
Total Rupees .	4,62,115	

Chapter VIII.

Crossing the river—Jehlam—The town of that name—Its revenue and population—Cultivation of the adjacent country—Timber—Boats used on the river—Coins and other Antiquities discovered by Generals Ventura and Court—Application to Ranjeet Singh for expediting the progress of the Mission.

Crossed the Jehlam on the 19th of February in five large boats built near Pind Dadan Khan. The river is about twelve hundred feet wide, and runs between well-defined banks, but both above and below, it is more wide and spreading. The depth of the stream is nowhere more than ten feet. It is occasionally fordable opposite the town, and almost always so for a few months in some part between it and Chowakan, and likewise below that place; but higher fords are preferred, on account of the stony bottom, and the absence of quicksands. They are sometimes as shallow as two feet. Like the other rivers of the Panjab, the Jehlam usually begins to rise about the beginning of March.

There appears always to have been a town on the banks of the stream on or near the site of the present Jehlam. Close to it there is a considerable mound, in which very old coins and fragments of stone pillars have been found.

Jehlam fell into the power of Ahmed Shah Abdali, and was subordinate to the government of the neighbouring fort of Rohtas. In 1767, when Charat Singh, Ranjeet Singh's grandfather, took Rohtas from the Afghans, Jehlam had a small but very weak brick fort, containing about fifty houses, and there were besides some thirty houses outside the walls. Charat Singh took Jehlam at the same time as Rohtas. It was plundered and burnt by Shah Zaman, who remained forty days near the town on his first expedition to India. On his second expedition he again destroyed the place, and it was on his return from Lahore that he was here obliged to leave his guns. The greater portion of his troops had crossed, and the guns had been brought to the banks of the river ready for embarkation, when the river suddenly swelled, and swept away the sand on which the guns stood: two or three of them were afterwards recovered by Ranjeet Singh. Jehlam was a third time plundered by Abdullah Khan Shahanchi about forty-two years ago.

Charat Singh appointed Dada Ram Singh his manager, and afterwards Sulia Singh, Kathri, held the office for twelve or thirteen years singly, and for five or six years in conjunction with Kan Singh. They paid six hundred manees,* or about three thousand mands † of grain to Government.

About forty years ago the town was given in jaghir to Mith Singh, Bherania, one of the old Sikh Sirdars, who held it for about thirteen years, and after him his son, Jawala Singh, held it for about twenty-two years; but, in 1836, after his death, the Maharaja added it to the numerous other jaghirs of Raja Golab Singh of Jammoo.

The transit duties may amount to 10,000 rupees, and the land revenue from the adjacent villages, and the place itself, may be as much more. The neighbouring jaghir of Sangooree yields about 18,000 rupees per annum.

* A weight of about fifteen pounds.

† A weight of about eighty pounds.

The town now contains, they say, about two thousand people, but apparently a thousand more. Timber is brought from Aen on the Jehlam, and bamboos from Chowakan, on a branch of that river. Grain is brought here from various places, and sent to the south and west.

The bed of the Jehlam becomes rocky at Myee Mangul, about ten kos above Jehlam, on the left bank, where it is swept on three sides by the river, and has a fort, strong chiefly from its situation, held by Kharak Singh.

The river Jehlam passes through Kashmir. Before it enters that valley it is a very small stream in breadth. Below Islamabad, about eighteen kos to the north-east of Kashmir, it is joined by several streams, and assumes the name of Behat, by which name it is known throughout the valley. Five kos farther it is joined by another stream, and from thence swells into a large river. On its appearance in the plains it takes the name of Jehlam.

On the right bank to the south of the town stands the tomb of a Sikh Sirdar, who was killed by the men of Mr. Holmes's battalion in the Sikh service, when the former attempted to take away by force a boat in which the baggage of that officer was being crossed over.

Rice has been cultivated for many years: two years ago the sugar-cane was introduced, for which the soil is found favourable.

Boats can go as high up as Chowakan, sixteen kos; the country beyond is very lovely; Dhongah, twenty-nine kos.

The best kind of wood used in building is that called Diar. It grows in the Himmalya, and when the snow melts in the months of March, April, and May, it is brought down the various streams into the river Jehlam, and is now collected by Government and sold to the public. The trees are not felled, and only such reach the river as are torn from their roots by the force of torrents. It is calculated that the average annual supply may amount to a thousand pieces: some of these are sixty feet and upwards in length, and two such will make a boat of eight hundred *mands* burthen. The people do not appear to care about the age of the timber, so long as it is of good size; but for boats they prefer such as have been seasoned for four or five years. At Aen, the chief mart, a place about sixty miles above Jehlam, one of the finest logs costs sixty rupees: each timber pays a duty of two rupees at three places between Aen and Jehlam, and at Jehlam itself a duty of 25 per cent. is levied if taken below the town for sale, but if sold in the town the duty is about 18 per cent. only, while none whatever is levied on wood used to construct the boats at the place. The timber is not usually taken below Pind Dadan Khan, though some are sold at Khushah, and once in two or three years a few are sent down to Multan, where large timber is very scarce; but at Pind Dadan Khan three or four boats are annually built, and after being laden with grain, cotton, or salt, they are taken to the lower parts of the Panjab and sold; but though rafts are seldom taken below Khoshab, yet many pieces of timber are carried by the violence of floods below that place. At night they pass by the towns and villages on the river without being observed.

On the accession of Raja Golab Singh to the jaghirs of Aen and of the neighbouring districts, which he had long been wishing to possess, he monopolized the timber trade, and the price of the article is in consequence double what it formerly was.

Other coarse kinds of deal are brought down, but they are not fit to be made into boats. At present there are no logs collected or purchased; much depends on the supply of the present year.

At Jehlam a boat of 200 *mands* will cost 140 rupees, viz., wood 40, iron 40, and labour and sundries 60. A 400 *mand* boat will cost about 400 rupees, viz., wood 100, iron 100, and labour and sundries 200.

A boat is usually made in five or six months, and will last good for eight or even twelve years, after which repairs will keep it together for two or three years longer; but at the end of that time the wear and tear renders it useless and it is broken up. The boats are flat-bottomed, long, and capacious.

Halted at Jehlam on the 20th inst. to

enable the baggage to come across from the other side. Plenty of supplies procurable; water from the river and the wells close by. Ground of encampment amidst ravines. It is near this spot the battle between Alexander the Great and the Hindu monarch Porus is said to have been fought. MM. Ventura and Court have excavated many coins in the vicinity bearing Greek legends.

20th.—Halted. A letter was despatched to Ranjeet Singh acknowledging the receipt of two from his Highness, in which he informed Colonel Wade that, agreeably to his request, he had sent a copy of the tripartite treaty for the information and execution of his officers; and that his agent, Rae Govindjus, who had remained behind, had been strictly ordered to join the Mission. It was announced in reply to the Maharaja that the Shah Zada had crossed the Jehlam, and would soon arrive at Peshawr, when it was intended to encamp at about two kos from the city, in order to prevent the chance of squabbles between the citizens and the camp followers. It was requested at the same time that his Highness would be pleased to send a general *Parwana*, or order, in the name of all his officers in authority there, that in case of any requisitions being made on them for their assistance, they would comply with them at once, without the delay of a reference to the Maharaja; and that a prohibition should be issued to the inhabitants of Peshawr generally not to aid or hold any communications with the enemy, on the acknowledged principle that the enemies of one state were the enemies of the other, and warning them that any one found guilty of breaking the order should be exemplarily punished; and, lastly, begging that as Rae Govindjus was old, and had let the opportunity of coming with the two howitzers (on their way to join the Mission from India) pass, Lala Kishan Chand, who was heard to have come over to the right bank of the Satledge, might be desired to join the Mission and remain with it, that the transaction of business between the two states might not be delayed.

Chapter IX.

Rohtas—Anecdotes—The people of Kamlagarh—A halt —News from Kabul—Bakrala—Dhamuk—The *Khilat* —Kasi Nala—Ruins—The Ghakars—Jherar—Rawat Kee Sarae—Manakiala—Researches of General Ventura—The Sohan—Rawelpindee—Gardens of Jahanghir —Traditions—Afghans in the hills—The Indus—Operations of Lieut. Mackeson and Mr. Lord.

Started early in the morning of the 21st on the way to Rohtas. First part of the road good and level. About the fifth kos a ridge of low hills, where the route follows the course of the Bakrala *Nala* in all its windings through the hills, crossing the stream some five or six times, a heavy road for artillery from sand and stones, but practicable. The distance to Rohtas is said to be about nine miles. Just after leaving our encampment near Jehlam the site of the ancient town is conspicuous on the left hand. For a few kos the soil appears good and is well cultivated: there are but few trees and the hills look bare.

At about two miles and a half there is a

well, lined with masonry, and a short distance on the right a small village. Two kos further there is another small village, and then the site of a fort or Sarae, with a small village at the base of the hills, about a mile and a half to the north. About the sixth mile the ground is undulating, and though, as before stated, it appears to be generally good for crops, yet it is here and there stony: after which the sandy bed of a hill-stream is reached, and the road lies along it for about a mile and a half farther, when a sharp turn to the left is made, and the fort of Rohtas suddenly comes in view. The road continues to wind by it: wheel carriages proceeding along the same road for a short distance, turn to the right. About half a mile beyond the fort the road descends and again crosses the Bakrala, the bed of which is wide. Less than half a mile from its western bank stands a fine Sarae built by Shah Jahan, the Mogul Emperor.

The hills through which the road runs so far do not appear to be above two hundred feet in height, and the *Nala* has formed its channel by continued reflections from point to point. The secondary bed may be a hundred feet wide, but when in flood it extends from rock to rock, and may vary from four hundred to eight hundred feet in width. During the cold season there appears to be only a few inches of water in the *Nala*, but when in flood it is three, four, or five feet deep, and the communication between the plains and these hills is cut off. The hills are composed of sandstone, while the flat tops are frequently covered with pebbles and stones of various kinds. The sandstone is of a whitish or grey colour, very friable, and such as is generally found in all the streams of the Panjab. In many parts there is a layer of earth above the sandstone, as if the country had been the bed of a lake. One spot near the *Nala* looked like a volcanic irruption; the earth about it was red as if it had been burnt.

I went to see the fort of Rohtas, which is going to ruin. Within its walls is a mere village. In circumference it may be about two kos. It was built by Sher Shah, the usurper of the government of the Emperor Hamyun, about three hundred and five years ago, to prevent any invasion from Afghanistan into India. It is stated that Sher Shah brought people from various parts who were acquainted with such constructions, and followed in some measure the plan of the fort of the same name in the province of Behar, which he had taken by stratagem. It took twelve years and one month in building, and, including the pay of the soldiery stationed in it, is said to have cost 11,107,975. 6. 3. It was calculated to hold a garrison of three thousand cavalry and fifty thousand infantry, and to mount a hundred guns. It contains one tank, three wells, and two *Baolis*. One of the wells is about ninety cubits (a hundred and thirty-five feet): and one of the *Baolis* are about eighty cubits.

Ahmed Shah took the place; and towards the end of his reign, Baland Khan, who had been governor of Multan, held it on the part of the Afghans with a garrison of three thousand men, but no guns. Seventy-one years ago (1768) Charat Singh, with five hundred Sowars of his confederacy, Gujar Singh, with about four hundred Sowars, two thousand infantry, and a thousand people of the country, with a few guns, laid siege to it.

The artillery played with some effect from the adjoining eminence of Govindgarh ; but after an investment of three months, the place fell chiefly through famine. Himmat Khan, the chief landed proprietor in the neighbourhood, together with others of consequence, had been killed by Baland Khan, who appears to have been disliked. He was taken prisoner by the Sikhs, and sent to Ramnagar. Raja Ghiasuddin, the son of Himmat Khan, was left governor. His cousin, Nur Khan, succeeded him, and held the office for thirty years. He was succeeded by Faizdad Khan. In 1808 the Sikhs placed their own *Thana* or garrison in the fort, and gave Himmat Khan's family a fourth share of the revenues; but five years ago, in lieu of it, a jaghir in villages, worth about five thousand rupees a-year, was settled on them. Misser Jassa, of the *Toshekhana*, was then made collector on the part of the Maharaja, but two years and a half ago Raja Golab Singh succeeded in getting charge of the district himself. It consists of sixty-seven small villages, and extends six kos to the south, seven to the west, and about eight to the north ; to the eastward it is scarcely beyond the fort, which contains about three hundred and fifty houses and twelve hundred people, chiefly Mahomedans. Artificial irrigation is little known: sugar-cane has been lately brought to cultivation, and has been much encouraged by Golab Singh.

We encamped here on a fine open piece of ground to the south-west of the Sarae and opposite to the fort: supplies scarce; water good from the wells and streams. During the Maharaja's journey he occupies the same ground in a mud building, with a small garden erected by his order.

There is a person here named Rahmat Ali Khan, a zemindar or landholder of the district, who is a living history of it, and amused us by relating some stories. One of them was, that in the neighbourhood of Rohtas there are two mineral springs which possess a purgative quality. He gave us the following strange anecdotes:—

It is superstitiously stated and generally believed by people in this quarter that Sultan Mahmud of Ghazni, on his expedition against India, was accompanied by some saints, who always assisted him in his operations, and in consequence of their presence he generally gained many victories without any personal exertions on his part. Among others Imam Walihaq also attended him.

Mahmud laid siege to the fort of Sialkot; but the place was well defended, and the siege was prolonged for a long time, and the Sultan became much distracted. One night the Imam professed that he had dreamt a dream; that if Pir Kilk, one of his disciples, would cut off his own head and strike it against the door of the fort, the shutters would be battered in pieces and the fort would be captured. No sooner was the dream explained than the disciple cut off his head with his own hand and furiously struck it against the shutters of the fort; and it had the effect the Imam had told him! the place was captured, and the chief and the people in it voluntarily turned Mussulmans.

The people are under the impression that ancient monarchs not only ruled the world, but had some share in the Divine power also; as several stories regarding them are foolishly related and believed, and their noble and illustrious actions are ascribed rather to their miraculous power than to their wisdom and personal valour. It is also worthy of remark that one of them whose shrine is at Sialkot, being sent against the old town of Aknur, in the district of the same name, invited the people to submit at once to him, which they declined. Being irritated he invoked some curses on the place, and prayed that its inhabitants might be converted into stone. God accepted the prayer of the Pir, and the people were petrified as they were sleeping, walking, or standing, and in that state were to be seen at the present day!

Another story is that a tribe known by the name of Bhajnal, inhabiting the hills near Aknur, confidently believe that there are particular clouds on the tops of their hills which never move from them to any other, but pour out their rain only on their own land. There is a party of Jogis or Hindu Faqirs living in that quarter, who are supposed to have these clouds in their power, and whenever water is required they can make the rain to fall. For this reason, these Jogis exact a share from the produce of every field. If any refuse, the next year the bounty of heaven is either kept from his cultivation or the crop destroyed by a heavy fall of hail! Such is the extent of their superstition.

I heard also a very curious story of the inhabitants of the fort of Kamlagarh, which ought not to be passed over in silence. This fort is situated on the top of a high hill in the Chamba territory, and appears to have been erected rather by the hand of nature than of art. It is reported to be impregnable. Ranjeet Singh has often attempted to capture it, but in vain. There is no passage but through a narrow pass, which is strongly defended.

The inhabitants hold no kind of communication with any foreigners. They have posts all round the place. If any stranger approaches he is killed without hesitation. Once in a whole reign they take their ruler into the fort on his accession, and show him all the treasures and the public property inside, and then bring him back and send him to his capital. On this occasion none of the attendants of the chief is allowed to accompany him; they are all left at some distance from the place. The people inside grow and manufacture everything they require. The fortification is said to be about twelve kos in circuit. The inhabitants of it pay no revenue to their rulers, but put it aside, and only use the share of government on great emergencies.

There are some other tribes also subject to the Chamba Raja, who never allow the officers of state to enter their territory, and only pay revenue at pleasure. When their crops are ripe and cut down they collect the government share in some appointed place, and leave the Raja's people to take it away without exchanging a word with them. From these accounts it will be observed how cautious these people are of their liberty, and what little authority their ruler possesses over them.

22nd.—Halted at Rohtas on account of a heavy fall of rain the last evening. The tents got all wet. A letter was written to the Maharaja in consequence of a report having been received from Captain (now Major) Ferris that the two companies of Native infantry escorting two howitzers to the Shah Zada's camp had been detained at Harikee for some time, from no person belonging to his Highness, as had been requested, having been sent to conduct the party as was necessary through the Panjab. It was requested that some one might be deputed with the least possible delay.*

* "In the evening Ferris and I rode down to the Ghât to see what facilities there were in readiness for crossing the Sutledge to-morrow; but on our way we met with a sepoy, who had been despatched early in the morning to collect the boats, &c., and who was returning to inform us that the authorities on the other side of the river have refused us a passage, as no 'purwannah' (a written order) from the Maharaja, directing our admittance into the Panjab, had been received by them. We, nevertheless, rode on, and on our reaching the banks we sent a message to the chief at Harikee, the village situated opposite to the Ghât, requesting him to cross and confer with us; but after waiting an hour, our messenger came back, accompanied by a common sowar, whom the insolent fellow had sent over in his stead, and to whom, beyond a question, F. would have nothing to say. We accordingly returned to Makhoo, and a letter was immediately despatched to the assistant political agent at Lodianah, informing him of the treatment we had met with, and the delay that was likely to ensue."—*Barr's Journal*, pp. 50, 51.

The Maharaja was also reminded of the stipulation in the treaty which required the nomination of a Mahomedan officer of rank to command the contingent for the service of the Shah Zada, and requested to relieve our anxiety on that as well as with regard to other important points to which he had already been urged to give his earliest attention.

News was received from Kabul stating that the alarm of Dost Mahomed Khan was increasing at the rapid progress of Shah Shuja, accompanied by the British army on one side, and Shah Zada Taimur, assisted by the Sikhs, on the other. Symptoms of disaffection on the part of his people are also announced, in consequence of which he is said to have sent messengers to recall his son Akram Khan from Khulam. Strict orders were also sent by him to his son Mahomed Akbar Khan on no account to proceed beyond Jalalabad. The Candahar Sirdars are reported to have been engaged in removing their property and family to some secure place; and that they were anxiously looking for assistance from

Persia, on the arrival of which they would contend with the Shah, otherwise they would not make any resistance. Dost Mahomed is said to have sent a copy of the proclamation issued by the British Government against himself to the Persian monarch, urging him to send an army without delay to his support.

A deputation has arrived in our camp from the Logar people, consisting of four respectable persons, viz., Fateh Ullah Khan, Zohuruddin Khan, Zainulabuddin Khan, and Kamal Khan. The Logaris are a numerous tribe, and occupy the hills about seven miles to the south-east of Kabul. They are the first who have declared their devotion to the cause of the Shah in that distant quarter.

23*rd.*—Marched before sunrise, and encamped at Bakrala, distant ten kos. The general direction is north-westerly. At about a mile passed a *Baoli:* about two miles a small *Nala,* which has cut a track for itself in the valley, within which it winds. The road lies along the *Nala* for nearly two miles, and then ascends some hills about five hundred feet high, leaving the *Nala* on the right hand. Between the fifth and sixth mile there are two tanks, on the right hand; the first is an old one, the second is now being dug by order of Raja Dhian Singh, the prime minister, for the accommodation of passengers. There are also a few shops close to these tanks. Between the sixth and seventh mile the *Nala* is again seen on the right hand, at the distance of less than half a mile. It joins the Rohtas *Nala* about a mile and a half above the fort. About the seventh mile there is another appearance of a volcano. At the ninth mile the road descends rapidly, and at the base of the hill runs the Rohtas *Nala*, about four hundred feet wide in sand, and in a ravine of very variable dimensions; the hills are covered with low bushes, and there is scarcely any cultivation except close to the two tanks above mentioned. Every spot available in the ravine of the *Nala* is, however, under cultivation. The road, as it is now, is quite impracticable for wheel carriages; but they can reach the place by the bed of the *Nala,* which may be four or five miles longer than the straight road.

Bakrala is a small village, and belongs to Misser Beli Ram, the *Toshekkhana;* no supplies, bad encamping-ground; water is from the stream. The village is about half a mile from our encampment, and on the summit of a hill.

A part of the Bakrala road was made by General Ventura, but the Sikh Government is averse to such works, being of opinion that improving them only prepares the way for a foreign enemy from the west, who would thereby be able to enter their country without obstruction. Formerly the passage was very dangerous from freebooters, and travellers could not pass but by *kafilas.* A single traveller cannot now pass with safety: the neighbouring hills are inhabited by a wild, predatory race of people.

To the north-west of this place lie the districts of Dhani and Gheb, celebrated for a breed of good horses and mules.

Owing to the difficulty of the road the baggage had not entirely arrived late in the evening, and we therefore halted on the 24th at Bakrala.

25th.—Started at sunrise, and encamped at Dhamuk, distance about eight miles. Route following the course of the Rohtas stream, which flows in a ravine with very steep sides. It is by no means an easy passage, from rocks and stones being strewed over the sandy bed. The strata are quite perpendicular, and run north-easterly and south-easterly. About the fifth mile the *Nala* bends to the left, and the road leads straight across the projection round which the stream winds: in one part of which the road is precipitous on both sides. Between the sixth and seventh mile the Rohtas *Nala* turns to the left, and the road, which is good though narrow, within a mile of the village, after a sudden and steep ascent along the side of a hill, leads to a fine table-land, on which the village is situated, but the land about it is cut into deep ravines. Excepting across the ridge at the ninth mile, the road is practicable for wheel carriages, but the ridge may be avoided by following the course of the *Nala.* The summits of the hills are about three hundred feet above the *Nala;* there are no signs of population in these hills.

Dhamuk is a small village; its supplies are scarce. Water is obtained from a neighbouring stream, and is good. The place is held in jaghir by Chatar Singh, Atariwala, and was bestowed on his family by Ranjeet Singh's grandfather. Wheat is cultivated, and grows well. No irrigation from wells. At present it is subject to a good deal of oppression from the Sirdar's managers; the Jaghirdar provides two hundred and fifty horsemen, but is liable to occasional exactions, which obliges him to oppress in his turn. Being on the high road to Attok, the Sikh troops frequently alight here, and destroy everything, like a flight of locusts. Old coins are found in the vicinity, of the time of Alexander the Great and his successors.

To-day being the festival of the *Eeduzzoha,* the Shah Zada held a darbar. All the

Khawanin who had joined his Royal Highness were admitted to his presence to make their *salam*, as customary on such occasions. They were presented with *khilats*, according to their respective rank. Goats were also distributed among them by Lieutenant-Colonel Wade for their dinners, a present which the Afghans are pleased to receive on the *Eed.*

Every Khan, on joining the camp, expects the present of a *khilat*, or he considers himself disgraced. In consequence of the small supply of articles which we had in the *Toshekhana*, or treasury of the Mission (the Shah Zada having none of his own), and the few additions which had been made by purchase during our stay at Lahore, they began to fail. The Maharaja was therefore requested to send a supply of various articles from his own *Toshekhana*, such things not being procurable in the country, on receipt of which his Government would be duly credited for their amount. On our arrival here a person was sent on to Peshawr, to prepare clothing for the new levies; and General Avitabile, the governor of that territory, was addressed at the same time, to afford him every aid in executing his commission.

A Qasid, who arrived with friendly letters on the part of Mir Alam Khan of Bajour, was dismissed with a reply, desiring that chief to depute his son to pay his respects to the Shah Zada on his arrival at Peshawr. By the same opportunity, and in consultation with the prince, a letter was likewise written to Sadat Khan, the chief of the Momand tribe, inviting him to tender his allegiance to the Shah Zada, either in person, or by deputing his son.

It ought not to be omitted that a Qasid had arrived in our camp at Jehlam, who professed to have been sent by Hafizji, a person possessing great religious influence in Kabul and the Kohistan, where he was said to be engaged by Dost Mahomed Khan in exciting the people to a religious war against the Shah. He brought a message from Hafizji, stating tha although he and others were forced by circumstances to appear hostile to the Shah, yet their real intentions towards his Majesty were as sincere as before. The man, having brought no letter, was disbelieved, and desired to leave the camp and return to Kabul from Dhamuk, with a verbal assurance to Hafizji of being treated with consideration and favour if he proved faithful to the Shah's cause.

As a condition of entertaining them, a written pledge of fidelity was taken here by the Shah Zada from all the *Khawanin*; on their execution of which a fixed allowance was assigned to each for the support of himself and party. Hitherto they had only been receiving daily rations.

26th.—Started early in the morning to Pakake Sarae, about twelve miles distant. At the fourth mile crossed the Kasi *Nala*, which has formed an immense ravine in the high land, which is undulating and broken. The ravine may be three hundred and fifty feet from height to height; but innumerable small ones run into it, which bring the water of the plains on either side into the *Nala* below. There is not much cultivation, but a few small villages to the right and left of the road. Near the tenth mile is a *Pucka* well.

Encampment in the ravine of the Kasi *Nala*: we reached it at the end of the twelfth mile. Country intersected by ravines of the same character as those we had previously crossed. Encamping ground very indifferent, close, and confined; supplies scarce; water good, from a stream.

The aspect of the surrounding country is very wild and bare. Near the camp the ruins of large Sarae of brick and stone, built by Aurangzeb, the Mogul Emperor. Here was an old city named Paka, some traces of which are still visible. The city was burnt by the Afghans; afterwards by the Mahrattas, seventy years ago; and then a second time by the Afghans. Neither Charat Singh nor Maha Singh, the ancestors of Ranjeet Singh, extended their conquests to Paka; but Sirdar Gujar Singh of Gujrat took the place from Sultan Mukaram Khan, Ghakar, whose chief place was Perwala, twelve kos to the north. Shadman Khan, his son, is now a pensioner in Jammoo. He was seized by Raja Golab Singh, who suspected him of instigating Shamsuddin

Khan, a conquered dependant of Golab Singh, to rebellion. Shamsuddin owed the Raja 17,000 rupees as arrears of tribute, which he refused to pay; and, in the absence of Golab Singh at Peshawr, seized some places which had formerly belonged to him. On the Raja's return, Shamsuddin Khan fled, but was betrayed by a Gujar, in whose house he had sought safety; for which act the Gujar was rewarded with a horse, a pair of bangles, and a pension of two rupees a-day.

Sugar-cane was formerly cultivated in this part of the country, and rice in large quantities; now wheat and Indian corn only. There are no wells about the place. Golab Singh has held the village for twenty-four years. The frequent passage of troops has led many people to leave the place from the destruction which is caused to the cultivation. The soil is strong and fertile.

The Kasi *Nala* rises near Megra, about ten kos distant. Two miles below Paka it is joined by the Gir *Nala*, and after passing within four miles of Dhamuk, and near to Bishandour, it finds its way into the Jehlam, at Sultanpore, near the hills. Kasi means any low place.

The Ghakars are a very numerous and hardy tribe of high repute; their sway extended from Gujrat, near the Chinab, to Attok and Muzzaffarabad. Ahmad Shah Durani married a daughter of one of their chiefs. The hilly parts were taken from them only eight years ago. Saw a small cupola called the tope of Megra, about five kos north-east.

Several villages round about Paka belong to different members of the Atariwala Sikhs, of whom Sham Singh is the present head.

27th.—Jhirar, a distance of seven miles; the first three miles northerly, the remaining four westerly. The surface of the country irregular.

The *Gir Nala* falls into the Kasi at Paka, and rises immediately to the north of Manakiala. The water from the snowy range falls into the Sohan, which is rather a large river.

There is a tradition that a king named Manak Rae possessed a city which extended from Manakiala to Dhamuk. Near the villages of Mandar, Dehar, Janala, &c., between Paka and Jherar, large square blocks of stone are found lying as in a wall. Janala, one kos from Jherar, left bank of the Nala; similar stones are seen to those between Jherar and Pindi.

About Manakiala pipes of earthenware, three or four inches in diameter, lying horizontally, are also found. The tope is said to be near a spring of water.

It is said that a nephew of Mahmud of Ghazni was taking horses for sale to India, and that the King of Manakiala demanded a tax from him, which he refused. The King took it by force. The Prince went and complained to his uncle, and Mahmud came and plundered the place.

The story is that Ghakars came and settled here eight hundred years ago, from Canaan, in Egypt (the Scriptural Canaan). They were then called Maliks: their chief was Malik Ghula, whence Ghuliana, the place to which they first came. He had four sons, Malik Feiroz, Sultan Hatta, Sultan Adam, and

Sultan Sarang. They then spoke Persian. Malik Ghula, from Ghuliana, came to Dhani Ghebi, and then to Perwala, and built a fort.

Gujar Singh Gujratia took Jherar. It now belongs to Chatar Singh and Karam Singh Atariwala. They got possession of it thirty-two years ago. Raja Golab Singh's lands adjoin.

The usual kinds of grain grow at Jherar; but for the last twelve years the people have not been able to rear grain: they say it becomes scorched before arriving at maturity, but can give no reason for it. Cotton cultivated, but no sugar-canc.

Jherar is a small village. Supplies scanty. Water good, from a stream. Good encamping ground.

Here the Hindu festival of the Holee commenced. The Hindus began to make merry, and have *Natches* to-night.

A letter was addressed by Sir Claude to-day to Ranjeet Singh, informing him of the receipt of news in our camp, that his Highness had been pleased to order his legions to encamp at Shahdera, on their way to Peshawr, and expressing the satisfaction it gave; but that no account had yet been received of the collection of the Mahomedan contingent of five thousand men, which he was to provide according to the treaty for the assistance of Shah Zada Taimur. It was intimated to his Highness that, as the time was short, and did not admit of new levies, it was advisable that he should make a selection of Mahomedans from the whole of his army, and that if the selected number fell short of the five thousand men, he might issue an order to his officers at Peshawr to complete the deficiency by enlisting people in that territory. His Highness was requested that he would send particular injunctions to his Mussulman vassals in that quarter (excluding the Barakzai, who were not perhaps to be implicitly trusted) to assemble at Peshawr, and to entitle themselves to their rights and claims by serving the three Governments on the present occasion with zeal and fidelity. It was suggested also to the Maharaja to send an order for a part of his force now at Peshawr to proceed to Dera Ismael Khan, so as to co-operate on that side with the Shah Zada's troops, by which means the enemy would be alarmed and their attention divided. It was necessary that the Maharaja should be reminded of the necessity of producing his contingent, as we had heard with surprise that nothing had yet been done to collect it; and the plan of creating a diversion by Dera Ismael Khan was one which it was expected that Ranjeet Singh would approve.*

28th.—Rawat Kee Sarae, distant about eight miles. Supplies scarce; water good. West, inclining to the north between two and three miles, is the tope of Manakiala; and about the seventh mile cross a small *Nala*, which joins the Sohan. Very little cultivation, but the country looks less bleak and dreary than that between Dhamuk and Pakaki Sarae. Layers of sandstone are frequent. Burnt red earth seen in the ravines. At Rawat itself a ridge of sandstone rises in upright blocks in

* Both he and Shah Shuja had suggested the importance of such a movement.

some places as high as twenty feet above the surface. These blocks are from four to ten feet square, and the ridge fifteen feet wide. Manakiala appears to be built of the same tough kind of stone as the blocks I have described.

Jagutpore, a village built by the Ghakars, at the same time as Perwala and Dhangali, one kos to the south. Perwala is six kos northward towards the hills. In Perwala is a fort like that of Rohtas, built by the Ghakars about twenty-five years ago. Since the hills were completely subdued by the Sikhs about ten years ago, it has been deserted, and is ruinous. Gujar Singh Gujratia took Jagutpore and Perwala, and went as far as Khanpore, where the Ghakars drove him back. At Jagutpore is a tank in ruins, built by Sultan Mobarek Khan's wife, one hundred and twenty years ago.

Rawat Kee Sarae was built by Sher Shah. The tomb is that of Sultan Sarang Ghakar. He died about one hundred years ago, or more. Sultan Sarang was the chief of Perwala, and is buried to the boundary line of that district and

Jagutpore, which belonged to the Edwal tribe of Ghakars, the largest of all their tribes.

The Sohan river rises twenty kos distant at the Dewat hills on the left bank.

Rawat is included within the jurisdiction of Rawelpindi: no sugar-cane cultivated. Little rain falls here during the months of March, April, and May (as often happens in other parts of the Panjab), during which it is exceedingly hot.

Before the country was conquered by the Sikhs, there was a prolonged famine, from the effects of which it greatly recovered under the good administration of Malka Singh, who was left in charge by Gujar Singh.

On looking at Manakiala it appears to be a hemisphere, perhaps fifty feet in diameter, with a neck of about six feet in height, and springing from a circular base, ornamented with pilasters; one of which, on the east side, is something, it is said, in the Grecian style. The basement, however, as it stands now, is not the lowest story of the building. It is said to rest upon another with a platform of about twenty feet, ornamented with pilasters, &c., in the same manner as the upper one. These pilasters are plain, but well proportioned, and appear only to have been brought to light since General Ventura dug to the bottom, in order to reach the vault in the centre of the building. He likewise cleared away the ruinous parts on the top of the tope, and discovered a well of about ten feet square, which is regularly built of squared stones, and looks now about fifteen or eighteen feet deep. General Ventura penetrated through the bottom of the shaft to satisfy himself that no further relics than those which he had found there were forthcoming.*

The tradition at Rawat is, that on the outside of the hemisphere there was a flight of steps leading to the top, and that on it Manak the king used to review his troops. The outside wall of masonry has nearly all fallen off or been torn away, and much of the upper portion has been removed, which has destroyed the

* They were afterwards offered to Sir Claude Wade, who forwarded them, in the General's name, to the Secretary to the Asiatic Society in Calcutta, the late lamented J. Prinsep, Esq.

regularity of the dome. Most of the stones of which the tope is built were brought from the neighbouring hills, though several of the blocks are of the sandstone common on the spot.

A little to the south of the tope and between it and the village there is a large square well of masonry which has existed from time immemorial; the water in it is good and abundant, and capable of supplying a large encampment for days together. It is ten feet square, and is said to have been built in that shape, in order that each of Manak's four tribes might have a separate place to draw water. The villagers say that the neighbouring ravine exposes every now and then the foundations of buildings. The road passes immediately to the south of the tope; it serves as a haunt for robbers who lie in ambush for a single or two or three travellers, there being no village near it.

Rawelpindee, March 1st.—Marched before sunrise, distance twelve miles, the road winding westerly as far as the right bank of the Sohan, and afterwards north-westerly. The general direction about west-north-west, and the direct distance may be eight miles; the ground gradually falls until, the second or third mile, a range of low hills is reached.

These hills consist of pebbles cemented together; the road over them is passable for wheel carriages, but with great difficulty, it being a high and steep ghat. Above the fourth mile from Rawat, we came to the valley or bed of the Sohan river, which is very picturesque after the bleak plains through which we had been passing. It was bounded by sloping hills sprinkled with green bushes which grew luxuriantly in the ravines; its sides were bounded by precipices more than a hundred feet high. The stream itself spreads over the valley when flooded, and now rolls along over pebbles. Shortly after ascending, we quitted the hilly or broken ground. On the left, a small tower or dome is to be noticed on a hillock which was opened by General Ventura in search of antiquities.

On leaving the banks of the river the town of

Rawelpindee appears in sight, situated on a cultivated plain stretching to the hills, which may be four miles off. There is a higher range of hills about seven miles distant to the north, and one hill with a patch of snow about ten miles. The country is broken here and there by the small *Nalas* which lead in to the Sohan.

The valley of the Sohan may be six hundred feet where narrowest; the stream was about two feet deep, and about two hundred feet broad. In the broken ground between the plain of Rawelpindee and the river, the sandstone again appeared in ridges and perpendicular strata.

Rawelpindee is a small town, and an abundance of supplies procurable; dry Kabul fruits are to be had in plenty. It is surrounded by a mud wall about a mile in circumference: the buildings are generally of mud. Shah Shujah, after his flight from Peshawr, took refuge here, and remained for several years. The house erected by him is still extant, and serves as a residence to the governor of the district, named Bhae Dal Singh, the elder brother of Bhae

Maha Singh, the Sikh officer who attends the Mission.

I may here enumerate that there are about five hundred shops in Rawelpindee:—fifteen blacksmiths, ten goldsmiths, twenty confectioners, ten shops for iron and brass, pots, &c.; twenty shoemakers, fifteen shops of besatis, that is, sellers of combs, scissors, thread, &c.; four hundred shops of cloth merchants, grain merchants, ghee dealers, &c. The entire revenue of the town is 150,000 rupees per annum, including land-tax, transit duties, &c. The town is known for its manufacture of ornamented shoes: there are somewhat more than four thousand people in the town. Bhae Dal Singh is liked by the people, and has had charge of the town for six years.

To the west of the town, five kos distant towards the hills, there is a shrine of a Saint Latif Shah, where a fair is held every year in the month of May or June, where numbers of people are collected from the neighbouring villages and towns, even as far as Peshawr.

2nd.—Halted at Rawelpindee. A vague report was received from Kabul of the intention of the Persians to renew the siege of Herat, to make a diversion in favour of Dost Mahomed Khan. It was further reported that Mahomed Akram Khan, the son of Dost Mahomed Khan, who had been sent towards Kunduz, had concluded a treaty of amity and alliance with Mir Morad Beg, and that Dost Mahomed had illuminated the city of Kabul in honour of the event. It is said that the Amir has failed in his attempt to obtain support from the king of Bokhara, unless one of his sons be allowed to share in the government of Kabul! His troops are reported to have become disaffected towards the Amir, on account of being kept in long arrears of pay, and the citizens to be much alarmed on hearing of the advance of the invading armies. Nightly meetings are held to concert measures the most favourable for their interest.

Letters were received from the Khaibar chiefs declaring their attachment to the Shah. Among others there was a letter from Alam Khan of Bajour, expressing a wish to form a separate alliance with the British government; but as it was not its policy to enter into alliances with the several chiefs of Afghanistan for its own benefit, the proposal was of course declined. The offer of his service was, however, accepted, and he was assured of the confirmation of his existing authority from his Majesty, if he would display his fidelity and adherence to his cause by joining the Shah Zada opportunely.

Lately the brother of Sadat Khan Momand, named Nawab Khan, has joined the camp; but he has not been formally received either by the Shah Zada or Sir Claude, nor distinguished by any marked consideration, as he is known not to be on good terms with his brother, and a letter having been addressed to the latter chief inviting his allegiance, pending the receipt of his reply, it was not considered just to give his brother the usual reception.

Jani Ka Sang, *3rd.*—About twelve or thirteen miles distant, direction westerly, slightly inclining to the north. Outside of Rawelpindee cross a *Nala*, with water running rapidly. About seven miles, cross a smaller *Nala*, and at the twelfth mile cross another stream, country undulating, the latter half stony. Cultivation near Rawelpindee, elsewhere scanty. A few villages here and there. The soil very barren, but in the last few miles large bushes are frequent, among which the olive may be noticed, of the wood of which the natives make beads. The hills are about two miles north of Jani Ka Sang. Between nine and ten miles a Mahomedan tomb. Close to the *Nala*, which runs by Jani Ka Sang, there is a quantity of the hard stone similar to some seen at Rawat.

Sheikh Jam, a rich and pious Darweish, is buried in the village; but his grave is only marked by the earth, according to his own desire. He died about two hundred years ago.

Bahnadra *Nala* rises at Shahditta three kos off.

Jani Ka Sang is a small village, containing about twelve houses of Khatris and twelve houses of Mussulmans. The supplies very scarce. Ground for encamping indifferent; water good.

The Kajri hills about twelve kos to the south.

4*th.*—To Hasan Abdal. At about three miles came to the Pass of Margalla, which is now a paved roadway about twenty feet wide. It was cut through by Akbar the Great, as an inscription on the side of the pass shows. No water near the pass except what is collected from rain in small pools. On the summit of a hill to the right is a tower where a party of ten or twelve matchlockmen is stationed to guard the pass. Formerly the road hereabouts was much infested by robbers; but since the establishment of the above party their depredations have been partly prevented. From hence a road branches off to the Hazara country, about twenty-five kos distant. Another road goes off to Burhan, leaving Hasan Abdal to the right.

The ascent is now slight, and appears never to have been great. The hills are bare, except in the dells to the right and left, where the trees attain to some size. About the sixth mile is a small stream, running between high broken banks, and with a single-arched brick bridge across it. Between seven or eight miles on the left hand is a brick Sarae in tolerable repair, and of a good size. Here the country opens out with hills on all sides: to the north-east the view is very fine, as the valleys and hills appear more wooded on that side. To the north, at the foot of a hill about three or four kos off, there is a small tope in ruin, called the tope of Burhan, which is also said to have been opened by General Ventura. To the west the hills are dry, and rise at once abruptly from the plain.

Formerly the Sarae of Kala formed the frontier post of the Sikhs to warn them of any invasion from the west. The Sarae was strengthened and repaired by Kala Singh, after whose name it goes. He was a converted Sikh from the lowest caste, and was in the service of Sirdars Ganda Singh and Janda Singh, the former chiefs of Lahore, who after the conquest of Rawelpindee appointed Kala

Singh their Thanehdar. Kala Singh, being a bold and desperate character, soon extended his authority all around, and carried his incursions as far as Hasan Abdal and Gandgarh, and harassed the Mahomedan tribes of that quarter. Many years ago, when the Daud Potras despatched a party of their troops to expel the Sikhs from this country, Ganda Singh carried war into Multan, met the invaders in their own country, gave them a desperate battle, and put them to flight.

In the meantime Charat Singh took advantage of Ganda Singh's absence, and reconciled Kala Singh to his own interests, which originated hostilities between Ganda Singh and Charat Singh, and led to a battle in which both the combatants lost their lives; the one was killed by the enemy, and the other, Charat Singh (grandfather of Ranjeet Singh), died by the bursting of his own gun. Maha Singh was thus left the sole owner of the estates of both. Soon after, Maha Singh, being suspicious of Kala Singh's conduct, took Kala Sarae from his charge, and put it under the superintendence of Jiwan Singh, whom he soon after also appointed the Governor of Rawelpindee: but Ranjeet Singh was not so kind to Jiwan Singh as his father. The latter was accused of having combined secretly with the Afghans, on which plea he was deprived of his possessions, and since that period Rawelpindee and Kala Sarae have been governed by officers under the Maharaja's own special selection.

I believe I have made an intrusive digression, and must now return and resume my path. About the twelfth mile cross a *Nala*, named Jabat, a clear stream running between two hills and close to the foot of both. Shortly after crossing it the ruins of a garden built by Jahanghir, a little way down the *Nala*, come in sight. These ruins are extensive, and the plan of the gardens, even in their present state, was much admired by some of the party, who visited them, from the natural scenery of the situation as much as from the work of art. So pleasing, indeed, is the scene around that Jahanghir is reported to have exclaimed "*Wah! Wah!*" (an expression of admiration) on first beholding it, whence the name of the present village near the gardens.

The story is, that the climate of Kashmir and Kabul being highly agreeable to Jahanghir, he frequently visited those places and proceeded by Hasan Abdal. There also resided a Faqir named Hyat ul Mir, who was held in great reverence by Jahanghir; which, besides the shady beauty of the spot, induced his Majesty to pass many days at Hasan Abdal. After a time he erected a pavilion and a garden, and likewise had dug a large tank in his Shikarjah or hunting-preserve, which still exists in a ruinous state. This monarch has erected many other buildings on the road to Kabul and Kashmir; *en route* to the latter place Saraes and seraglios were built by him at each stage.

At fifteen miles Hasan Abdal, a small town, overlooked by the hills, especially by one which was the residence of the pious Faqir mentioned above; there is a clear pretty stream running between the village or town and the hills. Close to the stream there is the tomb of the Faqir, ornamented with two large cypresses.

Hasan Abdal has a fine bazaar where plenty of supplies can be procured. Water good.

To the eastward of the place is a large spring situated in a grove of shady trees. Just above the spring is the impression of a hand which the Sikhs say is that of Baba Nanak, their first Guru, and hence Hasan Abdal is called *Panja Saheb* by the Sikhs. This is another instance of the truth of the observation, that people appropriate traditions and legends to their own faith.

They say that Nanak, when proceeding about the country, being wearied one day, asked the Faqir on the hill to give him a cup of water and some food. The Faqir was surly, and an altercation ensued between them, when the Faqir told him that if Nanak was a man of any miracles he would supply his wants without any assistance, and would even move the hills. Nanak put out his hand and stamped his fingers on the rock, where the mark still remains; and in commemoration of the Baba, the late Sirdar Hari Singh built a small temple, which he named *Panjá Sáheb*, from the five fingers.

The Mussulman story is that one Hasan, a Gujar, had many buffaloes; that a Faqir named Abdal came and asked him for a draught of milk. Hasan said, "I would gladly give you some, but my buffaloes are at present dry." Abdal laid his hand on one of them and said, "Now milk it." He did so, and soon gave him a copious draught. Abdal expressed his gratitude to Hasan, and asked what he could do for him. Hasan replied that they were much straitened for want of water, on which Abdal struck the neighbouring hills in two places, from which the two streams of Hasan Abdal have come forth. On the departure of the Faqir, Hasan said the spot should hereafter be called after them jointly.

Another story about the impression of the five fingers is that the Akalis of the fraternity of Sobah Singh Nehang, who held a jaghir near Hasan Abdal, being desirous of promoting their own interests, one of them engraved the five fingers on a piece of stone. It was soon given out by these artful fanatics to be the stamp of Nanak's fingers, from whence the springs issue. At present, all the Hindu and Sikh pilgrims make many offerings at the spot, which are taken by the Akalis. In a small tank which has been built round the spring are kept a number of fish which are fed daily by the visitors.

The *Nala* in Jahangir's garden, named Jabat, joins the stream which comes from Khanpore—the Kalapani, so called from the blackness of its waters, having previously joined the Jabat close to the bridge. The *Nala*, which comes from Khanpore, rises sixteen kos beyond that place, which is ten kos from Hasan Abdal. All these fall into the Indus at Jasua, about eighteen or nineteen kos distant.

There are some tribes of Afghans in the hills immediately to the north of Hasan Abdal. The Ghakars, in Khanpore and its immediate vicinity, are some of the Shia sect. The district of Khanpore is managed for the Maharaja by a son of Dal Singh. Bhae Maha Singh has had the management of Hasan Abdal four years. Before him it was held in jaghir by Lehna Singh, Sindhanwalia.

Ran Singh Pada, a Sikh, held the plains between Margalla and the hills west of it, about one hundred years ago, independent of others, and it descended to his sons, nephews, and their heirs till 1811, when Ranjeet Singh took Attok.

There are said to be twelve *Tappas* or cantons on the left bank of the Indus near Attok, viz., Chach, Sathgarh, Haru, Panjghatta Khatar, Panjghatta Khanpore, Khatar, Gandgarh, Sirikot (inhabited by *Halalkhors*), Hasanza, Salar, Mansur, Namlot. These cantons are chiefly peopled by Afghans, who are generally in a rebellious state; they pay very little revenue to the Sikhs, and that not without the assistance of troops. Among others the Gandgarhias, the head of whom is Khanzeman Khan and the Tanoul people, another district held by Paendeh Khan, are the most noted. They are very brave but turbulent characters. Occasionally they attack the villages in the plains of Hasan Abdal, and retreating with all they can find lay the country waste: the presence of troops alone can keep them within their limits, or otherwise they would infest the roads night and day. They hate the authority of the Sikhs, and do not like to submit to their rule. The late Sirdar Hari Singh was always at war with them. The inhabitants of the villages situated in the plains are rather more obedient than their brethren, and are more favourable to the English than the Sikhs. Several letters have been received from them, offering their services in the ensuing campaign, but they being nominally subject to the Sikhs their offers have been rejected.* The Hazara territory, consisting of seven Tappas, lies to the north-east of Husan Abdal twenty-five kos distant. It is managed by Sirdar Lehna Singh, Sindhanwalia, and appears rather peaceful.

The territory of Khatar is also managed by Mahu Singh. He is of a very respectable

* Some who were afterwards entertained made excellent soldiers.

Sikh family, and is a good, frank, and plain-spoken person. The following are some of the extraordinary legends of the place. Near the shrine of Hyatul Mir every Thursday a lamp containing about a seer and a half of oil is lighted, and remains so the whole night in the open air: it has never been known to be extinguished during the highest storms. I suspect the miraculous power of the lamp is owing to the thick wick inserted in it, which I hear is made of five chittaks of cotton.*

There are some small white stones to be found at the shrine, which are considered highly beneficial for the eyes, and pilgrims generally carry away some of them for their own and their families' use. There is also a block of stone measuring three or four yards in height, which when struck with another stone sounds like a bell. Visitors generally amuse themselves by ringing the stone, which is called the Shah's *gharial* or bell. I did not myself try the experiment, nor did I visit the tomb.

* Chittak, an Indian weight, the eighth of a pound.

Near another height, named Gup, there is said to be a bottomless pit, which has existed from time immemorial. It is stated that in the Bhimber territory, near a fort named Makanpura, there is a solid mass of rock, ten or twelve *bighas*, or two acres, in extent, and about a hundred yards high, on the top of which is an old and deep well, having no sign of being artificial.

The Hindu mythology says that when the Karwans were victorious over the Pandwans, the latter were transported to the above place, where they were condemned to pass a solitary life for twelve years. There was no water in the place; and from the want of it the poor exiles suffered much. One of them, Bhim, at last struck an arrow with all his might into the rock, and then took it out. No sooner did he do so than a spring of pure water issued from the hole, and they all quenched their thirst; ever since which the water has continued to flow.

To return to my narrative. The Afghan chiefs, who had lately joined the Shah Zada, began to advance high claims on the liberality of the Shah. They demanded an extravagant personal allowance, and urged that it might be soon settled, as the time for operations was approaching. Their demand was denied, and a moderate sum offered to each for himself and retainers; on which they applied to retire from the service. As the rapacity of the Afghans is well known, and it would have been difficult to satisfy their expectations, they were informed that they might depart if they liked. Accordingly they left the camp, and went about a kos on their way to Peshawr; when finding that they had thwarted their own object, to save their credit the Shah Zada sent a message to them, telling them that if they agreed to accept the rates which had been fixed, they might return. They assented to them without objection, and were readmitted to camp.

9th.—Baoli; distance fourteen miles; general direction north-west. About the third mile cross a stream running from left to right, that is, to the north-west. It is the united stream of the Hasan Abdal *Nala*, which afterwards falls into the Haru. At about six miles is the town of Burhan, within a kos of which there are three or four other small villages. *Nahib* Khan, the late chief of Burhan, fought many bloody battles with the Sikhs. He was at length killed, and the Sikhs introduced their authority in the place. At Burhan the people assume a change in their aspect and dresses. They are almost all Mahomedans of the Alizae tribe. Immediately after passing through the town, I was surprised to find one of my schoolfellows, named Ahmedgul, had been waiting for me on the road. It was highly gratifying to my feelings to meet a friend in a foreign land. He is a native of Islampore, near Burhan, and had gone to Delhi for his education. As we had still some distance to travel, and the sun was getting hot, I was obliged to leave my friend very unwillingly.

About the ninth mile we crossed the Haru, which was running rapidly, and is here two feet deep: the water is bluish. To the left of the stream the ground is broken by the valley, or the broad beds of the little ninth which fall into it. The Haru itself runs in a ravine thirty or forty feet deep, with the sides cut into smaller ones for three hundred yards inland. It is subject to very sudden inundations.

On leaving the Haru, the ground rises gradually for two or three miles, and then descends suddenly to the plains of Chach, which lie stretched before us. The ridge over which we passed is not fit for cultivation; but the plain is vast, and is dotted with villages. Five or six miles from the Haru is situated the *Baoli*, near which we encamped. To the south-west is a long isolated hill, on the inferior slopes of which stands the fort of Attok (but not visible from the *Baoli*). To the north can be traced the course of the Indus, chiefly by the mist overhanging it; and the hills are discernible in that direction, as well as to the south, from fifteen to twenty miles distant.

The usual encampment is between the *Baoli* and a village called Sydan. Supplies are scarce. Water is procured from the *Baoli*. On reaching the encamping ground, crowds of people came to see us, and several of them offered themselves for service.

From Hasan there is another route leading direct to Attok, *viâ* Hydro, a large village about two miles to the right of the course we followed; but it is said to be practicable only for horses. Hydro was some years ago attacked and burnt by the late Syed Ahmed.

One of the principal men of the place, named Ashraf Ali Khan, was entertained in the service of the Shah Zada, with his followers. He has been ordered to raise a Toman from the people of his own town, who are a brave race.

6th.—Started at the usual hour, and encamped on the left bank of the celebrated Attok, or Indus, distant six kos. The road is good and smooth. It lies across the plain, leaving the long isolated hill noticed above, on the left. About the fifth mile the offshoots of the hill on which the fort is situated are reached, and the road then turns to the river. Two kos from the last ground we passed a *Baoli*, lately dug by Ranjeet Singh, which is a great blessing to passengers in the hot season, as there is no village nearer than four kos. At the fourth kos crossed the bed of a *Nala*. It is celebrated for the battle fought between Diwan Mohkam Chand, the famous Sikh general, and Vazir Fateh Khan, in which the latter was totally defeated and repulsed with great loss. From that time the Sikhs have been constantly victorious over the Afghans, and either taken their territory or invaded their tributaries.

On approaching the camp, the Shah Zada and the Mission were met by the Thanehdar of Attok, and conducted by him to our tents, under a salute from the ramparts of the fort. After reaching our encampment, which was pitched about a kos and a half from it, we went to see the stream of the Indus, of which we had heard so much, and the roaring of which we heard at half a kos off; but on our arrival at the banks, we found that it was merely a branch of that river, and that the main stream ran at some distance. The bank on which we stood was only six cubits high. It is said that on the rise of the river it is overflowed. The water appeared very clear and cold, and the progress of the stream rapid.

While standing on the bank we amused ourselves by throwing stones across the stream, and observed several pieces of shining stone, which convinced us that there was a coal mine, or some beds of it, in the neighbourhood. If scientific researches were made, it is believed that they would meet with success. Letters arrived from the people in the Peshawr territory, expressive of their anxiety for the arrival of the Shah Zada. Among others, a letter from Mir Afzal Khan, residing near Gandamuk. He offered to excite his tribe, and to harass Mahomed Akbar Khan at Jalalabad, but that he was straitened for want of means. A reply was sent by Colonel Wade, admiring Afzal Khan's devotion and zeal in the royal cause, and informing him that on the Shah Zada's arrival, measures would be taken to meet his wishes.

Halted eleven days in the plain of Attok, to obtain some news of the army of the Indus before we arrived at Peshawr, and to open a communication with Lieutenant Mackeson, now Major, who was coming by the Derajat to raise the Afghans in that quarter, and to combine his movements with our own. Crossed the river Indus by a bridge of boats, and encamped on the opposite bank near the fort of Khairabad, three kos distant. Road good till within a mile of the fort of Attok, where it becomes narrow, and passes over a hard polished rock to the town: it then descends to the bridge of boats. The wheeled carriages proceeded round the rock. After leaving the carriage-way, we passed by the ruins of an old Sarae, where *Kafilas* use to put up. Shah Shujah, during his sojourn at Attok, occupied the same place. Two shrines to the left are also visible. They are dedicated to two Mussulman Darweishes Sultan Sudruddin and Hazratji. Close to them is the tomb of a celebrated courtezan. There are also a *Baoli* and a well within the fort.

On our way to camp we went to see the fort of Attok, within the walls of which is contained the town. It is built, as I have said, on a spur of the hill, which rises behind it, and slopes towards the river, consequently the inside of it is seen from the opposite bank. It is likewise commanded from one or two eminences on the left bank; but it is a well-constructed fortification for the time in which it was made, when the use of artillery was little known in these countries. The western side of it is formed by the outline of the rock, which is washed by the river. There are ravines on two sides and the river on the third; but such are the changes of the world, that Ranjeet Singh and his unlettered Sikhs are improving the works of Akbar the Great! The dimensions of the fort and other details have, I believe, been accurately laid down by Major Leech of the Bombay engineers, who accompanied Sir Alexander Burnes to Kabul. The hills have been occupied by various tribes at different times, and I saw some ruins near the summit of one of the peaks which are said to belong to the Kafirs, and are from time immemorial.

The hill of Attok may occupy with its spurs about two miles each way, or four square miles. It consists of several heights; the lower portions are of slate rocks, and some of the highest peaks are likewise slate. Others again are limestone, of the spongy kind which we saw in several other places. At the base of the hills, but at some length above the plain, there are quantities of pebbles of different sizes.

There is no well inside the fort of Attok, but water is supplied from the river through a passage called *Abduzd*, which communicates with the river through a bastion about fifty feet high from the surface of the water. It is said the river once rose so high that it overflowed the walls of the *Abduzd*, and a boat ran into it. A story is that there was a *Baradari* or pavilion close to the *Abduzd*, but lately pulled down. Nadir Shah, the Persian Emperor, on his return from India, stayed a night in this fort, during which a notorious thief came into it through the *Abduzd* from the other side of the river, and, climbing up the walls by means of striking nails into it, slowly glided into the room where the king was sleeping, and, finding him in a sound sleep, carried away his crown. In the morning the conqueror of India was astonished not to find his crown. Every search was made for it in vain. At last his Majesty proclaimed that if the robber would appear in person before him with the crown, he would not only be pardoned, but amply rewarded; and the thief actually came and delivered the crown. Nadir Shah was highly pleased with his bold conduct, gave him a large reward, and exalted him to a high rank in his own service.

The stream of the river is very rapid, deep, and narrow below the fort. It is very dangerous to be crossed in floods. If the boat is carried down between the two ledges of rock named Kamalia and Jamalia, there is little probability of its safety from the fury of the waves which throw it against one or other of them and it is dashed to pieces. Scarcely a year passes that one or two boats are not wrecked on them. The Indus, four or five kos above Attok before it receives the waters of the Kabul river, is divided into three or four branches, and is full of islands and dry banks. There the river is a ford. Ranjeet Singh forded it twice or thrice at the same point; but the Sikhs have an idea that it never becomes fordable, and the fording of Ranjeet Singh is ascribed by them to a miracle wrought by the favour of their Guru, or patron saint. The Indus, after leaving its rocky channel below Attok, and entering the plains of the Derajat, becomes very calm and gentle. Its banks above Attok are not above twelve feet high, and it evidently overflows annually the plains of Chach. The stream, in each of the many channels it has there, is rapid, and flows over a pebbly bottom with the noise of a cataract.*

* "We watched this deeply interesting picture from some overhanging rocks, which bear on their surface such a high state of polish, that they have the appearance of being perfectly wet; but it arises, I conjecture, from the constant trituration of the sand, washed upon them during the rainy seasons. From the sharpness of their angles and the darkness of their hue, I concluded they were composed of an extremely hard stone; but a few blows from a stick easily separated a portion, the fractures assuming regular shapes of a slaty substance."—*Barr's Journal*, p. 199.

It is obvious that the plain of Chach was formerly a large lake, the outlet from which was through the chasm formed by the hills east and west of the fort of Attok, which have been gradually worn away, and the present deep and narrow channel of the Indus formed. The river washes the hills on both sides, and becomes very confined immediately above the fort, yet the stream is there two hundred and fifty feet across, with precipitous banks.

There are traditions connected with the place about some ancient kings, which it might be worth while to gather together.

In the reign of Akbar, and during the wars of the Great Mogul general, Man Singh Rahtore, with the Afghans, there being no boats, Akbar caused them to be built, and induced some of the people with him, soldiers, and others, to become boatmen, on whom he settled a piece of ground near at hand yielding five hundred rupees per annum, and agreed with them that they should maintain the ferry with six boats. This land is still the property of the boatmen; but the Maharaja has built many other boats, and every year has a bridge formed of them to keep open his communication with Peshawr. The bridge lasts from seven to eight months in twelve; but from the violence of the torrent in the rainy months it is frequently broken and again put together. During the cold weather it is constructed just above the fort; but in the spring and summer it is removed to a spot rather lower down, where it lasts till the stream becomes too strong for it. The banks of the river are inconvenient of ascent and descent; the boats are small; the anchors are dropped at a great distance—perhaps four hundred or five hundred feet above where the bridge is to be formed—on account of the depth and rapidity of the current, to allow them to settle at a considerable angle. A boat will cost 300 rupees, viz. wood 150, iron 60, labour 90. It is built in one and a half or two months, and will last seven or eight years, and then with repair four or five longer. The anchors are six cubits long, five broad, with eighty or one hundred mands' weight of stone enclosed in a basket. The cables are made of a tough smooth bark like that of the palm in texture, procured from a tree which grows wild about the neighbouring hills. They wear away, however, on the rocky bottom in twenty-five or thirty days, and fresh anchors are then dropped.

The river generally rises forty cubits; the extraordinary rise talked of as having happened about the year 1800, was forty-six cubits.* A boat, during the cold weather, will reach Kalabagh (seventy-two kos) in three days, and in the rains in six hours! The boatmen are required to be very expert, and are better skilled in their profession than those of any other river

* Another great rise took place, 1840, which overflowed the country to a considerable extent. These inundations are common to the rivers of the Panjab from their beds within the mountains being frequently closed by a sudden avalanche of the precipice adjacent to them, which chokes the channel for many days; and when the water has formed a passage for itself it rushes into the plains with awful force, and, sweeping everything before it, spreads to a great distance over the country. Dr. Jameson, who visited the Attok a short time after the last great rise, has published the result of his observations in an interesting paper in the 'Journal of the Asiatic Society' in Calcutta.

of the Panjab. The fort of Khairabad, which is situated opposite to Attok, is of long standing, but was destroyed and subsequently repaired by Firoz Khan, Khatak, of Akorah. Its construction is of mud, and may be about a quarter of a mile in circumference. On summits close to it are three watch-towers, which entirely command the fort of Attok. Jahandad Khan, the Afghan governor of Attok, betrayed his master and delivered it over for a bribe to Ranjeet Singh. Since that time it has remained in the unmolested possession of the Sikhs.

The neighbourhood of Attok is the scene of several bloody battles between the Afghans and the Sikhs, before the latter had taken final possession of Peshawr.

Our encamping ground was spread over with stones, and confined; supplies abundant, and procurable from the town in the fort. The right bank of the river is within the jurisdiction of Peshawr.

While here we received news from Sindh of the rulers of that country having accepted the terms offered to them by the British Government, and that the army of the Indus would now advance on Candahar without further delay. Ranjeet Singh was informed of the event, and urgently requested by Lieutenant-Colonel Wade not to defer answering the letters which had already been addressed to him on several important points, and also to despatch the Mahomedan contingent of his troops, commanded by a good and wise officer, either European or Mahomedan, and to give him particular injunctions to adhere strictly to the conditions of the tripartite treaty. In the same letter Ganda Singh, the *Thanehdar* or commandant of Attok, was praised for his good behaviour towards the Mission and the Shah Zada; but Peshawra Singh, one of the supposed sons of his Highness, who is the governor of the place, was blamed for his inattention.* The Maharaja was likewise informed of the intention of her Britannic Majesty to despatch for his Highness some

* He afterwards behaved in the same manner to Major Ferris's detachment; and on the further representation of Colonel Wade was removed from his situation.

presents from England; and that among other things expected were a number of guns. The Maharaja was further requested to issue the necessary orders to his officers towards Derah Ismael Khan to facilitate the progress of Lieutenant Mackeson, who was on his way from Bhawalpur to join the Mission.

Intelligence was received that Mahomed Afzal Khan, who was sent to Kuram by his father at the same time that Mahomed Akbar Khan was despatched to Jalalabad, had returned to the latter place and joined his brother, and that the chiefs of Kuram were more favourable to the royal cause than that of Dost Mahomed Khan, and would do their best to throw off the authority of the latter.

News was likewise received from Peshawr to the effect that the merchants of Kabul, for fear of the arbitrary exactions of Dost Mahomed Khan to meet the expenses of the war, were removing the whole of their valuable property to some secure place, and had written to their agents in foreign towns and cities to stop the despatch of any merchandise to Kabul. It was further stated that in Turkistan, as well as in Kabul, there was such a heavy fall of snow on the 9th of February that the oldest persons had never witnessed any like it,—an event which had further alarmed Dost Mahomed Khan, as it would delay the return of his troops from Balkh, who had to cross the Hindu Koosh.

We learn that General Avitabile has issued a proclamation to the effect that if any traveller from Kabul should put up in the house of an inhabitant in Peshawr, and go away without the General being previously informed, the host would be liable to a severe penalty.

During the time that we were halted near Attok, instructions were sent off to Lieutenant Mackeson, to join the Mission, informing him of the intended plan of operations, and directing him to proceed, *viá* Dereh Ismael Khan, to Kohat, and to await there for further orders. By advancing along the hills in that direction, it was thought that he might create a diversion in favour of our own advance from Peshawr, when the time came to act in concert with Shah Shujah and the army of the Indus to lay open the road to Kabul. It was expected that the best mode of promoting that object would be for Lieutenant Mackeson to open communications with the Afghan chiefs inhabiting the country lying directly south of Khaibar, for the purpose of conciliating and inviting them to co-operate with us in destroying the influence of the existing government of Kabul.

In order to produce the desired impression on the minds of the people, Lieutenant Mackeson was recommended, before leaving Derah Ismael Khan, to engage the service of four or five hundred matchlockmen, and about half that number of horse, composed chiefly of the natives of that town, who were known to be a brave and well-affected race of men. The chiefs themselves were to be invited to join him either in person or by the deputation of some influential member of their families, and such of them as accepted the invitation would receive an allowance for their daily support with reference to their rank and importance; holding out to them, besides pecuniary benefits, a confirmation of their established rights and privileges in the event of their services proving of real utility in securing the restoration of the Shah. The principal object of recommending Lieutenant Mackeson to follow the plan proposed, was to show ourselves in a part of the country where active operations were not likely to be expected by the enemy, and to relieve, by the presence of a British officer, the power which Mahomed Akbar Khan at Jalalabad, and Mahomed Afzal in Kuram, partly possessed by their position, of controlling the actions of the chiefs, who were well affected to the royal cause in that quarter. Although it was not yet certain on what plan we might be obliged to act with a view of making our co-operation on the side of Peshawr as effective as possible with reference to the advance of the Shah and our troops from Shikarpore, to which we were told that every other plan was to be subsidiary, yet, from the present state of our information, the following is the mode which was explained as most likely to be carried out with the head-quarters of the Shah Zada.

1. After our arrival at Peshawr, Sir Claude was to proceed to the reduction of Ali Masjid, either by the agency of the Khaibaris or that of the Sikhs, to secure the entrance of the pass of Khaibar.

2. While engaged in effecting that object, with a view of distracting the attention of the enemy, and of keeping the Khaibaris in check, Mr. Lord and Lieutenant Mackeson were to be employed in the country on either side of the pass; Mr. Lord proceeding ultimately towards Bajour, and the other to Kohat, and each regulating his advance according to the intelligence he might receive of our movements. To insure as much as possible the success of these diversions, and to pay for the levies ordered to be made, it was proposed to send with each party a sum of fifty thousand rupees, the expenditure of which was to be left to the discretion of the officers in charge to engage the services of the chiefs and tribes lying in their respective routes.

With each party, exclusive of the peasantry of the country, were to be detached two companies of the Maharaja's Najibs, who are old and generally trustworthy soldiers, and a corps of matchlockmen, then being raised by Lieutenant Dowson and Ensign Hillersdon.

From the assurances which had been received by the Lieutenant-Colonel and Mr. Lord from the various chiefs on the Peshawr frontier, there was every reason to believe that both diversions, especially the one towards Kohat, would be cordially supported.

Chapter X.

Akora—The Khataks—Firoz Khan—Sayed Baha-uddin seized by Akbar Khan—State of Kabul—Pabhi—The Momands—Chamkani—Irrigation—Shukhan—Machni—A flood—A robbery—Retinue of Shah Zada—Duplicity of the Court of Lahore—Ill-health of the Maharaja—The Khaibari Chiefs—Assistance afforded by General Avitabile—Pir Mahomed Khan—Nawab Jabbar Khan—Tura Baz Khan—State of Kabul.

On the 9th of March we arrived at Akora; distance, ten kos; direction, north-westerly. Immediately on leaving the encamping ground near Khairabad, we passed through Gidargalli, or Jackal's Path, a narrow defile through a low rocky range of hills, and nearly two miles in length.* It is not very difficult,

* "Its whole extent may be from one and a half to two miles; and in the more exposed parts, Ranjeet Singh has erected a few castles, which are garrisoned by troops stationed there for the purpose of securing the pass, as well as for the protection of travellers. The scene was one of great wildness, and fraught with excitement; whilst the guards, armed with long matchlocks, and perched on the

since it has been used and improved by General Avitabile, the present governor of Peshawr, who, having no further occasion for the pioneers whom he had been employing there and at Attok, allowed Lieutenant-Colonel Wade to take them from him; and they proved of the greatest service to us in erecting stockades and clearing the way through Khaibar for artillery. They were afterwards increased to two hundred and fifty men, and put in charge of an officer. About the middle of the pass is situated a Burj, or tower, on a height to the left. A party of sepoys is always established here to protect the road, which formerly was infested by the Khatak people who occupy the neighbouring hills; but they are apparently now on good terms with the Sikhs. The rest of the road was good, but here and there spread over with stones. About three and a half kos from the last encamping ground we passed the dry bed of a *Nala*. During the floods it swells very

extremity of a jutting crag, paced to and fro on their elevated and confined posts, and added much to the picturesqueness of the effect."—*Barr's Journal*, p. 200.

high, and stops the communication for some time. Midway passed by Jahangira, about half a mile off to the right. It was raining very hard, and I stayed for a few minutes with my friend, named Haidar Ali Khan, commanding a party of four hundred Sowars, and one piece of cannon, belonging to Sirdar Nihal Singh Aluwalia, who is stationed here, and has a small katcha fort, near which the Sowars are pitched for the protection of the road, and to overawe the neighbouring tribes.

When the rain had ceased, we proceeded to the camp at Akora. The celebrated battle between Sayed Ahmad and the Sikhs was fought on the plains of Jahangira and Akora, on which occasion the Sayed was totally defeated, and retired to the Eusafzai country. The Sikhs had not much reason to be proud of the victory which they had gained, as they lost a great many men, and their general, Budh Singh, one of the finest Sirdars of the Sindhanwalia family, and a great favourite of the Maharaja.

We are now in the Khatak territory, which begins at Khairabad, and ends at the village of Zarah, near Naoshera, as far as Haran, on the Eusafzai frontier; and on the south is bounded by Lachi and Dherian, the frontier of Dour Banoo. It is a large tribe, consisting of many thousand families. They were long in enmity with the Sikhs, and fought many battles with them. The ground is covered with graves.*

* "After quitting it (Gidargalli) we emerged on to a fine champagne country, which, however, bears but few marks of cultivation—a measure soon explained to us by the thousands of tombs spread on every side. These are constructed with much care, and particular attention seems to have been paid to preserve their individuality, each grave being marked out by a row of white pebbles encircling the mound, and crossed in its breadth by two or three bands of the same; beneath them lie the bodies of countless numbers who have fallen in battle, and the vastness of the collection displays the bold spirit with which the Afghans opposed the encroachments of the Sikhs. Although several years have elapsed since these engagements occurred, the same spirit of animosity still exists between the two nations; but from the circumstance of the Maharaja having obtained the entire ascendancy of the country, nothing beyond a solitary assassination is now heard of unless when the hill-tribes of the Khataks descend from their fastnesses for the purpose of plundering an escort, and then a partial affray is sometimes brought about."—*Barr's Journal*, p. 201.

As long as Firoz Khan, their enterprising chief (a native of Akora), was alive, they did not allow the Sikhs to gain a permanent footing on the right bank of the Indus on the Peshawr side; but after his death they were able to establish themselves across the river. The sons of Firoz Khan, who were formerly with Sultan Mahomed Khan, the ex-chief of Peshawr, were among those who joined the Shah Zada at Lahore, and are now serving him.

The Khataks now pay a certain annual revenue to the Sikhs, and their chief is Najaf Khan, the cousin of Firoz Khan. At heart the Khataks do not like the Sikh authority, but they are subdued. On the approach of the Shah Zada, they expressed their readiness to join him and to shake off the yoke which has been imposed on them by the Sikhs; but, agreeably to the existing treaty, they were prevented by Sir Claude Wade from doing so. The Khatak hills produce nothing remarkable, with the exception of a grass called *Haran-latia*, which is used by the natives to improve the sight of their eyes. There is abundance of fuel also in this quarter, and Peshawr is much dependent on these hills for supplies of it.

We encamped on the right bank of the Kabul river close to Akora, which is rather a small and confined town chiefly inhabited by Mussulmans, there being only a few Hindu shopkeepers in the towns west of the Indus. The tract of country along the bank of the river is called *Tari*, or a morass, and irrigation generally is by wells. The district is farmed to a Hindu named Piara Mal: his rule is not said to be very oppressive, like the other Sikh officers.

I have hitherto omitted to mention that lately Sayed Baha-uddin, the ruler of Kunar, has been seized by Mahomed Akbar Khan on the charge of holding a secret correspondence with the Shah Zada.

It appears on further inquiry that he was apprehended by a stratagem when he was on a visit to Mahomed Akbar Khan at Jalalabad. The Sayed, being suspicious of the young

Sirdar's want of faith, did not, however, go to him without previously exchanging solemn pledges on the Koran, viz., that he would not be molested either in his person or territory; but these were merely idle words, for, as soon as the Sayed fell into the hands of Mahomed Akbar, he was treacherously seized, and troops sent to take possession of his territory. Such acts of treachery are commonly followed throughout the whole of Afghanistan, especially among persons of high rank. The Sayed is said to have been sent to Kabul, where he remains in confinement in the fort of Bala Hisar; but the circumstance of his being a Sayed will most probably secure him the safety of his life.* The territory of Kunar has been subsequently occupied by the troops sent by Mahomed Akbar Khan, and the family of the Sayed, after a bold resistance, expelled. It lies on the eastern frontier of the Kafir Siahposh, and has now been farmed to Sayed Hashim, a rival of the ex-ruler. So gross a breach of faith in the Amir and his son

* A descendant of the Prophet.

has offended all his vassals: among others, Sadat Khan Momand, who is allied to Sayed Baha-uddin by some family connexion, appears highly displeased.

News was received here of Lieut.-Col. Stoddart's arrival at Bokhara, and of the refusal of Mir Morad Beg of Koonduz to abide by the treaty which he had lately concluded with Akram Khan, which is gratifying intelligence.

10*th.*—Halted at Akora on account of the heavy rain yesterday having made the roads impassable.

Numbers of people are now joining the Shah Zada. If the chief of any party now arrives, he comes with some state. A party of native musicians plays before him, and he proceeds very slowly, surrounded by a large party of followers, to show that he is a man of some consequence.

A letter was again despatched to the Maharaja, informing him that the escort which was promised by his Highness for the Shah Zada was not yet complete; that among others, Jamaluddin Khan, of Mamdot, who was ordered to join him at Hasan Abdal with a party of one hundred Sowars, had failed to do so, and had only arrived at Attok, and with a party of fifteen or sixteen Sowars; that these delays at such a critical time were highly detrimental to the object in view; that neither had any account yet been received about the Mahomedan contingent; that it was advisable to instruct the officers at Peshawr to make a selection from the various corps under their command of all the Mahomedans in each, and on the arrival of the Shah Zada to place them at the disposal of the Lieut.-Colonel, for the protection of the Shah Zada, now that the prince was about to arrive on the enemy's frontier. He was further informed that a letter to the same effect had been lately addressed to General Avitabile, apprizing him of the Shah Zada's near approach, and requesting him, agreeably to the treaty and the paper of conditions exchanged between Lord Auckland and the Maharaja at Lahore, to receive the Shah Zada and the Mission on their arrival with proper consideration. It was also intimated to his Highness that no information had yet reached of the nomination of a Mahomedan commander, and he was urgently requested to appoint one.

11*th.*—Naoshehera.* Distance nine kos; road good; lying on level ground. The country open, and better cultivated than the last march. The town of Naoshehera is situated on the left bank of the Lundi or Kabul river, but our encamping ground is close to a small fort opposite Naoshehera, and on the right bank. Supplies easily procurable. Water from the river. Near this spot was fought the great battle which took place between Ranjeet Singh and Sirdar Mahomed Azim Khan, Barakzai. The main army of the Sikhs was situated on the left, and the Afghan chief with his troop on the right bank; but the brunt of the action was sustained by the Eusaf-

* "As we neared the town of Nao Shehera, the scene became almost English; the sloping banks on either side of the stream being covered with verdant grass, and fringed with mulberry and other trees, and the distant views bounded by ranges of hills enclosing the expanding valley." —*Barr's Journal*, p. 208.

zais, and other neighbouring tribes, the peasantry of the country, who came down in masses to oppose the Sikhs, and attacked them with such boldness that for a time they were victorious, and the Sikhs were seen retreating before them; but Ranjeet Singh rallied his troops, and sent General Ventura with a large party of infantry to their support; which led to the enemy being defeated with great slaughter. The French officers had not at that time been long in the Maharaja's service. General Allard was watching Azim Khan with the cavalry on the right bank, who retreated before him almost without fighting.*

To-day we received news from Jalalabad that near Soorkhab the snow was so heavy that a party of merchants who were on their way from Peshawr to Kabul, and took shelter under a loose ledge of rock, were buried under

* "One mound in particular was the subject of severe fighting. Three times did the Sikhs gain its vantage ground, and three times were they driven back. The Maharaja at length advanced in person at the head of his guards, and drove the Afghans from their position; the day was then his own."—*Barr's Journal*, p. 209.

it, the projection having sunk down under the weight of the snow with which it was covered. Only an infant of a year old was saved out of ten or twelve lives.

Dost Mahomed Khan now distrusts all the Kabul people, except Hafizji, to whom he has lately married one of his daughters. He intends to send him with the peasantry of the Kohistan to defend the Khaibar pass. Dost Mahomed has lately received an explicit reply from the agent deputed to Persia that Mahomed Shah would not comply with the Amir's request, as the Shah could not assist him till he had made himself master of Hirat.

Letters were also received by Dost Mahomed Khan from the Candahar chiefs, asking his advice how to proceed in the present exigency. The Amir replied that he could not go to their assistance, but that they had better make preparations for a protracted siege.

News was likewise received from Lahore to the effect that the province of Kashmir had been lately farmed out to Kharak Singh; a circumstance which convinced us that Ranjeet

Singh considered his end very nigh. Golab Singh, taking advantage of the Maharaja's declining health, had been actively exerting himself of late to prepare the way for the establishment of his own authority in that quarter; which having come to the ears of Ranjeet Singh, he thought it prudent to confer it at once on his son, which gave great offence to the Jammoo family, and they began to intrigue with Nao Nibal Singh for the subversion of Kharak Singh's power, whom they knew to be popular with the Sikhs, as the only legitimate heir to the throne.*

12*th.*—Pabhi, a small village, situated on a rising and sloping ground; supplies procurable, and the encamping ground extensive, and abundance of good water. The description of the road the same as yesterday.†

* Golab Singh's ambition has at length been gratified by the almost total destruction of the family of his benefactor and the ruin of the Sikh government to secure his own power.

† "The country, during the latter portion of our morning's march, exhibited many more traces of cultivation than we have hitherto seen in the valley, but the graves

We are now in the territory of the Momands. Their possessions commence at the village of Badarshi, five kos from Akora, on the road to Peshawr.

The Momands are a large and very influential tribe, and occupy two distinct tracts of country. One portion, the head of which is Sadat Khan of Lalpura, inhabits the hills to the north of the Khaibar Pass; while the other occupies the country which is now the subject of our observation. The last possess five tappas, or cantons, viz., *Badarshi*, *Musazai*, *Badaheir*, *Musa Khail*, and *Musrazae*. With the exception of Badarshi, the other four are situated on the banks of the Bara stream, which

were still sufficiently numerous to remind us of the severe contests that had been fought in it at no very distant period; they were, however, as nothing compared with those of the two preceding journeys. In some parts, where the plain had been left undisturbed, and was covered with a thick green sward, it was delightful to observe the profusion of wild and sweet-smelling flowers with which it was bedecked, and many of which forcibly reminded us of the fields of England, the most common being the dandelion, which, however, does not attain to the size of that at home."—*Barr's Journal*, pp. 212, 213.

chiefly supplies water both for drinking and irrigation. The head of the Momands, who are estimated to amount to many thousand families, is Karim Khan, of the Kela of Mohsou Khan. He is said to be a good man. This tribe and the Khalils, who lie between it and the other Momands under Lalpura, are generally in difference with each other, and the one secretly tries to baffle the interest of the other. The tribe of Karim Khan has an extensive range of territory, commencing from Badarshi.

There is a story at Pabhi that a saint who is buried here is well known to have cured many persons afflicted with leprosy, and canine convulsions; and that at present also many are known to have recovered from distempers of that nature, merely by resorting to the tomb of the Saint.

On the 13th of March we came to Cham Kani, distance seven kos—road good. Crossed several small canals cut from the Bara for the purpose of irrigation. To the north of Chamkani crossed the Bara by a bridge, and encamped on a fine level spot of ground. About two kos off from Chamkani the Shah Zada and the Mission were met by a deputation from Peshawr, at the head of which was General Avitabile, which conducted them with due honour to the camp, and a salute was fired from the city in honour of his arrival.

No sooner had we arrived, than numbers of people came to visit us from Peshawr, four kos distant, and several from the neighbouring villages voluntarily came and entered the service of the Shah Zada. Among the former were the Shah Zadas Jamhur, and Mahomed Saleh, the sons of Shah Zada Mahomed Hashim, who joined the camp with a view to serve their relative the Shah in the present expedition for the recovery of the Sadozai throne.

The Bara takes its rise in the Tirah country, in a hill named Rajzal; immediately after issuing from which it is divided into three branches: one of them, called the *Rodsoorkh,* or the red stream, from the colour of its water, passes through the Ishpin country, and joins the Kabul river near Sultanpore, seven kos above Jalalabad. The second branch is the Bara, which name, I am told, it takes on its entrance into the Peshawr territory. After many windings it falls into the Kabul river at Zakhi, five kos below Chamkani. The cultivation of Peshawr entirely depends on the irrigation of Bara. Several artificial canals are cut from it by the zamindars and villagers for the purpose of irrigating their cultivation. The water is also red in colour, and exceedingly good and digestive. On a particular piece of ground in the village of Sanja, just within the three tappas occupied by the Khalil people, the best rice and remarkably fine, called Bara, is produced. In a season of drought the water of the Bara is sometimes exhausted altogether, and then the people of Peshawr and its vicinity are very much distressed. The only course to which they resort on such occasions is to assemble in large crowds near a temple dedicated to a Mahomedan Saint in the village of Sheikhan, seven kos off, to the south of Peshawr, and sacrifice several oxen in the bed of the Bara. The tradition is that no sooner is their offering made than it rains in torrents, and the bed of the river is again filled with water, and even overflows its banks. I do not credit the story, but it is superstitiously believed and related to be so, by the natives. In the village of Sheikhan, on the banks of the Bara, there is another temple belonging to the Hindus, where a large fair takes place on the festival of the Bisakhi. There are many caves which have been dug for the use of the Joghis, many of whom reside there. The third stream, the name of which I forget, takes its course into the Kohat and the Bangish country, and falls into the Indus, twelve or thirteen kos below the fort of Attok.

These three streams are said to be nearly equal in their breadth, and to possess equally good water, and of the same colour; but it is not until it has been kept in a pot for some time that it turns out clear.

Machni is a thriving town of the Momands. Loads of Kabul fruits are brought to it. The merchants, either from the Panjab or Kabul, alight there. The latter generally come in the cold weather, as they are not able to brook the hot climate of Peshawr in summer. The transit duties levied in Machni amount altogether to twenty-one thousand rupees per annum. Rice, wheat, and barley, are abundantly produced; also *jawari** and the sugar-cane are cultivated.

A report was received from Mir Alam Khan announcing the intention of Mahomed Akbar to proceed against him, and requesting our assistance; he stated that the troubles in his territory were owing principally to the family divisions between himself and Mir Khan, Naowaghi; that it was never supposed Mahomed Akbar would engage in another quarter, when the Shah Zada arrived at Peshawr with the avowed object to open the pass of Khaibar. Mir Alam Khan's application was not complied with, but he was desired, in case the enemy should advance against him, to collect the people of his tribe and make a vigorous defence, and that on receiving intimation of the

* An Indian corn.

event means would be taken to make a diversion in his favour.

14*th*.—Remain at Chamkani. Last night it rained very severely, and continued so during the day from time to time. Our camp being pitched on a tilled ground, we could hardly move out of the tents on account of the deep mud about them. The Bara rose very high, and its current was exceeding rapid and noisy. One of the arches of the bridge before mentioned gave way, and was carried down by the fury of the flood. The communication between the town and the camp was cut off, and we were much straitened for want of supplies until the swelling of the river was lowered and the people could ford it.

We heard that last night a gang of Dacoits, or thieves, broke into the city of Peshawr, and carried away some valuable property belonging to a wealthy Hindu merchant, one of whose men was killed, and one severely wounded. General Avitabile prevented the deceased from being burnt, on the plea that his family deserved to be punished for not repairing the wall, through which the party of Dacoits came. After much discussion, a fine of 2000 rupees was exacted from the family before the deceased was allowed to be burnt. Such fines are set apart to improve the fortifications of the city. Some idea of the manner in which justice is here administered may be formed from the above anecdote; but the people require to be governed by very severe laws.

A reply was received to-day from Ranjeet Singh to the letter regarding the detention of the detachment, with the two howitzers, at Harikee for two days, in which it was attempted to lay the blame on the officer commanding it by those who had now begun to interfere with the just views of the Maharaja, when the delay was known to have proceeded from the neglect of the Sikh authorities, of whom reports were now received from every quarter that they were trying secretly to thwart us, and throw every possible obstacle in the way of our progress.

15*th.*—Still at Chamkani. The day was employed in preparing some necessary equipments, and completing the household of the Shah Zada. Four officers were added to his personal retinue, viz., a *Zabtbegi*, an *Amlabashi*, an *Arzbegi*, and a *Nasakhchibashi.** They were directed to employ twenty-five Sowars each of those who had offered, and to accompany the Shah Zada, whenever he went out, as his body guard. Proper dresses were provided for these, as well as his other respectable servants in attendance, so that his Highness might assume a becoming importance in the eyes of the people of Peshawr when he entered that city as the representative of his father.

16*th.*—Camp, as before, at Chamkani. Wahab Malik, accompanied by some influential persons of the Kukikhail tribe, arrived in camp. He offered his services in opening the pass, with the assistance of a part of the Shah Zada's troops. Wahab and his companions occupy the lands immediately to the right of the pass between Jamrud and Ali Masjid. They are in enmity with Abdurrahman and

* Offices of state.

some others, the chief persons of the tribe, from not being allowed to share the allowance settled by Dost Mahomed Khan on their tribe. Wahab further proposed that he and his men would go and bring back to the camp one hundred and fifty Jazailchis stationed in the fort of Ali Masjid, whom he had previously consulted; and at the same time desire the rest to join him; and that, if they refused, he would attack the fort, which contained a very small garrison, and take it. He also begged that, if he were successful, all the Afridis who had joined Mr. Lord might be sent to assist him in maintaining his ground; and requested an advance of three hundred rupees for distribution among his partisans.

As the time for operations had not yet arrived, though the opportunity was favourable, Wahab was only desired to return to his place, and quietly gain others of his tribe to his side, and also to try and induce the garrison to deliver over the fort to the Shah Zada, for which they would be liberally rewarded. The man was accordingly dismissed, and presented with the money he demanded, besides being honoured by a *khilat* from the Shah Zada.

Another circumstance which prevented us from profiting by the present opportunity was the information which we were surprised to receive from General Avitabile, on our arrival at Chamkani, that neither he nor any of the Sirdars at Peshawr had yet received the instructions of their master to co-operate in the present expedition, although deceitful assurances to the contrary had been given. This news was, of course, very vexatious, especially as but slight aid was then required from the Sikhs at Peshawr to effect the object of seizing the fort of Ali Masjid before its garrison was increased, there being then only about fifty Jazailchis all together in it, and they could not have long held out against a large and disciplined force; but the Sikhs, as I have stated above, seem resolutely determined to defeat rather than assist us in our operations. The Maharaja alone appears somewhat sincere to his pledges and engagements in the tripartite treaty. We hear, however, that he is too sick and feeble to do any business, and is said to have entirely lost his speech. Public affairs are consequently managed by Raja Dhian Singh and his other courtiers, who are strongly opposed to the scheme, and know that we are too far off to counteract their opposition in person; and they have succeeded in bribing the news-writers of our government at court, on whose reports no further dependence can now be placed. The Governor-General has been requested, therefore, to adopt the only course left, viz., of deputing an officer to Lahore, to give full effect to our requisitions.*

Letters were received from the Khaibar chiefs, in reply to those which were addressed to them from the Jehlam to join the Shah Zada. They expressed their sincere devotion to the cause of the Shah, but begged to be excused from attending his son, as their hostages were still in the hands of Mahomed

* In consequence of which Mr. G. R. Clerk, who had been appointed to act for Sir C. M. Wade on the frontier of the Sutledge, in the absence of the latter with the Shah Zada, was sent to Lahore.

Akbar Khan. They were informed in reply, that if they could not attend in person, they should depute their sons or relations, or testify their fidelity in other ways by serving him secretly, by which they could be in no risk from the other side. They were further encouraged to persuade the garrison of Ali Masjid to join the Shah Zada, who would take them into his own service at ten rupees *per mensem*, besides rewarding them with *khilats* and a bounty of twenty-five rupees each on their arrival; and were told also that the person who exerted himself most in bringing them over should receive in addition a present of five rupees per head.

It appears that the Khaibaris were alarmed on being misinformed that the pass would be forced and Ali Masjid garrisoned by the Sikh force. To remove these impressions from their minds, an explanatory letter was written to Abdurrahman Khan, the head of the Kukikhail tribe occupying the pass near its entrance between Ali Masjid and Jamrud, (the only people considered of importance in opening the way,) who was assured that, agreeably to the tripartite treaty, the Sikhs could not interfere in any affairs beyond their boundary; that, if surrendered, Ali Masjid would only be occupied by a garrison of Mahomedans from the Shah Zada's force; that if the Sikhs, contrary to treaty, ever attempted to enter Khaibar, it would be resented by the British Government as well as by his Majesty the Shah. In case of Abdurrahman himself joining the Shah Zada, he was assured of the settlement on him and his tribe of the allowance which they enjoyed from Dost Mahomed Khan, besides other royal favours with which he would be distinguished for his services. On the other hand, if he held out, he was threatened with every misery which the invasion of a formidable army could inflict.

A letter was also received by an agent from Inyet Ulla Khan, the chief of Sawat, expressive also of his sentiments of devotion to Shah Shuja. He was requested in reply to wait on the Prince, and informed that if he could not attend himself he should depute his son to the camp.

17*th*. — Chamkani. General Avitabile, though yet without any instructions from Lahore, being well informed of the articles of the tripartite treaty and his master's will, professed his own readiness to assist the Mission in forwarding its objects, but of course without incurring any responsibility which might exceed the ordinary exercise of his authority. In compliance with the request of Sir Claude Wade, he issued a proclamation to the people of the Peshawr territory, declaring the terms of the tripartite treaty, with an assurance that there was no objection on the part of the Sikh Government to any Mussulman joining the Shah Zada; in short, that the interests of the two states in the present enterprise were identical. Such a manifesto was much required to remove suspicions from the minds of the Mahomedans about Peshawr, who feared incurring the displeasure of the Sikh Government from joining the Shah Zada—to such a degree had the opinion got abroad that it was averse to the measure.

An agent on the part of the Prince was at

the same time sent into Khaibar to inform the people there of the real views and intentions of the Shah assisted by the British Government, and also to induce if possible the garrison of Ali Masjid to desert and come over to the Shah Zada.

Letters were received from several people of the Afridi and other tribes that they wished to join the Shah Zada, on condition of not being molested by the Sikhs. Such of them as were thought worthy of consideration were desired to come, and the rest directed to await further instructions.

It is customary with these people, when they offer their services in camp, to advance extravagant claims, and "Kharechbadeh" (Give money) or "Gursana-am" (I am hungry) is the exclamation in every mouth. Being so avaricious, no present is sufficient to satisfy them. We are exceedingly plagued by their greedy demands. Many of them come with no other view than to make money. It is difficult to draw a distinction between the good and bad. They all solemnly declare their fidelity by oaths, yet think nothing of betraying their masters. Some of the Afridis who joined us at Rawelpindee lately deserted the camp after they had filled their pockets.

The Barakzai family of Peshawr is still suspected of treachery, though they have been trying to cleanse themselves of the reproach. A letter was received from Pir Mahomed Khan, the brother of Sultan Mahomed Khan, who expressed in strong terms his good will. In consequence, however, of his connexion with Dost Mahomed, no implicit faith was placed in his word, and no answer has been returned.

News also came to-day from Kuram that Mahomed Afzal Khan, in his retreat from that country, was attacked by the natives, and a large booty carried off from his party; a proof of the inclination of the people towards the Shah, and of the hope of assistance entertained from them.

Dost Mahomed Khan seems to be much alarmed. He is said to have taken away his artillery from the natives of India in his service, and to have put his guns in charge of the

Ghilzais, the only people in whom he places much confidence. Mahomed Akbar Khan is stated to have ordered a collection of supplies to be made in Dhaka, but the report requires further confirmation, as he is said, by good authorities, to have no intention of proceeding so far towards Khaibar.

A very important letter was received to-day from Nawab Jabbar Khan, brought by one of his own trustworthy men, viz., after acknowledging the receipt of a letter which had been addressed to him, the Nawab stated that, on the occasion of Captain Burnes's visit to Kabul, that officer had at first adopted a conciliatory line of policy, but in the end had changed his tone, which had not given satisfaction; that the Nawab had then offered his humble advice, which was not, however, accepted; that now when matters had come to their present crisis, lakhs of rupees would be expended to carry out the enterprise, and it had been learned from the *Akhbars** that Sultan Mahomed Khan had been excluded from the scheme. He was of

* The Persian term for newspapers.

opinion that the plan was not a right one; that although his country and the Afghans were not remarkable for their power of discrimination, while the English were a very acute race, and eminent for wisdom, and had probably come to a just conclusion, yet the accuracy of their decision had eluded the penetration of the Afghans; but from a regard to the welfare of every party it had occurred to him that before an actual collision took place, negotiations should be re-opened with the Amir, that he would engage to conclude them, and, please God, peace might yet be satisfactorily established; that an intimation to that effect was alone wanting, and it would be to the credit of all parties; whereas, if the dispute continued, it was impossible to foresee the consequences to which it might lead.

Right or wrong, these sentiments accorded neither with the policy of the British Government nor that of Shah Shuja. The settlement of the affair on the expected terms appeared very improbable; as nothing short of the continuance of the government of Kabul in Dost Mahomed's possession was likely to satisfy him; but as the Nawab had previously professed a desire to come over to Peshawr, and it was supposed that he could not effect his escape without hindrance, the present seemed a favourable opportunity to aid him in his project. He was therefore requested, in reply, to come to Peshawr, as the time for correspondence had passed; and that, on his arrival, the subject of his letter could be verbally discussed better than by writing. It was thought that such a letter would give the Nawab a good excuse to effect his escape if that were his object.

18*th*, *Chamkani.*—Continued here for the arrival of Captain Ferris's detachment of two companies of infantry, and the howitzers under Lieutenant Barr. The enemy have been trying to incite the Khaibaris to make night attacks on our camp as well as that of the Sikhs.

Some of the Nihangs or Akalis, who were returning in the evening from some water-mills, were attacked by these freebooters, who were lying on the road in ambush for them;

one of them was killed, and two or three wounded, and the rest had a narrow escape, throwing down, of course, the burthens of flour which they had with them.

19*th*, *Chamkani.*—We had copious showers, during the last few days, which made a great havoc in the city of Peshawr, and a part of the Bala Hisar or Sameirgarh, as it is now called by the Sikhs, also fell down.

20*th*, *Chamkani.*—Tura Baz Khan, the *tarbur* or cousin of Sadat Khan Momand, wrote, requesting permission to join the Shah Zada. As the security of the Abkhana route (so called from lying along the heights on the left bank of the Kabul river) to Jalalabad, through the Momand territory, was considered of high importance in case the Khaibar people should refuse to open their pass; and Tura Baz was an influential man of the same tribe, and in enmity with Sadat Khan, it was deemed advisable to accept his overture, as the latter was the only chief on the Peshawr side who had not yet given any proofs of attachment to the Shah's cause: and it was believed that if, as was feared, he persevered in his adherence to the enemy, Tura Baz Khan, together with his cousin and brother, who had already joined, would be the best tools to open the Abkhana route, and to harass their kinsman.

As usual in such situations, reports became frequent that our camp would be attacked by a party of Mahomed Akbar's troops. In consequence, as we were only within a few miles of the enemy's frontier, the necessity of a well ordered camp, and a strict system of vigilance, became indispensable to our protection. Additional measures were therefore taken, and pickets so posted every night round the camp as to prevent surprise. To the present day no instance of theft has happened in our camp, though they have been of frequent occurrence in that of the Sikhs, who are not always vigilant, and encamp in a loose way. Our encampment is a compact square, divided in half, with the Shah Zada and his establishments on one side, and the British Mission with the Sikh escort on the other, the *Khawanin*, with their irregular retainers, being pitched outside. Captain Ferris, being on his way to join with treasure, was warned at the same time to be careful.*

21st, *Chamkani.*—General Avitabile entertained the members of the Mission to-day at breakfast. On his own part he is very attentive, and has been providing the whole camp gratis, since we entered his jurisdiction, with every necessary, such as fuel, forage, &c., though he has been repeatedly requested to discontinue these supplies.

Some of the *Qasids* or hired messengers have been lately in the habit of forging letters in the name of any one whom they think most likely to have some interest with the Shah Zada or

* "Colonel Wade had sent us word that once in Afghanistan it would be necessary to keep stricter guard than usual over the treasure, as the hills around swarm with a population who act upon

——— 'The simple plan
That they should take who have the power,
And they should keep who can.'

Almost every individual whom we have seen has been armed with sword and shield, or in some other manner; and all around bespeaks the unsettled state of the country and its population."—*Barr's Journal*, pp. 196-198.

the Mission, with a view of exacting presents from us; a trick which, I believe, has been greatly owing to the liberality with which they had been treated before our arrival. Besides rations while they remain in camp, which is a custom of the country, a sum of money is presented to them on their dismissal. Some forged letters were received to-day from the Khaibar chief Khan Bahadar Khan, and his son, by a Khaibari, who called himself one of his relatives. No sooner were the letters delivered, than his wickedness was discovered merely by a perusal of them. They were written in a different style to that which is generally used by the Khaibaris, whose letters are usually expressed in very rude and ungrammatical Persian. The man was disgraced and turned out of the camp.

A letter was received from Ranjeet Singh enclosing a detailed list of the five thousand Mahomedans who were to form the contingent, which he said he had ordered to assemble at Peshàwr; but it appears that these troops, with the exception of a party of about four hundred

Sowars, were to come from a long distance. A portion was ordered from Multan, and another from the Doaba of Jahlandar, and some places not less than two hundred and fifty kos distant from Peshawr! This dilatory and evasive mode of producing the force, on the part of the officers who now ruled Ranjeet Singh's darbar, gave much vexation. It had months before been stipulated in the treaty that these troops were to be collected in Peshawr before our arrival. In consequence a reply was returned in very strong terms to his Highness, requiring the particular attention of his officers to the immediate fulfilment of his pledges. He was urged to send the troops without delay; but as their early arrival was now quite impossible, it was again intimated to the Maharaja that a portion of his troops forming the usual garrison of Peshawr should at once be transferred to us; that General Avitabile and General Court had engaged to give us a Gorkha battalion, with two pieces of artillery and a howitzer and mortar, if his Highness had no objection

Had General Avitabile, like the Sikh officers of the Lahore Government in general, been averse to aid us, our camp would have been entirely exposed to the incursions of the Khaibaris, and our other predatory neighbours. The helpless state in which we had reached the frontier had been reported by our enemies to Dost Mahomed Khan, which had shaken the confidence of the Shah's friends in our power to support their demonstrations in his favour.

22nd, *Chamkani.* — Intelligence was received from our agent, to whom I alluded above as having been sent into Khaibar, stating that the Khaibaris of the Kukikhail tribe, whom he had only just seen, were willing to adopt the cause of royalty, provided their old rights were previously confirmed to them. They also recommended that some sepoys of the enemy in Ali Masjid should be invited to join the Shah Zada, on an assurance of getting a higher rate of pay than they drew at present. A reply offering to confirm them in their actual rights was immediately returned. It ought not to be omitted here that these people, as well as all rude nations, place great faith in their Pirs or religious patrons, and are guided or deceived by them according to their views and wishes; but the Khaibaris are notoriously a wicked race, and will mind their Pir only as long as their own interest is concerned. On the other hand, their Pirs are not less treacherous than themselves, and, to use a native adage, "are bricks of the same kiln." The person whom we have employed as an agent to go amongst them is also a Pir, and we were inclined to place more confidence in his influence than in that of his disciples. The reason why he has been sent is that no one else could be found to communicate with them in safety.

News was received from Kabul that Dost Mahomed, finding himself incapable of coping with the English, appeals to God, as people generally do in time of despair, to save him from impending destruction, and that he had employed a number of Mullas in the temple of Ashqaniarf to pray to the Almighty in his behalf.

CHAPTER XI.

News from Herat—Remissness of the Sikh Authorities—A Darbar—Movements of Dost Mahomed—The Khaibaris—Delays of the Sikhs—The Khataks—Review of the Sikh Troops—Further Delays—Arrival of the Sikh Army—It halts at Attok—Force at Kabul—Excessive Heat—The Shah Zada at Peshawr.

CHANGED ground on the 23rd of March to Shah Dand, within half a mile east of the city of Peshawr, for the convenience of drawing supplies and facilitating the equipment of the Shah Zada's personal guards, in which Lieut.-Col. Wade, aided by Mr. Lord, was engaged, to enable the Prince to enter the city, and pass through it with that pomp and state which it is thought desirable to give him for the sake of popularity.*

* "The prince's personal guards consist of a rissala of horse, composed of one rissaldar, four duffodars, one nissanchie, or standard-bearer, one nikarchie, or trumpeter, and ninety-eight troopers, and two companies of Rohillas, each having one jemadar, four naibs, or corporals, one

Lieutenant Dowson and Ensign Hillersdon, with their two levies, the battalion of Jazaelchis, and two guns, besides the Maharaja's escort of irregular cavalry, were directed to-day to encamp on the other side of the city in advance of our party. These officers had been very busy since their arrival in equipping their men with uniform sets of clothing and accoutrements to make them look respectable.

On the 25th intelligence was received from Herat, stating that a personal dispute had occurred between the British officers at that place, and Shah Zada Kamram and his minister, the receipt of which excited some suspicion of the fidelity of Kamram, and that he

nissauchie, and ninety-nine sepoys. These are under Maule's superintendence and command, and he also performs the duties of what may be termed the Shah Zada's principal assistant. The other regiments and detachments (except the British) belong to Ranjeet Singh, and have been placed at Colonel Wade's disposal. Two guns (six-pounders) are respectively attached to the Ghoorka and Nujeeb regiments, who, with the Poorabees, are dressed in red; but the Aligols wear white jackets and blue trousers, and the Goorcherras retain their native costume."—*Barr's Journal*, p. 222.

had been influenced by the Persians. We are anxious to advance as soon as we can; as we have an impression, and not without strong reasons, that if the Persians renew the siege of Herat before the Shah's arrival at Candahar, there would be a vast change in the aspect of affairs favourable to the views and interests of the enemy.

27th.—Much to our satisfaction, Captain Ferris's detachment, which had been long expected to join the Shah Zada, arrived in camp to-day. It appears that on their arrival at Attok (where, owing to the late heavy rains and consequent swell of the river, they found the bridge of boats broken), the authorities there had given them no assistance in crossing the Indus, although repeatedly pressed to do so by the officer who had been detached by the Maharaja to accompany the detachment. They at last effected the passage by their own exertions without any accidents.* The conduct of

* "The governor of Attok, on being applied to for assistance, refused to give us any; but he was bound to facilitate our transit across the ferry, which, instead of

the Sikhs at Attok was immediately reported in a letter to Ranjeet Singh, and is another proof of their systematic opposition. Generals Avitabile and Court are the only exceptions we have hitherto found. They have since our arrival been giving us the readiest aid in

doing, he appeared to throw every obstacle in our way, and declined to issue an order that the boats should be collected for our use. There were but three boats to pass the guns across the river, and these were small, and so much out of water as to render them but little adapted for the transportation of artillery. Nothing in the shape of a plank to run the wheels upon was to be procured, and the men had to lift the pieces a perpendicular height of from two and a half to three feet, ere they were lowered on board, each boat taking a gun or waggon and its lumber. Two trips were made, and I embarked in the last boat. We pushed off from the ghat formed on the edge of a narrow channel of the river, and separated by a stony bank from the main stream, which was flowing like a sluice; and once within its influence we were carried down with great rapidity, in spite of every exertion made by the united efforts of six rowers and two steersmen, who struggled hard with their oars, and displayed much dexterity in avoiding the huge rocks on either side, and on which, had the boat once struck, nothing would have saved it from being dashed to pieces."—*Barr's Journal*, pp. 192–194.

their power. The former had, before our arrival, had the families of the Afghan chiefs, who had been seized, together with their property, by order of Sultan Mahomed Khan, released; but one of them, Jafir Khan, the son of the late Firoz Khan, Khatak, being found still in confinement, on a representation of the case to the General, he has been equally prompt in supporting the credit of the British Government, and in ordering the release of that individual also, who has since joined the Shah Zada with his retainers.

28*th.*—Lieut. Maule busily engaged in preparing for the darbar which is to be held to-morrow.

On the 29th of March the public darbar,* on which occasion the Durranis and heads of tribes who had either joined the camp or Mr.

* It was to have taken place on the 25th instant, but owing to the Moharram, which is a season of mourning with the Mahomedans in memory of their martyrs, Hussan and Hussein, after consulting the Peshawr Mullahs, who did not approve of offending the prejudices of the common people, the Shah Zada decided on postponing it till the expiration of that festival.

Lord, and those from Khaibar, and the neighbouring mountains, before the Prince's arrival, were presented to him. The Sikh officers then at Peshawr, headed by Sham Singh, Atariwala, were likewise introduced on the same occasion, including the civil functionaries and citizens of Peshawr, who were presented by General Avitabile. Every one received a *khilat* according to his rank and merit. Distributing them to the Afghan chiefs was a difficult task, as some of them advanced claims to consideration beyond their due. At length the matter was settled by serving them out as they had been previously arranged by the Shah Zada's own officers, without yielding to their groundless pretensions.

Among others who came to the darbar on that occasion was Shah Zada Mahomed Hashim, one of the Saddozai family, and a half-brother of Shah Shuja, who has been living for a long time at Peshawr on the Sikh bounty. Formerly he was the governor of Candahar; but after the fall of the monarchy he went to Bombay, where he was very respectably received by the Honourable Mr. Elphinstone, then the Governor of that Presidency. Since his return from Bombay, he has settled at Peshawr. He is about sixty years old, and looks in good health. He has three sons, by whom he was accompanied, as well as by Shah Zada Jamhur, his nephew, a very unassuming and intelligent person. Lieut. Maule, who was personally attached to the Shah Zada's household and in charge of his various establishments, was sent to conduct these distinguished visitors into camp, who, as well as General Avitabile and the Sikh officers, were received with the salutes due to their respective ranks by the Prince, seated on his *Guddee.**

* "His Guddee or throne consisted of a large square ottoman covered with khim khwab (or silk worked with gold and silver flowers), in the centre of which and approaching to the front were three pillows enveloped in a beautifully delicate-coloured silk to support his head and arms. Cashmir shawls were spread in front for us to walk on, and, as we did not take off our boots, seemed out of place on the ground. On either side of the guddee were arranged chairs, on which we sat, and, conformably with Eastern manners, did not uncover the head. In front of the Prince stood the old Vazir (Mulla Shakur), habited in

The son of Mir Alam Khan, the chief of Bajour, who arrived last night, was also presented. He was treated with distinction, as Alam Khan was the first chief who had openly declared his attachment to the royal cause; but he afterwards proved a faithless character and of a weak mind, as his conduct will amply show.

bright khim khwab with gold ornaments, and behind on his right and left were two attendants. The two French generals having been presented with all due form, we three, who had lately joined, passed through the same ceremony, making a salaam with our right hands as we were named to his Highness. A period was at last put to these proceedings by a few menials entering with the *khilats* or honorary dresses, and presents intended for the French generals. These consisted of *chogahs* or robes, some trays of shawls and American rifles. We shortly after took leave, a relief both to ourselves and to our host, who, although he looked a prince in every respect, yet being but lately drawn from comparative obscurity, seemed but ill at ease with this public exhibition of his greatness, and I have no doubt was glad when the ceremony concluded. We all salaamed to him, which he returned, and we then backed out, passing beneath a *semiana* or awning under which trays of flowers were spread out, and thence through the range of *ranauts* or screens that enclosed a large area in front of the darbar tent."—*Barr's Journal*, pp. 233–5.

Sayed Reza is another person of note who appeared on that occasion. He is a Sayed living on his own estate in Tirah, and is one of the old friends of the Shah. He came to Mr. Lord to prove his sincerity on hearing of the intended restoration of his Majesty. He says that he is the man in whose house the king remained when he sought an asylum from his pursuers in the Khaibar hills. Several of his relatives have been killed in defending his cause. Sayed Reza has ninety followers with him, who have been duly entertained.

It should here be remarked that the chief cause of holding a grand darbar was that it had been rumoured, nay, believed by the natives, that the Shah as well as his son were merely puppets in the hands of the British Government; and that they were produced merely to prevent the Mussulman population from declaring a religious war; and that as soon as the country was conquered, his Majesty would be sent back to Lodianah, to remain there as heretofore, while the British officers would be the sole rulers of the country.

The circumstances under which the present expedition was undertaken—the restoration of the Shah, after remaining so long unnoticed by the British Government; the liberal manner in which he was supported; the fact that he was entirely guided in his counsels by the British officers; and that his troops were almost altogether officered by them, naturally gave rise to these suspicions among the natives. To remove them was considered an object of the highest importance. In consequence a public darbar was held, to show the people that the Shah Zada had a court of his own, and could receive with honour and distinction those who flocked to his standard. At the same time proclamations were successively issued both by him and Colonel Wade, declaring that the Shah would be the sole master of the country; that the British Government would have no interference in his affairs; and that its object was only to see his Majesty restored and confirmed in the kingdom which had descended to him from his forefathers, and to which he was considered the rightful heir, although it had of late been usurped by his rebellious and disloyal servants. These declarations partly assured the Afghans, and prevented them from joining in a religious war, which Dost Mahomed was industriously proclaiming against the English. The Shah was called a Kafir by the Amir's partizans, by reason of being supported by Kafirs or infidels.

In the afternoon, when the darbar was over, the Shah Zada went out in state to inspect and show himself to the followers of the *Khawanin* and other chiefs who had joined his camp, reserving the inspection of his regular levies to another opportunity.

A Qasid, who arrived to-day from Kabul in eight days, stated that Dost Mahomed was engaged in collecting the Kohistanis, or people of the mountains north of Kabul; and that to the heads of each party he gave a present of five or six rupees and a *nanka chogha;* while to their followers he only made fair promises of reward; and that Hafizji was preaching the necessity of making the present a religious war, to carry on which every one was expected to depend on his own resources. The communications between our camp and Kabul, and the latter place and the Shah's camp, are almost stopped. All foreign messengers are being seized at Kabul; and if any papers against the ruling family are found in their possession, it is proclaimed that they shall be immediately sent to eternity. Dost Mahomed Khan is said often to observe that he was only the master of a sword, while the three united powers advancing against him were armed with wealth, and had many other advantages over him, but time would show in whose favour fortune would turn the scale of victory.

By intelligence received from another authentic source it appears that the Amir lately proposed to levy a contribution from the citizens of Kabul; but was prevented by his advisers, as it would give rise to discontent among his people. In lieu of it, he then proposed to demand the services of three men from each family; but this step also did not appear to meet with approval. It was said that Dost Mahomed was becoming very suspicious of the fidelity of his people, and that a number of spies were employed to watch their motions and inform him regularly of their conduct. Two Hindustanis had been seized and confined, on the plea that they had attempted to explode the magazine of the Amir. Some troops, consisting of the *Arbabs* of the city, had been ordered to proceed to Jalalabad: supplies were also to be collected at that place, and the roads had become very dangerous. Such is the state of affairs at Kabul at present; and its ruler, like a sinking person, is laying hold of everything within his reach to save himself.

30th: Shahdand.—Sir Claude Wade received the native officers of the Sikh escort who had accompanied Major Ferris from Lahore, and after acknowledging their services with his detachment in the usual mode, and promising to make a favourable report of it to the Maharaja, informed them that they would be dismissed the next day.

Several letters were received from the Khaibaris and others residing in the Khaibar mountains and its neighbourhood, in reply to those which had been previously written both by the Shah Zada and the Colonel. The letters which were addressed to the Khaibaris were written with a view to make them sensible of the situation in which they would be placed by continuing to serve the opposite party, after the arrival of the Shah Zada on their frontier. A constant correspondence had been kept up with them. It had been better if such an earnest desire for their conciliation had not at first been shown, as one of them, Bahadar Khan, returned Mr. Lord the *khilut* which that gentleman sent to him before our arrival; but his son Alladad Khan, who manages the affairs of the family, wrote at the same time to say that he had highly disapproved of the conduct of his father, and that they were now both ready to join Prince Taimur, when circumstances rendered it practicable for them to do so.

The other letters from the Khaibar chiefs were also written in the strongest terms, declaring their devotion to the Shah, and that they would not be found wanting when their presence was required; but strongly condemned precipitation and an indiscriminate expenditure of money until matters were in proper train for action, with every chance of success.

I was told by a confidential native that the chief object of the Khaibaris was to secure the good will of both parties until they knew the fate of Candahar, and then, like the bat of the fable, to join that party which might prove successful; and it was with reference to that policy that they had given the above advice.

Some of the Khaibaris, we heard, had already written to Dost Mahomed Khan to say that in consequence of the arrival of the Shah Zada at Peshawr, and the number of their tribes who had gone over to him, they would not be able to hold their ground unless reinforced by some of the Amir's troops. Without the support of their tribes it is evident that the chiefs have no real power; and although Dost Mahomed commands the passes to their territory, his troops could not protect them from their attacks if they chose to rise, but a common sense of danger would of course prevent them from running the risk of being ruined and persecuted, which had made the chiefs temporize and send messages to Sir Claude Wade by their secret agents to the effect, that, when the Shah Zada advanced to the entrance of the pass, they would countenance the desertion of their tribes and declare their inability to control them. Great confidence was not, however, placed in their promises, and it was determined that, if they did not fulfil them when they might safely venture to do so, they should be considered unworthy of further consideration, and the money which had been promised to them individually by Mr. Lord be employed in raising levies to be disciplined as well as time would allow.

It was believed by some persons that our delayed arrival at Peshawr had encouraged Dost Mahomed Khan to demand hostages from the Khaibaris; which seems a very groundless opinion, because when he has not exempted any chief of note in his country from giving them, it is not to be supposed that those who have been in open communication with us, and occupied the most important pass to Kabul, would be relieved from that exaction; but it is a demand which may be evaded in their case, though it will be difficult for those in the vicinity of Kabul, whose familes the Amir took the precaution of confining within the precincts of the Bala Hisar some time ago. It requires no force of argument, however, to show that any sway that he may thus acquire over the minds of the people cannot be preserved for any length of time, with a powerful enemy on two sides of his country. The Shah Zada's approach might have tended to confirm the measure of taking hostages; but Dost Mahomed had considered it good policy to do so as far back as December last.

As Ranjeet Singh has not yet authorized his officers at Peshawr to co-operate with the Mission in making any forward movement, which was much to be desired at the present moment, it has excited much vexation in camp. We must now sit inactive before Peshawr, until it pleases his Highness's officers to fulfil pledges the execution of which we have not ourselves the means of enforcing. Could the operations have commenced now, it would have shown the Shah's friends towards Sawat Buneir and in the Kohistan of Kabul that we were prepared to accept their services without delay.

The Amir is said to have expostulated very strongly with his son Akbar Khan for his treatment of Sayed Babajan of Kuner. He directed the Sayed to be released and dismissed with every honour and respect. The sagacity of Dost Mahomed had shown him that his reputation was likely to suffer seriously by the insult offered to a person of so sacred character, at a time when the hopes of the former of engrossing his countrymen on his side mainly depended on exciting their religious feelings: but the report afterwards proved groundless. Babajan was not released; he remained in arrest until the fall of Kabul.

In order to be kept regularly informed of the state of affairs at Ali Masjid, a daily communication was secretly established with that place. The garrison did not yet appear to have been augmented to any extent. Some of the people inside sent word to say that they were ready to enter the service of the Shah Zada. Liberal terms were offered to such as might like to come with their Jazaels, an arm which was much wanted by Shah Zada: but no immediate effect was anticipated from these offers.

31*st.*—Shah Dand. News was received that Dost Mahomed Khan intended to send one of his sons with a part of his troops towards Candahar, to make a diversion in his brothers' favour; but the report was not trusted, as the serious troubles which had already broken out in his own territory would occupy them at home. He was every day threatened by the advance of the Shah Zada; and the active preparations which were made by Colonel Wade with that view kept him fixed in his position, and showed him he could not move. Had he been at liberty to proceed to Ghazni, the Shah and the army of the Indus, it will be affirmed on all hands, would have met with more opposition. The Kohistan people, and other tribes about Kabul, who had been secured by the early exertions of the Colonel, had already revolted against him. Among others, the Logar people were the first who set the Amir's authority at defiance: they retired to their mountains, and refused to pay the revenue. A party of Jazaelchis was ordered by the Amir to march to Jalalabad. On the same day we heard that the road between Attok and Peshawr was infested by the Khataks; and that three sepoys, in the Sikh service, were killed on the other side at Margalla. General Avitabile took the necessary steps to prevent these outrages.

Numbers of letters were addressed to the Bangish people, deputing Mian Budruddin Musazae (the nephew of the holy man of the same name in whose house the late Mr. Morecroft lived for some days, and through whose influence for sanctity he was enabled to visit the Vaziri country, who had joined the camp on our arrival at Machni) to confer with them.

This individual is also a religious character, and his family has several disciples in that quarter. The object of his deputation was to excite the people of that country, and to hold a communication with Lieutenant Mackeson, who was now on his way from Bahawalpore *viâ* Dera Ismael Khan, and Kohat, to the camp, that, should that officer require the services of those people, the Mian was to procure them readily.

1*st April*, 1839.—Shah Dand. Early in the morning the Shah Zada proceeded to the Sikh encampment south of the city, where General Avitabile had invited him to a review of his own battalions and the cavalry and infantry of Generals Allard and Ventura; the latter we heard was on his way to join us.*

* "On the arrival of the Shah Zada the artillery fired a salute of twenty-one guns, the infantry presented arms, and the drummers and trumpeters vied with each other to produce the loudest sound in honour of the event. This concluded, we rode to the left of the line, and commenced the inspection. Here was a small battery of foot artillery, consisting of a large howitzer and two small mortars mounted on field carriages, and drawn by bullocks; the

After the review the Shah Zada and his suite returned to camp, and the members of the Mission went to the Gor Katra to breakfast with General Avitabile. Several arrangements were made regarding the medical establishment, the labour of which was much increased owing to the augmentation of our camp. Respective duties were assigned at the same time

men attached to them being badly dressed in old coats of divers colours, and the ordnance not having even cleanliness to recommend it. Two or three regiments of infantry came next, the soldiers being accoutred in red jackets and white trowsers, black cross-belts, and pink silk turbans. Adjoining them ranged some more foot artillery, bad in every respect; about as many more regiments of infantry, and three guns again to their right. We then reached the cavalry, the dragoons occupying the left. These were well mounted, and form a fine body of men and horses; their dress I have already described. On their right were two regiments of Allard's cuirassiers, the most noble-looking troops on parade. The men and horses were all picked, and amongst the former are to be seen many stalwart fellows, who appear to advantage under their cuirasses and steel casques. Many of the officers wear brass cuirasses; and their commandant is perhaps the finest man of the whole body, and looked extremely well in front of his superb regiment."—*Barr's Journal*, pp. 245–6.

to each officer attached to the Mission, so that everything might go on with regularity. Captain Farmer, who was in command of the detachment of British troops, was now also charged with the drill and general superintendence of the levies and the guards and pickets of the camp.

The Sikh Government having delayed to have in readiness the Mahomedan force to enable us to seize the opportunity of taking Ali Masjid, and as any preparations which the Maharaja had now begun to make were too late to be of use in the contemplated event of Dost Mahomed Khan leaving Kabul to oppose the Shah, Colonel Wade was obliged to apply to General Avitabile for his assistance in raising a battalion of Mahomedans, such a one as he had already promised from his own force, called by the name of Aligol by the Mussulmans and Ram Ghaul by the Sikhs. The General readily complied with his application, and soon engaged a number of men.

It will not be out of place to observe that General Avitabile, in reply to his report that he had placed the Ghorkha battalion and two guns at our disposal, had received a letter from his court, in which he was blamed for doing so, and directed not to allow the corps to pass the Sikh frontier. The Maharaja assigned as the reason for such an order that the men, who were partly Ghorkhas and partly Hindustanis, were murmuring and saying among themselves that they would only fight along with the Sikh army. No expression of the kind was used by these men; but it is very likely that some of the courtiers might have invented the story from an idea that it was calculated to gain not only the belief of their chief, but to deprive us of the services of an efficient body of men (intended only to be employed in the protection of the camp itself, and not on any detached duty), and to throw blame on one of the Maharaja's European officers exercising the chief authority at Peshawr, whose prompt attention to the views and interests of the British Government seemed not to be consonant with their wishes. It will be recollected that application had been made to Ranjeet Singh when we were on the banks of the Jehlam to place the Ghorkha battalion and a couple of guns on our arrival at Peshawr at the Colonel's disposal; and he wrote in reply that Nao Nihal Singh would furnish him with that force. His present disapproval of the measure did not therefore appear to be very consistent either with his previous communication, or his sincerity of purpose to assist the Shah Zada at the time when the aid of his troops and officers was chiefly required. The Sikhs had the same time to complete the provisions of the tripartite compact that we had, and repeated letters had been addressed by Sir Claude Wade to his Highness since our departure from Lahore, reminding him of the necessity of these preparations, and urging him to hasten their completion, without, as it has been seen, producing any other result than the assurance of orders having been issued which were not obeyed by his officers, while studious care was taken to inform the Mission that the Sikh forces were advancing, and might soon be expected to arrive at Peshawr!* Had the Maharaja himself been able to accompany us as he wished and intended, these vexatious delays and evasions would not have been tried; but as he remained at Lahore, his officers were aware that Colonel Wade had not the power of exerting his personal influence; who knew, from his intimate knowledge of their court, that it was only by repeating his applications that they were ever likely to attend to them.

We now heard of the near approach to Attok of the Sikh army, amounting to at least

* "Lieutenant-Colonel Wade arrived at Peshawr with the Shah Zada about the middle of March, 1839. His first object was, of course, to ascertain whether the Mahomedan contingent which the Sikhs were to provide was forthcoming; but, although nearly nine months had elapsed since the Sikhs were made aware of their obligation to fulfil that article of the treaty, and Lord Auckland in his conference with Ranjeet Singh had particularly pressed the matter on his attention, and repeated representations had been made by the Lieutenant-Colonel to obtain the production of these—the only organized troops on which he had to rely—yet he had the mortification to find that not only had nothing been done, but that no orders had been issued to assemble them."—*From the United Service Magazine* for 1842, pp. 477, 478.

15,000. The Colonel suggested to his Highness that it should be halted on the left bank of the river, and there remain until its services might be wanted. There was already a considerable Sikh force at Peshawr, perhaps 10,000 men; but the officers present with it, from a fear of acting contrary to the supposed views of their own court, declared their inability to join the Shah Zada in any separate enterprise.

In compliance with the Colonel's suggestion, Ranjeet Singh directed his army to halt at Attok, where it soon afterwards arrived. The reason for recommending that measure was to guard against an apprehended scarcity of supplies, as well as to prevent an outbreak of that religious feeling which might result from the continued presence of the Sikh army on the Afghan frontier; and as the Maharaja had made the arrival of Kour Nao Nihal Singh, of prior importance to the production of his Mahomedan force, and by treaty that force should have preceded and not followed the other, he gave a just plea for detaining his army at Attok until the Mahomedan force was actually produced.

2nd.—To-day we received a report in camp that there were about 3000 Sowars at Jalalabad, and that they were stationed along the road between Khasa Maidan and Dhaka, and that the protection of the passes of Tatara and Abkhana was assigned to the care of Sadat Khan and Khalu Khan, Khosta of the Momand tribe; and that their first object was to stop the communication between Jalalabad and Peshawr. It was also reported that Aziz Khan and other Ghilzai chiefs were about to be sent to Khaibar to oppose the Shah Zada's advance. Four Sikh Sowars are said to have gone to Jalalabad, and to have been converted to Mahomedanism, and taken into service by Akbar Khan.

The strength of the Kabul force was estimated at 10,000 Sowars, 5000 Jazaelchis, and 100 pieces of artillery and swivels.

Sadat Khan being now strongly suspected of his intentions, and hitherto having made no satisfactory professions of his loyalty to the

Shah, his brother Nawab Khan, present in the camp, was treated with increased favour, and desired to collect other people of his tribe, and to send for his elder brother Sadiq Mahomed Khan. At the same time letters were written to Tura Baz Khan, the rightful claimant to the chiefship of the Momands, as well as to Nawab Khan of Pindiali, another enemy of Sadat Khan, desiring them to join the camp without the least delay. It was known that Sadat Khan meditated an incursion towards Machni in the Doaba, and in case he or any other of his tribe should attempt to descend into the plains, we were preparing to repel them. From the excessive heat, the Afghans who had joined the camp applied for tents. As they were not allowed to take shelter in the town or villages, as is usual with them in the field, their request was complied with; and a large number of small tents of various sizes were accordingly ordered to be forthwith manufactured, as we had no British magazines to supply them.

On the morning of the 3rd of April we assembled in front of the tents of the prince, and moved to the other side of the city about a mile to the westward of it, and joined the new levies which were encamped in advance of us as already mentioned. The Shah Zada passed in procession through the city, on which occasion he was accompanied by the British Mission and the Sikh, European, and native officers, besides a number of the Afghan Khans or nobles, who had lately joined his Royal Highness. The crowds of men and women who were collected on the tops and balconies of their houses to have a sight of their old prince (Peshawr is his birth-place) expressed their pleasure by making exclamations of "Long live the Shah Zada."*

* "As our route lay through the main street of Peshawr, Colonel Wade directed our march should assume the form of a procession, in order that the situation of the Shah Zada, surrounded by British, Sikh, and Mahomedan troops, should be more fully displayed to the public, as a means of inducing some to blazon forth the irresistible grandeur of his position, and others to enrol themselves under the Durranee banner. A company of British troops, and likewise one from each of the Maharaja's regiments, under Lieutenant Corfield, were sent in advance to the new ground, there to be in readiness to salute the prince on his arrival. Twenty-

After passing the city we saw a number of the Khaibaris, who had been entertained by Mr. Lord, standing in line on the side of the road, who expressed their joy by firing their matchlocks and playing their rude music, which they continued till we reached the camp. Most of these people were collected by a person named Rahmat Khan Orakzae, a rather forward and loose character, who seemed alike rash and boastful. He is a pensioner in the Sikh service, and resides at Peshawr.

one guns announced the moment when his Royal Highness mounted his horse. A line of Sikh troops, stationed on either side of the road rising from the bottom of the hill on which Avitabile's mansion is situated, up to the gateway, formed a street, for the procession to pass through, both the French generals being present to receive the prince, and conduct him to the city. The eminence being steep, the horse artillery galloped up, and winding beneath the walls of the caravanserai, entered the main street of the town, which was just broad enough to allow a passage for the guns, and no more. Crowds were assembled to witness the scene, and the people in the distance eagerly stretched forward to catch a glimpse of the cavalcade as it appeared in sight."

CHAPTER XII.

Description of Peshawr—Taken from the Afghans by the Sikhs—Its Climate—Productions—Population—The Usafzaes—The Khalils—Revenue—Administration of General Avitabile—Hatred of the Mussulman population to their Sikh Rulers—Manufactures.

THE city of Peshawr is well known, and has been described by many travellers, Mr. Elphinstone, Mr. Morecroft, Sir Alexander Burnes, &c., and does not require a further description than of the changes which have taken place since it has been occupied by the Sikhs.

Some of the streets have been lately made much wider, and a high mud wall has been erected by General Avitabile round the city, which he has finished by levying a tax on the people for that purpose. He has also improved the city in other respects. A building called Gor Katra, which was formerly a sarae, has been converted by him into a lofty and magnificent dwelling-house which overlooks the city and commands a fine view of it and the suburbs. It is fortified and situated at the eastern extremity of the principal street which leads through the city. On the top of the gateway the General has erected a splendid pavilion, which he assigns to his European guests.

There is a temple still existing within the enclosure of the square dedicated to Goraknath. Some time ago there was a great dispute among the Mussulmans and the Hindus about the place. Each of them claimed the spot as belonging to their respective saints, which led to much bloodshed and frequent quarrels between the two parties. At last General Avitabile, to prevent future disturbances, caused a mosque also to be built for the Mussulmans close to the Hindu temple; and now the two parties resort to their respective places of worship without interfering with each other. The Hindu tradition about the place is that Goraknath, who resided on the holy spot and plunged into the earth, came out on the other side of the city near our present ground of encampment, and from that time a spring issued from it, which still continues flowing. A temple is also dedicated to Goraknath at that place, where a *Mela* or fair takes place every Sunday.

According to the Memoirs of the Emperor Baber there were several caves near the spot where the Gor Katra now stands, and that a large quantity of hair was visible near their entrance, from which it is said that the Hindus considered it very meritorious, on particular occasions, to be shaved there, but at present there are no traces of these caves to be found.

The palace of Shah Shuja, which is said to have been situated within the Bala Hissar, where the British Embassy, under Mr. Elphinstone in 1809, was received, is extinct. On the second expedition of Ranjeet Singh against Peshawr, one of the fanatic Akalis set that noble building on fire without his sanction. An exertion was made in vain to extinguish the flames. As the buildings in this part of the country are chiefly composed of wood, it is difficult to allay the fury of that destructive element. The fire continued burning for many days, and thus was destroyed the palace of Shah Shuja. Owing to the frequent incursions of the Sikhs, and the want of repairs, the walls of the Bala Hissar were also decayed and became level with the ground in the course of time. The Sikhs rebuilt the citadel on taking possession of Peshawr, and called it Sumeirgarh. It has been enlarged and much strengthened by General Avitabile, and is in complete order, with a clear space all round. State prisoners are confined here, and it also contains the arsenal, from which we were abundantly supplied by the Maharaja's sanction with powder, ball, and other articles, the Mission being provided with no stores of its own to equip the levies. In a military point of view the place is superior to any forts in the vicinity. The treasure with our Mission was removed there as the only place of security, and, with the General's permission, measures were also taken to form within it a depôt of grain for our future use.*

* "The governor having volunteered to show us the

The valley of Peshawr has natural boundaries on every side. On the west it is bounded by the Khaibar range, and the east by the river Indus; on the north by the high lands of Kashghar, and on the south by Bangish. It is a very fertile, productive territory, and hence has been called by all historians the

fort of Peshawr, four or five of us rode there in the afternoon, and found him in readiness to receive us. After proceeding through a street, formed by a squadron or two of dragoons, and passing beneath a lofty and castellated gateway in the northern face, we turned sharply to the left, and cantered up a paved camp that leads to the highest of the three stories, of which the fort may be said to consist—the causeway being of breadth sufficient to admit of the governor driving his carriage-and-four to the summit. Troops were stationed at the different angles, who turned out and presented arms as we rode by. In the second tier are ranges of very comfortable barracks; and wells to supply the garrison with water during a siege are to be met with every here and there. On the top compartment, in addition to an incompleted citadel, are buildings for magazines and store-rooms; the latter he threw open for our examination, and a vast number of ten-inch shells at one end of a gallery, and a complete hill of bullets at the other, besides lead and other requisites to make up material, plainly prove that a warm reception would be given to an attacking party."—*Barr's Journal*, pp. 266, 267.

Sheher-i-Sabz, or the green city. The exuberant crops which we observed on entering the plains of Peshawr, notwithstanding the unsettled state of the country, and the repeated invasions to which it has been exposed, were very striking, and showed the agricultural habits of the natives.

It is said that formerly there were many gardens and groves of trees about the town and in the villages, but since the establishment of the Sikh authority they have been cut down. The chief motive which led the Sikhs to commit such havoc in the garden of nature was that their settlement in Peshawr was regarded by the Mahomedans with the utmost jealousy, who took every opportunity of killing the Sikhs when they left their homes, it being customary for the most bigoted of them to hide themselves behind these trees, and when they saw a Sikh passing by, they used to attack and kill him. A want of fuel and wood for building was another motive with the Sikhs for destroying these groves; but a few gardens near the south-west of the town are still visible.

Among others, that of the Vazir Fateh Khan, which is the largest and best, and contains some old extensive buildings erected by the late Vazir of that name. It was now the *Karkhana*, or workshop, where cannons, rifles, and every kind of warlike implement was being made to arm and equip the Shah Zada's levies under the general superintendence of Mr. Lord; who resided there himself with the Khaibaris, whom he had been entertaining before we arrived.* The garden of Ali Mardan

* "Years have rolled by since the locality was first used as a retreat from the bustle and turmoils of the day; but its hours of repose and quiet have also long passed, and the clang of the hammer on the anvil, the vociferations of the workmen, and the ribald talk of mercenary soldiers, are now heard where formerly the joyous mirth of some lighthearted inmates of the *harem* was re-echoed, before 'grim-visaged war' drove their masters from home and country. Those from among the Khaibaris are quartered in this agreeable spot, and groups of them were to be seen sauntering along the terraces, their thick hobnail shoes jarring the ear as they scraped the smooth surface of the pavement; whilst their rough-looking features, and tall, gaunt, but athletic figures, armed with the jazail and long knife, or sword and shield, harmonized with the warlike preparations and the existing state of the gardens, in other

Khan, the famous maker of canals, is much neglected, and its buildings hastening to ruin A part of it has been converted by General Court into a dwelling-house. The Shahi Bagh (royal garden) is situated to the north of the Bala Hissar, and seems in a somewhat better state.

I need scarcely remind the reader that before the Sikhs established their government in it, the territory of Peshawr was possessed by Sultan Mahomed Khan and his full brothers, Pir Mahomed Khan and Sayed Mahomed Khan. On the arrival of the Sikhs, and after a short skirmish, the Sirdars retired to Jalalabad and Kabul, where they were supported by Dost Mahomed Khan, their half-brother, who shortly afterwards, having defeated Shah Shuja before Candahar, defied the authority of the Sikhs. Instead of offering terms of negotiation,—which would probably

days, would have been ill-suited to appear in a place evidently dedicated to peace, and where all ought to have been lovely, soft, and beautiful."—*Barr's Journal*, pp. 263-4-5.

have been very favourably received by Ranjeet Singh, who was at that time averse to continuing his authority in Peshawr, where many lives were lost among his people by the rancorous spirit of the Mussulmans,—Dost Mahomed appeared in the field to drive the Sikhs from Peshawr. He was soon met by Ranjeet Singh, who hastened from Lahore to give him battle at the head of his army; but before the two armies came to blows, the wily Maharaja secretly induced Sultan Mahomed to come over to him; when Dost Mahomed Khan, feeling his utter inability to contend successfully with the Sikhs, was obliged to hasten his retreat as quickly as he had advanced.

Ranjeet Singh, in fulfilment of the terms offered to Sultan Mahomed, settled on him the district of Kohat, yielding a revenue of three lakhs of rupees annually, in lieu of military service. The Doaba and the district of Hashtnagar were some time afterwards settled on Pir Mahomed and Sayed Mahomed, and the three brothers are now in the full enjoyment of their several jaghirs, while Dost

Mahomed is threatened with ruin. Whatever judgment may be formed of his wisdom and foresight in the despatch of ordinary affairs, the Amir has shown that want of prudence and discernment which only enlighten high minds in critical junctures.

Had he accepted the offer of the British Government to make terms of reconciliation for him with the Sikhs, and not have been deceived and misled by his self-interested councillors to rely on Persian aid, he would have now been safe in the actual possession of his power, and not have been compelled to throw himself on the mercy of others.

The climate of Peshawr is exceedingly hot, and very oppressive. There is a saying, that "the heat, the scorpions, and the flies of Peshawr are so bad, that it may be likened to the eye of hell." While we were there, the people said that the weather was milder than in the last year; but, in truth, we felt it more severely than at Lodianah, and were obliged to dig holes in our tents, where we generally passed the day, as it was almost impossible, from the extreme heat of the sun, to remain in them without such a contrivance, though well provided with *Jawasa tatties** (*khas khas*, or the scented grass roots, is very scarce in Peshawr, and people send for it from the Panjab). But, notwithstanding the affirmed mildness of the season, we heard of two or three instances of travellers being scorched to death in the dry stony plain between Jumrud and Takal, on this side of Khaibar. We were told that a *Simoom*, or hot wind, prevails for several days in midsummer between Dhaka and Bhati Kot, which quite stops the communication, and many persons are said to have fallen a sacrifice to it. The excess of heat at Peshawr is to be ascribed to its situation in the midst of low and dry hills. In the summer, the natives generally pass the day in the *zerzamins*, or cells, which every one has in his house for the convenience of his family; and the nights are passed on the roofs of their houses, which are flat. The winter of Peshawr is said to be no

* A thorny bush growing in deserts, on which camels feed, and remarkable for its verdure.

less severe than its summer. The *hamams* or baths are a great luxury to the inhabitants during that season.* The snow, however, seldom falls here; but the hills to the south-west are always covered with it in winter. In the month of June we received plenty of ice in the camp from the Tirah mountains. Kohat, the southern part of the Peshawr territory, is not so hot. On the whole, the climate is said to be salubrious. Several men in our camp were attacked with brain fever, from which they suffered much, and some died.

The rains are very scanty at Peshawr; but storms sometimes happen in the summer, which cool the air for a day or two. In rainy weather, which is severe in Hindustan, very few showers fall here. The cultivation rather depends on the Barah and the Kabul streams than the bounty of heaven; and those who inhabit their banks consider themselves very fortunate. The rains appear to be frequent in Tirah, from the

* It is customary in the winter for the natives of those countries to occupy the heated rooms adjoining their baths.

mountains of which the Barah takes its rise. Almost every day we heard peals of thunder, and saw flashes of lightning, and black clouds covering their summits. The more we go to the west, the less rains we find. In July, August, and September there is scarcely any rain, as we afterwards experienced in Khaibar, Dhaka, and Jalalabad, which in those months are dreadfully hot and sickly, and during which the winds are very strong and hot in the Peshawr territory, especially in the stony plain between Khaibar and the city. Towards evening, there are sometimes severe storms from the west and north-west.

The productions of Peshawr are such as belong to hot climates. The spring harvest chiefly consists of wheat, barley, Indian corn, and other inferior grains. The autumnal crops are rice, sugar-cane, cotton, and *kunjad* or sesame seed. *San*, or flax, which is used in making ropes, is also produced. There are fruits of every kind, but very inferior to those of Kabul, and neither transportable to foreign climates. The mulberry, peach, fig, *naranj*, and lemon, are of the best sort, and the two last are exported largely to Kabul, where they are much used. *Naranj*, a kind of orange, is generally used in seasoning a *pilaw* called *naranji*. Among the fruits peculiar to Peshawr is the *alcha*, or plum; it is double the size of a grape, and generally of a red yellowish colour, and very delicious; but eating too many of them causes dysentery or fever.

Taimur Shah tried his best to cultivate the mangoe; but all his exertions failed, and the plant did not take root. The Afghans, who have not seen India, have no idea of the mangoe. The tree ceased to be seen after we left Vazirabad.

The olive, *shisham*, and *blut*, or oak, &c., are the principal trees here, but they are not numerous. The *diar*, or cedar, is brought down by the Kabul river from Jalalabad, and by land from the Safeid Koh, or white hills, so called from being covered with snow. The people generally roof their houses with the *diar*, which is considered long-lasting. The *neem*, *kikar*, *babul*, *jandh*, *khar*, *sal*, and several other trees, which grow in India, are not to be found in Peshawr.

The population of the Peshawr territory consists of several tribes, and as I shall have occasion to use their names frequently, I will enlist them here.

The Usafzae is the largest of the Peshawr tribes, and, I dare say, of the Afghans generally; they occupy both banks of the river Indus to the north-east of Peshawr. Their possessions in the plains are partly included in that territory, but extend much farther, as far as Kashgar, Sawat, and Buneir.

The Usafzaes are a warlike and independent people. It was a long time, and after much bloodshed, that the Sikhs succeeded in establishing their authority over them, and then only in a few cantons, yielding an annual revenue of 45,000 rupees. During the monarchy the tribe had certain allowances settled on them for keeping the peace of their country, and the safety of the roads. They, like the Khaibaris, never paid any revenue to their nominal rulers. They were always in a state of war with the late Hari Singh, and harassed him very much. Fateh Khan, of Panjtar, Arsaleh Khan, of Zeida, and Paendeh Khan, of Derband, are the most distinguished leaders of their tribe. Paendeh Khan and Fateh Khan are very desperate characters. They never let slip any opportunity by which they can annoy the Sikhs. They are an exceedingly rude and ignorant people, but very strict in their national prejudices. An Usafzae will not marry his daughter to any one of a different tribe, or, without receiving some dowry, with a person of his own tribe. The late Sayed Ahmed, whom the Usafzaes at first revered highly, observed to them that many of their daughters, though advanced in age, could not be married without difficulty; he therefore preached to them to resign the usual custom, and even had one or two of their daughters married by force to some of his own followers. The Usafzaes were greatly incensed at the conduct of the fanatic, and made a conspiracy against him, killing nearly the whole of his party in one day in every village where they were living or had taken shelter. This incident will fully illustrate how jealous the Afghans are of their old customs and habits. Education can only eradicate them, but there is no chance of its light extending to them at present.

The Usafzaes in the plains are divided into nine tappas. Their villages are generally of large size, some containing no less than eight or nine thousand souls. It is said that in time of war they can produce nine lakhs of men in the field. How far this assertion may be true it is difficult to decide; but it is stated by every one that the Usafzae country is very populous.

The second tribe which is settled in the valleys and hills of Peshawr is the Khatak; and the third, the Momand, situated to the south-west and north of that place. They have been already described. Kugiani is the fourth tribe: they occupy the Daoba to the north, and are divided into six tappas. The Mahomedzaes inhabit the Hashtnagar district, which is to the north-east of Peshawr: they have eight tappas. The most influential and respectable of the tribes is the Khalil, who are divided into six tappas, three situated on the Bara to the west, and three on the left bank of the Kabul river to the north-west. They are a brave and warlike tribe, and have produced many good characters. Bahram Khan, one of the *Arbabs* of Takal, the principal town of the Khalils (whose son, named Gholam Khan, a very quiet young man, is present in our camp), distinguished himself highly in many battles against the Sikhs. He was one of the chief supporters of Sayed Ahmed in his religious war against them. It was a regulation, while the monarchy lasted, to assign to the Khalils the control of the Khaibar chiefs, for which duty they enjoyed a liberal jaghir. The Khaibaris cannot with impunity molest any of this tribe, as their wrongs could be soon avenged; the former being very dependent on the latter for procuring their livelihood from the plains, having generally to pass by Takal, which is on the roadside. Juma Khan, the brother of Bahram

Khan, who fled from Takal on the occupation of Peshawr by the Sikhs, and entered the service of the Kabul ruler, sent secret messages to Sir Claude Wade of devotion to the royal family; but did not join us until the flight of Dost Mahomed Khan. The present *Arbabs* of Takal are Mahomed Amir Khan, Gujar Khan, and Hamid Khan, who enjoy a handsome jaghir from the Sikh government. They were introduced to the Mission by General Avitabile, and from their knowledge of the country proved themselves very useful in our operations to gain and keep the entrance of the pass, and after the capture of Ali Masjid. Mahomed Amir Khan is a sensible and clever fellow, and appears to possess more influence over his tribe than the other two.

The eighth tribe is Daudzae, inhabiting the country between the Khalils and the Doaba. They are divided into five tappas, but have little influence, being the least of the tribes which inhabit the Peshawr territory.

To the north, about five kos distant, lie five tappas called Khalsa.* They do not belong to any particular tribe, but are occupied by various people, and farmed to the Khatris and others the natives of Peshawr.

Great enmity exists between the Khalils and the Momands of the plain. Their disputes chiefly originate in claiming the waters of Bara in the irrigation of their lands. Should a watercourse belonging to one be used by the other, a dispute is certain; and the matter is seldom brought to a settlement without a good deal of bloodshed on either side. An Afghan considers it highly honourable to fall in the field and distinguish himself by bold exploits. Old age does not command much respect among them; and to be killed in full manhood is considered a distinction. When an Afghan goes out in the field he is advised by his wife to behave bravely, and not to fly. Notwithstanding this high spirit, I have never heard of their fighting in a pitched battle against the

* A term signifying lands belonging specially to Government.

Sikhs, but on the contrary, that they have sought safety in flight; which is, perhaps, owing to want of discipline and proper leaders.

During the time of the Mahomedan rule Peshawr yielded a revenue of about nine lakhs: but since the administration of General Avitabile it has been much increased. It is said that it has been raised to about eighteen lakhs, including the jaghirs held by the late rulers. Formerly several grants of land were allotted to the Mullas and Sayeds; but since the introduction of the Sikh rule many of them have been resumed, which has added much to the revenue.

Among others, Mulla Najib, a pensioner of the British Government, has suffered great loss in the resumption of his lands. Poor man! in his old age, and with a large family, he deserved rather to be relieved than distressed; but the Sikhs, I believe, appear more willing to injure the Mullas than any other Mahomedans, because they are considered the only persons who inculcate war against the Sikhs. Mulla Najib, however, is not of these; and enjoys a small pension from the British Government for services performed to Mr. Elphinstone.

The Sikhs met with many difficulties in establishing their authority in Peshawr. Much bloodshed was occasioned, and Ranjeet Singh was against its permanent occupation; but the honour of his nation made him maintain it, though many lives were annually sacrificed. Since General Avitabile's appointment much tranquillity has been restored, but he has been exceedingly severe in exercising his authority by hanging many Afghans for small crimes. A thief can hardly ever escape with life; he is almost certain of being hanged. Both in approaching and leaving the city we observed a row of four or five gibbets on a height to the right, with corpses hanging from them.*

* Notwithstanding Avitabile administers justice with a strong hand, murders are still committed in the neighbourhood of Peshawr; and the other night, within a few yards of our camp, a poor grass-cutter was cruelly cut off. Such occurrences are, however, far too common in the district to create surprise, and the bloodthirsty disposition of the Afghan is but too manifest in the number of gallows that

The Mussulmans hate the Sikh rule, and every one of them who came to our camp inquired whether Peshawr would not also be restored to Shah Shuja. They seemed to wish for the restoration of the Shah or to come under the British rule. They prefer the English to the Sikhs, and entertain less re-

it has been deemed necessary to erect in the environs of the city. These are constructed of sufficient size to accommodate some five or six malefactors at a time; and after they have suffered the extreme penalty of the law, their bodies, instead of being cut down or removed, are allowed to remain on the gibbets until they either drop to pieces or are ransomed by their friends. The number of corpses, stiffened into the attitudes they assumed when convulsed with the last agonies of death, or suspended (as some are) by the feet, that are thus presented to the gaze of a stranger, renders a visit to the suburbs of Peshawr far from agreeable: but disgusting as these exhibitions are, it is to be feared that, without them, there would be safety neither for life nor property. Indeed, the benefit of this terrible severity is already being felt, as the unruly tribes under the governor's control are becoming sensible of the necessity of either subduing their evil passions, or of suffering the punishment that they now see will certainly follow the commission of crime; and the monthly average number of murdered victims, though still numerous, is nothing to what it was a few years back.

ligious animosity against the former than the latter.

Peshawr is not celebrated for any particular manufactory, nor is it a great mart of trade; but being situated on the high way to Kabul, the shawl-merchants from Kashmir and fruit-dealers from the latter place to India pass through it. Woollen *namads* or felts of a coarse kind, used for carpets, are made here, but they are of an inferior sort to that produced in Persia. A Persian *namad* or felt will last for several years, while those of Peshawr wear away in a year and a half.

Chapter XIII.

Distress of the Najibs — A Review — The Khaibaris — Sultan Mahomed Khan — A Skirmish — Measures of Akbar Khan—General Ventura—The Khaibar Pass—State of Kabul—Defeat of Tura Baz Khan—Kour Nao Nihal Singh—The Mahomedan Contingent—A Meeting —Proclamation of Akbar Khan—The Amir's Family removed from Kabul.

I think I have wandered astray from the road on which I was treading, and must now resume my journal.

Nothing of importance transpired on our arrival at the new ground. The day was spent in taking precautions to protect the camp, and in selecting advantageous spots for the pickets. Exclusive of camp followers we now mustered about five thousand men, which were pitched within thé square of a ruined garden, and occupied the smallest possible space.*

* "The Colonel's camp may well be termed a miscellaneous depôt, so various are the materials, and so incongruous is the mass of which it is composed, and its strength, exclusive of some Durranie horsemen under Mr. Lord, and the levies under Dowson and Hillersdon (about 1200),

The escort which Ranjeet Singh had provided for the protection of the Shah Zada being reviewed, was found to fall far short of the strength which was reported by the Maharaja's officers at Lahore to have been provided; and the battalion of Najibs, who were now upwards of three months in arrears of pay, began to complain of distress. It appeared on inquiry that the people at court had taken no measures nor provided any means for

is under 4000 men, and may be classed under the following heads, which will give their numbers as near as possible—

	No. of Men.
British troops:—Detachment of 4th troop, 2d battalion horse artillery; two companies of 20th N. I., and two companies of 21st N. I., about . .	380
Shah Zada's guards, one troop of horse, two companies of foot . . .	300
Ghoorka regiment	840
Najib ditto	840
Aligols (infantry)	840
Purabis ditto	200
Gorcheras (cavalry)	500
A party of lancers	50
Grand total . .	3950

—*Barr's Journal*, p. 221.

their future payment. A letter was therefore written to supply the deficiency in the number of the escort, and to take immediate steps to defray the arrears of pay; and that in case of delay they would be paid from our treasury, and the amount charged to the debit of the Maharaja's government in the account between his Highness and the British Government, as the troops might otherwise mutiny or desert the camp.

A few days after our arrival at Ali Mardan's garden, General Court paraded his troops, consisting of some fine pieces of artillery and three battalions of infantry, for the inspection of the gentlemen of the Mission, who were much pleased with their high state of discipline.*

* "The two guns on the right of the battery were six-pounders, and were the same that Lord William Bentinck had presented to Ranjeet Singh at Ropur. The rest were cast by himself from their model, and appear almost equally good. The precise number of pieces we saw I forget, but I think nine, including two small mortars for hill service. We then tried some of his fuzees, which are very good, and burn true; and his portfires are also tole-

As it will be necessary to mention the names of the Khaibaris and their tribes very often, I will give a brief account of them here, that the reader may be able to recognise every one without confusion. The extent of the pass of Khaibar is inhabited by five tribes, having the general name of Afridi. They have each their separate chiefs or superiors, and are named as follows:—

Names of the Tribe.	Names of the Chief.
Khuki Khail	Abdurrahman Khan
Malikdin Khail	Khan Bahadar Khan
Sipa	Salim Khan
Zaka Khail	Alladad Khan Feiztalab Khan

---

rable, but when compared with those in use with every other part of the Sikh army, admirable; as with the latter, they are nothing but cases filled with pounded brimstone indifferently rammed down. All the shot was formed of beaten iron, and cost a rupee each; and the majority of the shells were composed of pewter, which he told us answered uncommonly well. When it is considered that all we saw was the work of the General's own knowledge, and we reflect on the difficulties he has had to surmount, it is a matter almost of wonder to behold the perfection to which he has brought his artillery."—*Barr's Journal*, pp. 259, 260.

Names of the Tribe.	Names of the Chief.
Shinwari	Sangar Khan Ghalib Khan Mohallak Khan

These tribes occupy the pass in the order in which I have placed them, viz., the Kuki Khail lie between Jamrud and Ali Masjid, and have much influence in the pass from their position at its entrance. Next comes the Malikdin Khail, on whose ground the fort stands. Khan Bahadar, an old man at the head of it, is considered the principal chief in Khaibar. Shah Shuja, during his refuge in these hills, remained several days in his house. Next to the Malikdin Khail come the Sipas and Zaka Khail, and then the Shinwaris. The last people are generally traders, while the four other tribes are noted for living by plunder and the allowance they enjoy from the government of the country for keeping the pass open. In the cold weather the Khaibaris in the valley live in caves, which are dug on the face of the hills along the line of the road, and towards their summits, while in the hot season they retire with their families towards Tirah, where they remain during the summer. There is another tribe of the Afridis, called Orakzae; but they inhabit the mountains to the south, and have no place in the pass. Alam Khan is the head of the tribe, and a personal friend of Dost Mahomed Khan, who placed great confidence in him.

I must now proceed to give some account of our transactions with them.

I have mentioned that, before our arrival, a large party of the Khaibaris, with several Maliks* from almost all the tribes, had been collected at Peshawr by Mr. Lord, and handsomely paid, some at six and seven rupees a day, besides an allowance to their followers, amounting to about one thousand men of two rupees each. Besides these Khaibaris, persons from Tirah and other places had joined him, and been feeding on us for the last two months, which appeared a mere waste of money, as none of these people were of any influence, or engaged to perform any particular service.

* A Malik is inferior from the head of the tribe, and has only control over a village or a few families.

With the exception of some Maliks, almost all the rest were *chob farosh*, or dealers in fire-wood. Rahmat Khan Orakzae, the Sikh pensioner, alone had about eight hundred men, exclusive of the above number. He was not paid regularly, but only by occasional presents.

4*th.*—To pay these Khaibaris for doing nothing was absurd and impolitic; the Maliks were therefore invited by Lieutenant-Colonel Wade, in the early part of the morning after our arrival at Ali Mardan Khan, to wait on him. These Maliks, between forty and fifty in number, were some brothers, and others near relatives, of their chiefs, who had brought secret messages to Mr. Lord, on the part of the latter, that when the Shah Zada arrived they would support the cause of his father, and exert themselves in opening the pass. In consequence *khilats* had been sent to all of them by Mr. Lord, and they, with the exception, as I have already mentioned, of Khan Bahadar, readily accepted them. The time had now come to try their faith; and the present Maliks were therefore desired to adopt some course by which they would be able to prove their professions of fidelity and devotion, as they had previously often professed, and were informed that these of course were the terms on which they would or could be employed. Before they answered the question, they begged permission to hold a *Jirga* or consultation among themselves, to discuss the matter. Their request was granted; and, accordingly, they retired to hold a council. These people, though rude, yet understand politics so far that they will never undertake any important affair without deliberation, either in their own respective tribes, or with the Maliks of all the tribes collectively, as the nature of the occasion may require. After a long discussion they came to a conclusion, and one of them, Abdurrahim, Khan Sipa, the brother of Salim Khan, addressed Sir Claude as follows:—

"It is well known that the present Khans or chiefs of Khaibar are in the enjoyment of liberal grants from Dost Mahomed Khan, and possess considerable force and wealth; that he, seeing the Shah Zada and the

English before him, and dreading their designs, will not spare lakhs of rupees to secure their fidelity. We who enjoy none of these advantages, how can we compel them to act with us without a superior force? Now, you desire us to expel the enemy from the pass, and to secure it for the passage of the Shah Zada. You should send one of your confidential men along with us, with a large sum of money to expend among our brethren, as the occasion may demand; or, should you not trust to our sincerity, keep some of us as hostages in your camp, and order the rest with your assent to proceed to Khaibar to effect the object in view; otherwise, what can we alone do against Dost Mahomed, who is powerful, and has yet two-thirds of the Khaibaris on his side?"

The Colonel replied to them in the following terms:—"If the Khaibaris are faithful and willing to serve the Shah Zada, he will supply the five chiefs of Khaibar with sufficient means to enable each of them to employ one thousand men of his own tribe during the war, provided they send approved hostages to our camp;

while I, on my own part, pledge myself to apply to Shah Shuja, on his restoration, to continue to them the same allowances they at present receive. You know as well as I do in what the troops and wealth of Dost Mahomed Khan consist, and may rest assured that neither he nor his son will ever attempt to enter the pass; should they do so, we are ready to support you. If your chiefs decline my proposition, you cannot of course expect the same favours to be conferred on you."

The Khaibaris said:—"We are convinced that, if you offer even ten thousand rupees to each of our chiefs, they will never come while Dost Mahomed is in possession of the country. We, on our part, however, are ready to perform the service you require; but victory or defeat is in the hand of the Almighty."

After these discussions the assembly was dissolved, and desired to meet the next day. Accordingly the Maliks again assembled, when a long argument ensued. At length the Khaibaris came to the resolution of sending a deputation to their chiefs, to say that if they would not engage to expel the garrison of Ali Masjid, and to conduct the Shah Zada at once through the pass, they would undertake that service themselves. They sent their deputies, and a few days afterwards they returned. The result was the failure of their mission; and after further consultation the Maliks expressed also their own inability to act offensively. It now became perfectly evident that they had joined Mr. Lord with no other end than to gain money. They were therefore desired to leave the camp and return to Khaibar, and that, when their services were required, they would be recalled. Thus we got rid of these idle hands. They had been entertained in the idea that we should prosecute our operations from Peshawr without delay, when they might have been made of use; but the Sikhs took care that we should be disappointed in that object. The Khaibaris and other rude Afghans of the hills believed that we had a countless treasure, and that they had only to ask to be sure of receiving innumerable presents. Some of the Afridis who visited me, seeing a few tin cases containing records, supposed that I had a great deal of money in them. I unlocked the cases and showed them the contents, on which they exclaimed with astonishment that they had been grossly deceived. These faithless marauders and robbers do not spare even to rob those who feed them.

A letter was received from the Maharaja on the 5th of April, enclosing the copy of a bond delivered by Sultan Mahomed Khan to his Highness, renewing his declaration of allegiance to the Sikh Government, and pledging himself and his brothers at Peshawr to hold no correspondence with Dost Mahomed Khan, his sons, or dependants, or any other person, the enemy of the Sikh or British Governments. It was very satisfactory to receive such a document from a party which had been labouring under suspicions of favouring the enemy by secretly collecting troops and raising difficulties to impede or prevent the advance of the Shah Zada, and was regarded as a strong pledge of their forbearance from intrigues; and whatever may have been Sultan Mahomed's secret wishes, it is proper to state that we did not find him afterwards guilty of any breach of faith. Soon after the delivery of the paper the Sirdar returned to Peshawr, where he remained during the whole of our operations. His reassurance on the part of the British Government was considered by Sir Claude Wade an expedient course of policy, and he was treated liberally by him throughout; in consequence of which Sultan Mahomed spared no means in his power of conciliating that officer. He offered to co-operate in any way; but although his personal services were declined, his fidelity was tried by asking him for some camel swivels, &c., which he readily placed at our disposal; while Pir Mahomed Khan and Sayed Mahomed Khan visited the Mission in succession, and vied with their elder brother in offers of service. They were treated with every consideration, and Pir Mahomed Khan proved his good will by furnishing about fifty jazails, which he had in his stores, to arm a corps of jazailchis the Colonel wished to raise. It was considered prudent, however, not to rely altogether on these proofs of adherence to our side, as the natural ties of affection between the Sirdars and their half-brother at Kabul might perhaps, on some occasions, lead them to change. News-writers were consequently stationed in each of their jaghirs to watch their conduct and report current events regularly. The reports of these people, however, did not show any disposition on the part of these Sirdars to league with the enemy.

About the same time a deputation, consisting of Nawab Khan and Gul Mahomed Khan, respectable natives of Kalabagh, had been sent on the part of the Prince Taimur with some presents to the chief of Bajour, as a mark of distinction and favour, and in order to confirm him in his early declaration of attachment to the Shah. On their way they were molested and insulted by Amir Khan of Naowaghi, a chief in favour of Dost Mahomed, and in great enmity with the Bajour chief. Some notice of his misconduct was thought necessary, especially as the security of the three routes lying in that direction, viz., Kharappa, Abkhana, and Tatara, by which alone our friends beyond Khaibar could communicate with us while the pass was closed, was of importance to our success. Mir Alam Khan was, therefore, requested to collect his allies or tribes, and await further instructions. Inaetulla Khan of Sawat and Ghazan Khan of Dir, and Saheb Zada Murid Ahmed, as well as other people who had previously professed their loyalty to the Shah Zada, were at the same time required to join the Bajour chief, and conjointly with him to carry into effect the instructions which they would receive; and they were also informed that they would be rewarded hereafter according to their conduct in the pending affair. Soon after some of these persons arrived at Bajour, and Alam Khan having also reported the collection of his allies, Nawab Khan and Mahomed Sadiq Khan, the half brothers of Sadat Khan, were directed to proceed to Machni, and by the assistance of their retainers and a party of our jazailchis to secure the Kharappa and Abkhana routes. They were at the same time supplied with the means of collecting more troops, and a good number of *khilats* were sent with them also for distribution among the Momand Maliks, and such as might distinguish themselves in supporting them. The money and *khilats* were of course put in custody of an agent attached to the Mission, as it was impossible to trust entirely to the Khans themselves; and the sequel will show how ill they did their duty.

The 6th and 7th were passed in making these preparations, and the force marched from camp for Machni on the 8th of April, about seven kos distant, on the other side of the Kabul river. On the 9th we heard that they had been met in the field by the son of Sadat Khan; a skirmish ensued between the two parties. Nawab Khan and his brother retreated with a loss of some lives; and the enemy, having treacherously been joined by Dilasa Khan, who had accompanied our force from camp, defeated Nawab Khan, and then retired to their own high mountains, while our party remained at Machni and exerted themselves in collecting the wounded, and rallying their men.

10*th*.—When the state of affairs in the Doaba came to the knowledge of Mahomed Akbar Khan, he, supposing that the force sent to Machni was a diversion to deceive him and enable the Shah Zada to turn the Khaibar pass by taking a route to the left by Chora, invited the Maliks of the Sangukhail tribe, residing at Beshbolak, on the other side of that place, to wait on him, and desired them to guard that road. They pleaded their inability, without the aid of the Khaibaris: and so the young Sirdar failed in his design; but he wrote to his father, urging him strongly to remove the families of his uncles and others in Kabul, who were suspected of their fidelity, as he soon expected operations to commence in his quarter. He also recommended the hostages of the Khaibaris, &c., to be released, as it would encourage them to make a religious war; and said that he had sent his own family to Kabul.

The last accounts at Kabul, from Candahar,

are stated to be that the people of that quarter were every day going to join the Shah; that Mahomed Akram Khan, the son of the Amir, who had been employed at Qundooz, had returned with three thousand men on the 31st of March; but as they were fatigued by long marches, they would not be fit for service for some time. The return of these troops had revived a little the drooping spirit of Dost Mahomed Khan.

News was received from Ali Masjid that Yaqub Khan and Suleman Khan were soon expected there with one hundred jazailchis; while Rasul Khan, the uncle of the young Sirdar, who had arrived at Dhaka with some troops, would follow him; but another party of the Lamghan people, who had been collected from that country for the purpose of being employed in Khaibar, were said to have deserted from want of subsistence. The camels and carriages belonging to the merchants were being seized by Mahomed Akbar's people, in order to transport supplies to Ali Masjid from Jalalabad. From all accounts it appeared that he began to be alarmed, and to employ himself very actively to oppose our invasion.

11*th*.—A report was received that Azam Khan, the brother of Afzal Khan, who had been sent by his elder brother to punish some rebels in Kuram, had been defeated by them, and was wounded in the head. Another tribe, named Kadu Khail, in the vicinity of Jalalabad, had also revolted and infested the road, to the great annoyance of Mahomed Akbar Khan.

Since our arrival at Peshawr, Colonel Wade had, among others of the Shah's friends, been engaged in close correspondence with the Tirah people, who had declared their devotion from the beginning. Lately, Sayed Ahmed Shah, the son of Sayed Madad Shah, who possesses great spiritual influence with the tribes in that quarter, arrived in our camp in company with Mirza Hasan Ali, the son of Mirza Ghirami, who had before been sent to that country by the Sayed to secure the co-operation of these people. The Sayed also came accompanied by Sirfaraz Khan of Hingo, Nijabat Khan of Nariab, and Mir Alam Khan, Kakar; the latter a deserter from Afzal Khan's camp in Kuram, and the nephew of Haji Khan, Kakar, the man who deserted the Sirdars of Candahar and joined the Shah on his approach to that city. Sayed Ahmed and his companions were received with marked attention; but in consequence of the extreme heat of the weather, the Sayed, who lived in a cold climate, was dismissed to return to his country, leaving his son, a fine young man, in camp. On taking leave, he and the whole of his party engaged that they would join Lieutenant Mackeson with five hundred retainers, in his intended diversion, when he arrived at Kohat.

A note was therefore delivered to the Sayed for transmission to that officer who would inform him of his approach. From the reputation which the Sayed enjoys, and the high respect in which he is held by his disciples, every confidence was placed in his promises; He soon after wrote that he was employed in collecting his followers and preparing to forward the views of the British Government and the Shah. The relatives of Madad Shah, named Hasan Reza and Mahomed Reza, besides Sayed Reza, whose arrival has been already noticed, also joined the Shah Zada's camp. They likewise reside in Tirah, and are equally pleased to co-operate.

These Sayeds appeared more enlightened and civilized in their manners than their neighbours. They were a fine-looking and polite people. Madad Shah and his relations, and a considerable portion of the population about Tirah, are of the Shiah persuasion, particularly the Turis, while the Afghans are of the Sunni sect; and constant quarrels exist between them. Their religious enmity is so high that they each consider a person of any other faith much preferable to the other in point of good principles and morality.

12*th*.—Nawab Khan, of Pindiali, and Tura Baz Khan, were recalled from Machni, and joined the camp. The former is a very brave man, and has a high character in his tribe for liberality. The Kharappa route lies by

Pindiali, his native place, and of which he is the nominal ruler, as the people pay him nothing in the form of revenue. He and his retainers chiefly subsist on the income of the taxes which they levy on the merchants passing that way. It is considered by them a safer road than the Khaibar one, where, besides paying the established tolls, they run the risk of being plundered.

Tura Baz Khan is the son of Mazulla Khan, the late chief of the Momand tribe. He was killed by his cousin Sadat Khan, who usurped his territory, and his family became fugitives in the hills. Hence the claim of Tura Baz as the heir to the chiefship of the Momand tribe, and the condition on which he joined the Shah Zada was, that, if he distinguished himself in his zeal and devotion to the royal cause, he would be restored to his father's rights and possessions on the re-establishment of the monarchy, as his cousin had already evinced a determined opposition to the Shah's cause, notwithstanding the frequent overtures and letters which had been addressed to him both by the Shah Zada, Colonel Wade, and General Avitabile. Tura Baz Khan's proposal was accepted, and an assurance given to him of favourable treatment by the Shah. These partizans acquitted themselves satisfactorily, as will soon appear.

The latest accounts received from Candahar were that the Shah had advanced as far as Shal Mustang, and that the chiefs of that place were engaged in sending off their families for protection to Salu Khan at Lash, who was said to have been reconciled by them. Mahomed Akbar is reported to have sent three pieces of artillery back to Kabul from Jalalabad. The Amir had been trying as much as possible to strengthen his power, and to depend more on his own troops than the peasantry of the country; but he spared at the same time no exertions to excite a religious war. Letters were addressed by him to the Usafzae people to join his son at Jalalabad; but they treated them coldly, and appeared more anxious to join the Shah Zada. A proclamation was likewise issued by Dost Mahomed Khan, in concert with the Mullas of Kabul, contradicting the one issued by the Shah and the Governor-General of India, and on our side by the Shah Zada and Sir Claude, and alleging that the Shah was a Kafir, and calling on the Mussulmans to rally around his standard and commence a religious war against the infidels. A proclamation was also drawn out and issued on our part by the Mullas of Peshawr, refuting, on the precepts of the Koran, the tenor of Dost Mahomed's manifesto, and impressing on the minds of the people the obligations of loyalty to their lawful monarch. These diplomatic demonstrations, to the great vexation of the Amir, kept the people from being deceived; and to their effect, as well as to the exertions of some of the Shah's old friends in Kabul, which I am about to mention, the excitement against Dost Mahomed Khan was ascribed.

Gholam Khan, Popalzae, who was the first of those at Kabul to declare in the Shah's favour, was in close correspondence with us. He had induced several persons in Kabul, and the Kohistan, and towards the Logar country, to adopt the cause of the Shah. Emissaries were also sent to secure the fidelity of those people, and to tell them that they were to wait a little longer, when they should at once revolt in the Shah's favour. One of these emissaries was Shah Zada Yehia, of the Saddozae family. He is an intelligent young man, and who, with his family, had, as I have noticed, lately effected his escape from Kabul and joined Prince Taimur, his cousin, on our way, at Jehlam. Gholam Khan proposed that he should be sent to the Kohistan, where the deputation of a Shah Zada would in his opinion be considered an honour done to them by the Kohistanis and excite a rebellion among them. He was sent to them in disguise, and, having to pass through a hostile country, was exposed to many hardships and dangers to avoid discovery. On his arrival he became the guest of Shadad, the son of Mazulla Khan, a powerful chief in that quarter, who had been well affected to the interests of the Shah, and some years ago murdered by Dost Mahomed. It was owing to these direct measures and the exertions of our emissaries that the Kohistanis revolted and advanced to meet the Shah on his approach to Kabul.

On the 13th inst. General Ventura arrived from Lahore by express. He was requested by Ranjeet Singh to assist in arranging matters between the Mission and Nao Nihal Singh for the fulfilment of the tripartite treaty; and his arrival gave us every hope of the Mahomedan contingent being soon collected, in which we were not disappointed. His intimate knowledge of the friendship existing between the two Governments, and the character and disposition of the different parties on whose co-operation we were dependent, enabled him to fulfil his master's injunctions to produce that force better than any one else who could have been employed; and his control over the troops, as well as influence with the Sirdars, made his presence valuable to us as long as he remained. Jemadar Khoshal Singh, Raja Golab Singh, and Lehna Singh, were said to have arrived at Naoshehera, and Nao Nihal Singh was also soon expected.

General Ventura promised to visit the latter to expedite the production of the contingent.

14*th*.—The news from Kabul announced the arrival at that place of an express Qasid from Candahar, bringing a letter for the Amir from his brothers, who are reported to have informed him by that opportunity that he was to consider that letter as their last, as they had heard of the near approach of the Shah, and urged the Amir to send them a reinforcement with the least possible delay, otherwise their destruction was certain. Dost Mahomed expressed his inability to comply with their request, on the plea that his subjects were already in arms against him; and recommended them to meet the Shah once in the field, and if they suffered a reverse, to confine themselves in the fort and make a resolute defence. Mr. Harland, an American, in the service of the Amir, and lately absent at Qoonduz, was said to have been seized and confined in Kabul on suspicion of being a spy of Shah Shuja. Abdal Sami Khan, the secretary of the Amir, for whose return he had been exceedingly anxious, to secure the fidelity of the Gholam Khana people, had soon followed Akram Khan with the rear of the Qoonduz troops. Hafizji was still engaged in deceiving the people to give a loan to the Amir to support the expenses of the war, but without success.

It was also reported that some days before Dost Mahomed had collected all the Mullas and religious men of the city, and told them, by a solemn oath on the Koran, that he would not prevent any person from joining the Shah, who wished to go, as he was not a tyrant; but that, if any one deserted him or his son in the time of battle, his family were to be seized and his property forfeited; and then he would be exempt from blame, as he informed them beforehand. The Amir had no other object in view by addressing the Mullas so solemnly, than to impress on the minds of his people a good intention and love of justice on his part, and thereby to excite them to *Jehad*, or a religious war; but his endeavours were still of no use.

On the 15th one of the sentries of the Ghoorka battalion on duty in our camp stopped two *chupars*, or mounted messengers, belonging to the Mission, which created a great disturbance, but was fortunately quelled without any serious consequences.*

16*th.*—Sir Claude Wade, accompanied by General Ventura, went again to the tope on the other side of Takal, which he had before visited with General Avitabile, to take a view of the entrance of the Khaibar pass; as the Sikh officers were impressed with a belief that the occupation of Khaibar would be attended with impassable difficulties; while Colonel Wade from the beginning had been of the

* "The persons whom Colonel Wade usually employs as spies are his choopars, or mounted messengers, who disguise themselves inimitably; and it was only the other day that two returned from a successful visit to Jalalabad, whither they had gone dressed, or rather *undressed*, as faqirs; for I believe they were not encumbered with many clothes. Most of these men are wild and daring fellows, apt to quarrel, and by no means slow at drawing their weapons, especially when their opponents are either Sikhs or Hindus."—*Barr's Journal*, p. 281.

opposite opinion, and wished to explain his plans to General Ventura. Had he only had an efficient force on which he could have depended, he felt assured that he could have taken Ali Masjid at first; but the misfortune was there were then no regular troops.

The 17th and 18th were employed in inspecting the levies raised for the service of the Shah Zada and completing them with separate establishments of camp equipage, ammunition, &c. The cause of our delay at Ali Mardan Khan was chiefly on account of the formation and equipment of these levies. They were formed into two battalions of eight companies each, and Lieutenant Dowson and Ensign Hillersdon were incessantly employed in completing them. The formation of another party of cavalry and infantry, to form a part of the Shah Zada's guard, was assigned to Lieutenant Maule, who had besides charge of a small mortar and howitzer sent by General Court, and also of the camel-swivels, &c. aided by Lieutenant Barr.

The enrolment, payment, and organisation

of the Durrani Sowars into something like an efficient body of cavalry was managed by Mr. Lord, who had previously raised a rissala of irregular horse, well armed and clothed alike in uniform. These preparations were indeed attended with constant labour and vexation, and it was some time before they were brought to completion. The party of the Durrani Sowars amounted altogether to about a thousand men, who, from their independent habits and pride, gave more trouble than any one else. Many more offered, but it was necessary to fix a limit and pick out the best, as they were very expensive.

Besides these levies there were about two hundred Khaibaris, the residue of those who had been discharged the other day, who were placed in charge of Wahab and Slimo, the Kaki Khail Maliks living near Jamrud for a particular service. There were also about four hundred Terah people. These constituted the whole amount of our levies.*

* "Most of the mornings and evenings were now occupied in admitting volunteers into the service of the Shah Zada;

Some time was employed in collecting sufficient supplies also for the consumption of the camp: though nothing was wanted at present, as the bazar, now consisting of no less than a hundred shopkeepers, supplied all our wants; yet, in case of emergency, we could not depend solely on them. The difficult and tedious task of collecting these supplies, of keeping the accounts, and of performing every duty of the

and so many Durrani horsemen presented themselves to be enrolled, that it became necessary to select only those whose steeds and arms were better than of ordinary description. Several chiefs who came for this purpose, attended by their clansmen, formed fine specimens of the rude and predatory soldier; their manly and tall figures being generally enveloped in the folds of a crimson chogah embroidered with gold, which, opening in front, display a *crimson band* studded with pistols and knives, or an arm protected by a steel gauntlet which reached to the elbow, and was terminated at the hand by a flexible glove of chain rings. To Maule and myself fell the lot of instructing some dozen and a half of individuals in the British method of gunnery; and our crew consisted of a most motley group, enlisted by twos and threes, as we could collect them, the basis of the set being formed by three deserters from Dost Mahomed Khan, to each of whom the Colonel gave dresses of honour as an inducement for others to follow their example."—*Barr's Journal*, pages 268, 269.

Commissariat, was managed by Lieutenant Cunningham; and the active and regular way in which he performed it deserves the greatest praise. Every one in camp had plenty to do from morning to night.

On the 19th inst. further accounts were received of desertions and distractions from the enemy. The Kabul merchants, fearing that the Amir, having failed in procuring money by peaceable means, would now employ force, were said to have retired to the hills, where they could find themselves and their wealth safe and out of the reach of Dost Mahomed Khan. He was left now to depend entirely on his own resources.

Letters were again received from Gholam Khan Popalzae, &c., urging the expediency of despatching agents to other parts of the Kohistan and Zurmut for the purpose of raising the people. He stated that they were already in a state of disaffection towards the actual ruler, and required only the presence of the Shah's agents to excite them further and to make decisive efforts in his favour.

Gholam Khan's wish had been in part anticipated.

Mulla Jabbar, the bearer of Gholam Khan's letter, a native of Kohistan, and in full confidence with some of its chiefs, was soon remanded to that quarter with letters from the Shah Zada and Sir Claude. A sign was also given to the emissaries, both there and in Logar, by which the leading men were to act in communication with Gholam Khan, who left Kabul and joined Shah Zada Yehia in the Kohistan.

20th.—The repeated applications which had been made to the Maharaja for the production of his Mahomedan force were followed by successive orders to the Sikh officers with his army on the Indus, directing each of them to draft every Mahomedan from their corps, with the exception of the infantry which had already been furnished by the French officers and a party of their cavalry; yet no increase had been made. Kour Nao Nihal Singh had, however, arrived at Naoshehera, where a confidential servant attached to the Mission was deputed to meet him, and to remind him of the suggestion for the continuance of the Sikh army on the left bank of the Indus; that we were waiting with anxiety for the completion of the contingent to the requisite number, and trusting that he himself would come to Peshawr.

General Ventura, who went out yesterday to meet the Kour, had returned with every assurance that the remaining part of the force would be provided without delay; but he could not tell how long we might yet have to wait for them, as they had to be drafted from so many regiments.

21*st.*—To-day Colonel Wade received a visit from Raja Golab Singh, accompanied by Diwan Hakim Rae, the principal functionary of the Kour. They had been sent by him to consult Sir Claude as to his intentions, and their wish for the advance of the Sikh army to an intermediate position between Attok and Peshawr, to which the Colonel would not yet consent.

From the fourteen Sikh regiments encamped

on the Indus we were led to expect that there would be about two thousand Mahomedans, and being well disciplined were considered of much more value than double the number of irregulars.

The arrival of Lieutenant Mackeson was now looked for with great anxiety. He had been desired to come to Peshawr, in order that Sir Claude Wade might have the advantage of communicating personally with him before he proceeded to the execution of the duty assigned to him.

22nd.—A letter was received from Mir Morad Beg, the Kundooz chief, in reply to one addressed to him lately by Mr. Lord. A reply was also received by the same opportunity to the letter of the Governor-General, sent through the same channel. The Uzbeck chief regarded the destruction of Dost Mahomed Khan's power with satisfaction, as with it he hoped the conquest made by his son in that quarter would cease.

Intelligence was also received from Bokhara, giving information of the arrival of Colonel

Stoddart at that place; but that owing to some disagreement between him and the King of Bokhara, the Colonel had been put in confinement, since which it was not known what had become of him. We became very desirous to learn something farther regarding that officer's fate. It was stated that the ruler of Bokhara had lately despatched a mission to Russia, and that the Colonel was severely treated.

Our accounts from Ali Masjid are that there are now about a hundred Jazaelchis inside the fort, while four or five hundred are encamped outside on the *Nala* below its walls, who were living in temporary tents. The camels which had transported supplies and some swivels from Jalalabad had been sent back there, were said to be only seven Sowars in the whole party—two or three hundred more Jazaelchis were soon expected. The commanders of the party were Mahomed Shah Ghilzae and Sharif Khan, two well-known Sirdars, officers in the Amir's service. Forty Jazaelchis were also stationed at Kafirtangi, the bye path to Ali Masjid; but they remained there only during the day, and retired to the fort at night.

On the 23rd news was received from Candahar that the chiefs of that place having failed in their hopes of getting reinforcements from Dost Mahomed Khan, had called on the Western Ghilzae chiefs, Abdurrahman Khan and Gul Mahomed Khan, the son of Shahabuddin Khan, who are at the head of about twelve thousand families, residing near Makur, to join the Sirdar against Shah Shuja, who they said was coming with the avowed resolution to conquer the country of Islam for the Kafirs. Besides these arguments the Candahar chiefs offered them also a sum of money to assist them in their preparations; but they had not yet succeeded in obtaining their alliance.

The alarm of Dost Mahomed Khan increased with the nearer approach of the Shah towards Candahar. He was said to have nearly discharged all the Popalzae Durranis from his service, because they were distrusted, and supposed would desert him when the time for action came; but he scarcely anticipated any danger at such a juncture from Qazalbashes, or the Gholam Khana, in whom he had long confided as his friends.

The chief Sirdars with Mahomed Akbar Khan were Sadat Khan, Mahomed Alam Khan, Orakzae, and the Arbabs of Peshawr. There were besides about two thousand Jazaelchis directly paid by the Sirdar, who were commanded by Nawaz Khan and Aziz Khan, the Ghilzae chiefs, as well as by the cousin of the late Ismael Khan, Wardak and Faqir Mahomed Khan, Rahik. Each of these persons had five hundred men. The artillery consisted of seven horse and six foot pieces of ordnance, as well as two large rifles, which were drawn by horses and planted on a bastion. Two of these pieces were made of wrought iron, and the rest cast in brass. Shah Mahomed, a native of Hindostan, was the commander of the artillery. The gunners were also natives of that country, and ten men were allowed to each gun. Besides the artillery the young Sirdar had twenty-five swivels ready for use. A party of two hundred and fifty

Sowars formed his body-guard, which consisted chiefly of the people of the Gholam Khana.

The above was the whole strength of Mahomed Akbar's force, exclusive of the peasantry, of which he could collect about three thousand fighting men. The news from Kabul was still favourable. Dost Mahomed Khan one day went to the blind old chief Ata Mahomed Khan, Bamizae, to ask his sage advice, saying that he was in such perplexity that he had neither rest by day nor sleep by night. Ata Mahomed advised him to make peace, which the Amir said his honour prevented him from doing. Ata Mahomed then observed, "It is proper that you should remain in Kabul, as a stone remains firmer in its own bed; but send your sons in every direction to meet the enemy."

Since the return of the Qandaz troops, Dost Mahomed Khan has contemplated to send a reinforcement to support his brothers at Candahar; but his advisers opposed the scheme, and suggested the concentration of his troops at Kabul.

April 24.—Lieutenant Mackeson had not yet arrived, and we were waiting for him. In consequence of our inactivity the friends of the Shah on the side of Bajour, having too early thrown off the mask, the state of affairs in that quarter has not been so satisfactory, as in the country south of Khaibar; but every endeavour was made to counteract the designs of the enemy and establish that influence on both sides of the pass without which the advance of the Shah Zada becomes very difficult.

We were earnestly engaged also in bringing the Khaibaris to terms, but we have not yet had the satisfaction of doing so. Abdurrahman, the head of the Kuki Khail tribe, as well as Alladad Khan and Faeztalab Khan, the head of the Zaka Khail tribe, were the first parties with whom the negotiations were renewed. They were once more offered a confirmation of their present rights and the continuance of the allowance which they enjoyed from Dost Mahomed Khan, besides a certain number of *khilats* to the Maliks and Reshsafeid (or white-bearded people who assist in *Jirga* or consultation), if they would declare the authority of the Shah in their own tribes, and expel the garrison from Ali Masjid. At first they seemed to agree to the terms, but afterwards they gave reins to their avidity, and were likewise deceived by other Khaibar chiefs. As usual, they asked an exorbitant sum, which, of course, was refused; first, on that account; and, secondly, because it would reflect disgrace in these countries on the character of the British nation (which has so firmly established their name for military skill and bravery), to yield to a race of robbers.

It should be mentioned that the Kuki Khail people were paid three thousand rupees by the Sikh Government for supplying water to the fort of Fatehgarh, and a jaghir of fourteen thousand rupees per annum was held by Sadat Khan in the Doaba of Peshawr on the part of the same government. As both parties had proved themselves so hostile to us, and according to the treaty the enemy of one state was to be considered as the enemy of the other, their stipends and allowance were requested to be stopped. Ranjeet Singh readily agreed to the measure, otherwise it would have been affording means to the enemy to fight his own friends.*

* "Lieut.-Colonel Wade finding, from the rapacity of Abdur Rahman Khan and his party, who occupied the pass on the side of Peshawr, that it was difficult to come to terms with them, and that, while seeking to open a negotiation with him, he was sending agents to some of the officers in the Sikh service, principally to stipulate for the payment of the water supplied to the garrison of Fattehghur, as well as with a view of intrigue, that officer deemed it proper to inform him, that if he could not accept his terms with a certain time, his agents would be directed to withdraw. At the same time he spoke to the Maharaja's officers, who were aware of his desire to gain over Abdur Rahman, and stated to General Avitabile that the treaty with the Shah having left the provision of the water to the fortress, and the expenses attending it to his Majesty's Government, he would himself become responsible for the future regulation of that point. Finding that they could not carry on a separate negotiation with the Khaibaris, without risking the success of those which were confided to Lieut.-Colonel Wade, and that his injunction was promptly supported by a similar one from Ranjeet Singh himself, the officers then broke off their communication with Abdur Rahman."—*United Service Magazine* for 1842, p. 481.

The son of Sadat Khan Momand, having retired from Machni, applied for the assistance of his father. That chief, however, did not join him readily, but assisted him in sending a party of his Oolus, with which the young man was now thinking to come down again to the plains, when Tura Baz Khan and Nawab Khan Pindiali were provided with means to secure the services of their Oolus, and despatched to defend that frontier. At the same time Nawab Khan and Mahomed Sadiq Khan, &c., who were encamped at Machni, and had now been joined by other partizans, were directed to form a junction with Tura Baz, while Mir Alam Khan of Bajour was informed of the despatch of these leaders, and requested to afford ready aid to them whenever required. Tura Baz Khan's instructions were that, after beating the enemy, he was to advance to Naowaghi, which he was to attack on the east, while the Bajour chief was to make a diversion in his favour on the west.

On the approach of Tura Baz and his party,

young Sadat Khan retreated, on which the former continued advancing, and stationed himself at a place called Garang, about seven kos distant from Naowaghi to the east. When information of the meditated attack on Naowaghi reached Mahomed Akbar, he ordered Sadat Khan, the father, to proceed to that quarter. In the mean time Tura Baz Khan invited the Bajour chief to attack Naowaghi; but he did not attend to his request, nor did he make any movement to join him, stating that his Oolus was not yet collected. Every exertion was made by Mr. Carron, a British agent, who had been employed by Mr. Lord with Mir Alam, to stir him from his lethargy, but in vain.

He was, it is said, privately gained over by Sadat Khan, who, meanwhile, attacked Tura Baz, when a sharp skirmish took place between them. At first the latter gained some advantage; being overpowered, however, in the end, by the superior numbers of the enemy, who were about this time joined by the Naowaghiman, and being deserted by Nawab

Khan and Sadiq Mahomed Khan, Tura Baz was obliged to retire to Pindiali, where he halted a few days to collect and refresh his men, and endeavoured to get some succour from Bajour or Machni, but still without effect. His faithless brothers, no doubt, saw another pretender in Tura Baz to the rule of the Momand tribe, and had accordingly been persuaded by Sadat Khan that his rise would defeat their own interests. They had been well treated by the Shah Zada, but they wanted the spirit and firmness of their brother in the hour of trial. Deceived in them, and receiving no support on the side of Bajour, the latter defended himself as well as he could. A few days afterwards, however, Sadat Khan returned to the attack, and after firing a few shots and throwing stones from a height overlooking the camp (a mode of warfare generally used in these hills), he and his people rushed down and closed with Tura Baz, who, finding himself completely defeated, and his force diminished, partly by deserters and partly by the wounds which his men had received, retreated to a place of safety towards the outside of the pass, where he remained until he was reinforced from our camp.* Sadat Khan, after establishing his authority in Naowaghi, returned to Lalpura. These reverses may be entirely ascribed to the pusillanimous behaviour of the Bajour chief, and the treachery of Nawab Khan and Sadiq Mahomed Khan, the half brothers of Sadat Khan, who, ashamed of their conduct, asked to be forgiven, and did not continue long with the enemy; but they were not allowed to rejoin the camp.

In the mean time Kour Nao Nihal Singh, accompanied by Raja Golab Singh, Sirdars Attar Singh Sindhanwalia and Lehna Singh Majithia, arrived at Peshawr, while Jemadar Khoshal Singh had been left at Naoshehera in charge of such of the Maharaja's troops as had crossed the Indus, while the main body of the army, consisting, besides three regiments of

* "The chief brunt of the action fell upon fifty Jazaelchies from Dowson's levies; but many of them met their deaths, and the wounded were a few days afterwards brought into our camp in a most pitiable state."—*Barr's Journal*, p. 297.

cavalry and fourteen battalions of infantry, of about fifty pieces of artillery, remained halted on the left bank of the river by the order of his Highness. That part of the Sikh troops which had crossed consisted of some of the Maharaja's *Ghorcheras;* the personal troops of the Kour and of the Sirdars who attended him. These were estimated at about ten thousand men, viz. five battalions of infantry, and five thousand irregular horse, with about twenty-five pieces of artillery.

On the 20th of April the Mission paid Nao Nihal Singh a visit of ceremony, in the course of which no conversation of any importance occurred. The place being crowded with people, Sir Claude Wade did not discuss any matters of business. Among those present was Sirdar Sultan Mahomed Khan, to whom Nao Nihal Singh turned and said that he had asked him to establish a communication with Candahar, to procure news from that quarter, but that the Sirdar had reminded the Kour of the pledge he had given the Maharaja to hold no correspondence with his brothers, either at

Kabul or Candahar, and asked the Lieutenant-Colonel whether he should employ Sultan Mahomed to effect his object, or do it by his own means. That officer agreed in the force of the objection stated by the Sirdar, and recommended the Kour to employ his own agents, though there might be no harm in Sultan Mahomed Khan providing him, as the Kour said he had offered to do, with experienced messengers, which his connexion with the intervening country would probably enable him to do better than others. The Kour, however, was informed that he himself would be held responsible for the employment of the Sirdar's agency in any way, to which he agreed, and said that he would station two moonshees on the road to Candahar, and hoped soon to be in the receipt of regular and rapid intelligence from that place about which both himself and the Sirdars began to betray some anxiety, which we also felt, having only once heard from Mr. (afterwards Sir William) Macnaghten, the envoy and minister with the Shah since our departure from Lahore. No other point worthy of notice transpired, and the Colonel took leave.*

On our return to camp the Kour sent word that he was not empowered to execute any important affair without the Maharaja's permission; a discovery of his real views which, after all that had been done by the Governor-Gene-

* "Colonel Wade having intimated that it was his desire to pay the Prince a visit in the evening, the Sirdar Lehna Singh, with three elephants and a large train of horsemen, was sent to conduct him to the darbar tent, situated about four miles distant. At six P.M., attended by a large escort, and all his officers in full uniform, the Colonel left camp, our cortege forming no inconsiderable body, increased as it was by the presence of the Sikh Sowarree. On nearing the royal tents, where a large assemblage of troops, comprising artillery, cavalry, and infantry, was drawn up, the soldiers presented arms, and the batteries fired a salute. At the entrance to the darbar court a deputation, consisting of General Ventura and a party of nobles, received the Colonel, and conducted us to the chiefs, who advanced to the edge of a white cotton carpet, and shook hands with Wade, who afterwards introduced us. On extreme left sat Rajah Golab Singh, one of the best of Ranjeet's officers, and second in command. Next in order was Sultan Mahomed, brother to Dost Mahomed Khan, the Amir of Cabul, but at enmity with him, increased, I believe, by the latter having retained one of his favourite wives."—*Barr's Journal*, pp. 273–4.

ral in the presence of Ranjeet Singh, at Lahore, and the letters which had from time to time been written to his Highness, on our way, and since we came to Peshawr, was very provoking. No time was lost, however, in despatching a letter to the Maharaja to remind him of the necessity of investing the Kour with full powers, as the terms of his engagement with his Lordship demanded, which he immediately granted; and at length, after much vexation and delay, these letters and remonstrances had the desired effect. The Mahomedan contingent was produced, the best portion of which was that selected from the French legion, amounting to six companies, and formed into a separate battalion, besides a selection of about fifteen hundred men, which was made from the army of reserve encamped on the left bank of the Indus, under General Teij Singh; of these, two more battalions were formed. A party of matchlockmen was provided also by Sirdar Lehna Singh, Majithia, and some Kohistanis were sent in addition from Lahore, by Ranjeet Singh, from an idea that they would prove useful in our hilly warfare. The only thing now wanting to complete the force was artillery, a proper quantity of ammunition and stores, and an officer to command the whole; which caused further delay. Including two battalions of Najibs, and the one of Ramgol, there were now altogether six battalions. The whole of the infantry, regular and irregular, amounted to five thousand two hundred and eight men, the cavalry to one thousand and sixty-seven, and gunners and swivelmen to one hundred; making a total, including the escort, of six thousand two hundred and seventy-five men from the Sikh Government. The Lieutenant-Colonel applied to have each battalion furnished with two pieces of horse artillery, and ten swivels for the irregular horse, which might be of use where guns could not be taken. His Highness now promptly gave orders for the provision of everything, and M. La Font, one of General Ventura's subordinate officers, was appointed specially to command their infantry.

When these preparations were completed, it

was reported that Dost Mahomed Khan intended to detach a part of his force, under the command of one of his sons, towards Candahar. As it had been stipulated that, in case such a movement should be made, the Sikhs were to support the Shah Zada, and to lay siege forthwith to the fort of Ali Masjid, the Kour was asked to hold his force in readiness for such an event. General Ventura, being also consulted, readily offered his services, and said that, agreeably to his master's order, his own corps was the first to be employed, but that the views of the darbar and the Sirdars were not strictly the same as his own. He was assured that by the agreement made with the Maharaja, the Sikhs were undoubtedly bound to aid us when we advanced beyond their frontier, and to act in cordial concert with the Shah Zada in the capture of Ali Masjid. The General replied that he would look at the treaty, and prepare his own corps, if authorized, to proceed with the Prince. Much discussion then took place with Kour Nihal Singh, as to the extent of assistance to be given by his Government, which ended in a promise from him to hold a part of the Sikh army in reserve to support our advance in case of any reverse.

It was deemed necessary that every precaution should be taken before leaving the Peshawr frontier, to secure the execution, on the part of the Sikh Government, of the preliminaries required to be performed by them.

Being apprehensive, not only from the state of the Maharaja's health, which now began to be very precarious, but from the secret desire of some of his Sirdars to impede our progress in order that we might be left to ourselves, that the object of our expedition might be defeated, no means were omitted from the first to keep the Sikhs to their engagements. By those not present to judge of our difficulties it might be thought that Sir Claude Wade was more urgent than necessary in calling their attention to them: but the delay which had been experienced at Lahore, even in the trifling matter of completing the personal escort of the Shah Zada to the proposed strength; and his experience of the inactivity and reluctance of the Sikhs in such matters; convinced the Colonel that it was only by a continued reiteration of his demands, and by letting the Maharaja see, in plain but conciliatory terms, that any omission might risk the benefits to be derived by him from the tripartite treaty, that there was any chance of moving him to an energetic support of our operations, or of restraining his people from interfering to prevent the execution of his orders.

At the same time it was desirable by such a decisive course to let his Sirdars also see the possible injury they might themselves do to their master's interests and credit with the British Government, and the result showed the correctness of these arguments; for no sooner had Sir Claude been compelled to place the subject in its true light before the Maharaja and his officers than he issued the most peremptory injunctions to them to complete the contingent, and give us every other aid in their power.

Now everything was ready to commence

operations. Had we proceeded without these preparations and the assurance of being supported by the Sikh army held in reserve on the Attok, the Prince, as well as the British detachment, might have been exposed to that hazard which was directed above all things to be avoided, and we might at the same time have exhibited the singular spectacle of being powerless, either for attack or defence, with the army of a declared ally at hand.

On the 3rd of May we received another letter from Gholam Khan, reporting the state of affairs at Kabul. The position of Dost Mahomed Khan was represented to be more dangerous than before; that the people had become impatient to declare their adherence to the Shah; and that strong declarations of support had been received from the Kohistanis, on whose defection every reliance was to be placed. By the same letter a correspondence was also said to have passed between Ranjeet Singh and Dost Mahomed Khan, but there was no proof of its truth.

The next day the arrival of the Shah at

Candahar was confidently reported and generally believed in Peshawr. A letter was also received from Nawab Jabbar Khan in reply to the one which had been written to him, inviting him to come to Peshawr. The Nawab appeared unwilling to come, but expressed the readiness of the Amir to acknowledge the supremacy of the Shah, provided he would remain at Shikarpore, where one of his sons should be in perpetual attendance on His Majesty! We were surprised to receive such overtures at a juncture when the Shah was supposed to have reached Candahar. The bearer of the Nawab's letter, Mahomed Qasim, was therefore dismissed with a mere acknowledgment of its delivery.

Further accounts had been received from Kabul announcing that great and active exertions were making by Dost Mahomed Khan to raise the population of Kabul to join him in resisting the Shah as a religious merit. Every report now bore concurrent testimony to the sense which he entertained of the desperate nature of his situation. Failing in his own resources, and his attempts to conciliate the affections of his people, it appeared that he was anxious to guard against the probability of a conspiracy to seize him, and be allowed to retire from the country in safety, as he dreaded an insurrection on the one hand, and was sensible of his inability on the other to resist the combined attack directed against him from without. He was well aware that he could not leave Kabul without the consent of the people, or he would expose himself and family to insult and injury; and it was the general opinion that he wanted to make his escape in a quiet manner. It was said also that the people of Kabul, rather than subject themselves and their families to the horrors of a foreign invasion, would seize the Amir, and deliver him up to the Shah.*

On the 7th of May, we were highly rejoiced by the receipt of information from Kabul and Jalalabad of the occupation of Candahar by Shah Shujah, assisted by the army of the Indus, on the 11th of the Mahomedan month

* These events actually came to pass.

Saffer, corresponding with the 27th of April, 1839; and that the Sirdars of that place had fled to Persia.

Having every reason to trust to the accuracy of the report, the event was proclaimed by a salute from the British and Sikh artillery in our camp, and congratulations were poured from every one in the city of Peshawr to the Shah Zada. The news was likewise conveyed to Nao Nihal Singh, who declared his satisfaction by ordering a salute from the Sikh artillery under his command; and the city of Peshawr was illuminated by his orders in the evening. A darbar was also held on the occasion by the Shah Zada to receive the congratulations of his adherents and of the members of the Mission. Studious endeavours were made by the enemy to conceal the fact, and, in consequence, the report reached us two days later than it ought to have done. Mahomed Akbar Khan was said to have immediately engaged himself in selling his grain at a cheap rate, which circumstance was regarded as a proof of his intention to fly. It was supposed that Dost Mahomed intended to follow the steps of his brothers of Candahar, and to retire to Persia *via* Hazara or Kundooz.

Letters were addressed to various quarters in Afghanistan, informing our friends of the fall of Candahar, mentioning the immediate intention of the Shah Zada to advance, and inviting them to join him on his way.

8*th*.—We now began to prepare to move to Takal, a place four kos distant to the west; but before we did so, the presence of a competent officer to command the Sikh force was sensibly felt, as Colonel Wade, who had hitherto looked after their troops alone, could hardly attend to them and his other important duties at the same time with satisfaction; consequently when Nao Nihal Singh paid him a return visit, that measure was urgently pressed on his attention. The Kour proposed to refer to the Maharaja, but was told that, as we were about to move, there was no time for such a reference to Lahore; that his Highness would no doubt sanction the Kour's nomination, who then said that he would send his answer in the morning. Accordingly, on the morning of the 9th of May, I was directed to wait on the Kour, and express to him the desire of the Lieutenant-Colonel for his decision. The Kour at first declared that he had no power to appoint an officer; but proposed to direct General Ventura to join the force, pending the sanction of the Maharaja: but that in the mean time he could not proceed farther than Takal, to which place our camp had now moved. The Kour was informed that, in that event, the presence of a commanding officer with our camp was of little more use than if he remained at Peshawr; that he ought to give us credit for requiring no more than we were entitled to ask by the terms of the treaty. These arguments changed the mind of the Kour; and, after consulting his courtiers, he said that, although he could not take the responsibility of nominating one solely on himself, yet if Sir Claude Wade would give him a letter of assurance in the name of the Maharaja, he would comply with his wishes. I assured the Kour that the Colonel would make no objection to such a reasonable request, and reported the matter to that officer, who readily agreed to it, and a letter to the effect desired was given to the Kour. So this simple affair was at last settled after long discussions, and an officer joined the camp the following morning. The above will fully illustrate the objections which the Sikh officers raised in every instance to accede to our requisitions.

The occupation of Candahar by the Shah was not believed by the Sikhs until the fact was confirmed by reiterated proofs. They said that the public announcement of that event by the Shah Zada and the Mission was merely a political act to secure or raise the Afghans in favour of the Shah. Disgraceful rumours of the total defeat of his Majesty and the British army were studiously spread among the people. I heard several declare that the Shah had been killed, and that his remains had arrived in our camp, where they had prudently been concealed to prevent any defection. However, time cleared away all these gloomy clouds, and the people were soon convinced of their deception.

Before leaving our last ground, I omitted to mention a mutiny which broke out in the Najib corps.* They ejected their commandant,

* "A mutiny occurred in the Najib regiment, which but too plainly showed how slight was the discipline that existed among the Sikhs, and very forcibly exhibited to us the qualities of the allies who are to co-operate with us when required. I have already alluded to the little authority possessed by Colonel Jacob over his men. They had now become altogether dissatisfied with him, and taking the law into their own hands, had turned him and his adjutant out of their camp, levelled their tents with the ground, and declared they would have nothing more to do with either of them. As a mark of *respect* for their Colonel they inverted his chair on the spot where he usually sat, and then, having shotted their guns, quietly awaited the results of their misconduct. Dislike to the officers they had thus summarily got rid of, want of pay, and the unfair manner in which they had been sent to Peshawr (their present appearance in this province being the third within a very short period), were amongst the alleged causes of grievance; but, to show they had no ill-will towards us, they planted their sentries as usual at sunset; and when directed to parade by Colonel Wade did so at once. He, however, told them they could no longer form a part of his camp; and in a few days they removed from their ground, I believe, to the Sikh cantonment."—*Barr's Journal*, pp. 270, 271.

a country-born European, Mr. Jacob Thomas, the son of the celebrated officer of the same name in Sindhia's service, and said that they would not serve under him, as he abused and ill-treated them. They stood to their arms and performed the duties of camp as usual, but would allow no one to enter their lines or interfere with their mutinous conduct. The Ghorchera Sowars also treated the kotwal of our bazar in an insulting manner, because he had prevented them, according to the regulations of the camp, from distilling spirituous liquors on the Afghan frontier, as it was considered very offensive to these people. Their leaders, Pir Doulat Khan and Jalal Khan, Bhatti, the latter a very rude and boisterous fellow, were summoned to Sir Claude's tent to explain their conduct. They came in a large body, well armed and with their pieces or matchlocks loaded; on seeing which, they were prevented by the sentry from entering the inclosure of the receiving tent. The poor sentry was knocked down, and they entered the tent, when, observing their excited state, the Colonel declined holding any conversation with them, and ordered them back to their quarters. These occurrences were brought to the notice of Nao Nihal Singh, and in two or three days peace was restored in both parties, viz., the Najibs and the Sowars, by putting the ringleaders into confinement; which was a great relief to us, as the former were encamped close to our tents, and we could not move out of them without passing their sentries.*

10*th*, 11*th*, *and* 12*th*. *Camp, Takal.*—On hearing of our further advance, Mahomed Akbar advanced also to Chahardeh, a village

* "On the 9th of May our camp was moved to a spot of ground just beyond the deserted village of Takal, which is situated about eight miles to the west of Peshawr. The right front of our position was formed by the ruins of the Badshah's tope; one of those singular constructions which, like that at Manikiala, are attributed to Alexander the Great, or his immediate successors. As it had been confidently asserted on all sides, that as soon as ever we took up a position at Takal the Khaibaris would attack us in force, every precaution that is necessary to guard against a surprise has been put into requisition, and it is now his orders that the subaltern officer of the day shall go the rounds twice during each night."—*Barr's Journal*, pp. 290, 291.

midway between Dhaka and Jalalabad, to encourage the Khaibaris, and had stationed his troops along the line of the road. Dost Mahomed Khan, on being informed of the diversions which were to be made by the troops with the Shah Zada in three different directions, resolved also to abandon his design of detaching any of his force towards Candahar.

Our present ground of encampment, lying between the village of Takal and a ruined Grecian tope similar to that at Manikiala, was confined, and besides the two camps, the Sikh auxiliary force of Mahomedans and our own were intermixed, and caused much confusion; in consequence of which, on the 13th instant, the Shah Zada moved to Koulsir, about a mile off to the westward, while the Sikhs occupied the ground close by, their left flank resting on the village of Safeid Dheri.*

* "On the 13th we marched to Koulsir, a mile and a half in advance of our position at Takal; but the Sikhs remain on their old ground. In front of our new encampment, an arid and stony plain, seemingly unspotted

Our ground was very rugged and uneven, the crops having been only just cut down; and it was divided by several aqueducts and mounds, which took some time before they were cleared off by our party of bildars or pioneers. Small wooden bridges were also made by them over these canals, to cause a free communication in the whole camp; and as we were now in front of the pass, and likely to remain here a long time, some heights and an old tower near our camp were fortified, and parties of jazaelchis placed in them.

On the day we reached the last ground we were joined by Lieutenant Mackeson, who arrived alone, leaving his levies and camp at Kohat; but he was afterwards directed to send for them, and was retained with us to supply the place of Mr. Lord, who, on account of ill health, had been allowed to return to Peshawr.

by a single patch of cultivation, extends to the base of the Khaibar range, whilst directly before us the white citadel of the Sikh fortress of Fatehgarh is occasionally to be seen through the thick haze, and marks the entrance to the celebrated pass."—*Barr's Journal*, pp. 293, 294.

The diversions which were to have been conducted by these officers were therefore assigned to others.

The want of a plan of the Khaibar Pass had been exceedingly felt, and we remained in extreme ignorance of the topography of it from any authentic source. It was therefore arranged on the 15th of May, that General Ventura, accompanied by Lieutenant Mackeson, should reconnoitre its entrance, which, together with a native map kindly supplied by General Court, in a degree obviated the want of a plan. Colonel Wade was prevented by sickness from accompanying them.

It has been already stated that Tura Baz Khan and Nawab Khan, Pindiali, having retired from that place and taken shelter in the Alamzae tribe, were about to be attacked there also by the sons of Sadat Khan and Khalid Khan Khosta; but the latter were prevented from attempting such a measure by the Alamzae people, who, on the well-established rule of hospitality, would not allow their guests to be molested. When these altercations were pending between the two parties, Tura Baz and Nawab Khan applied for reinforcement; and as to draw off the attention of the enemy from the side of Khaibar before we advanced was considered of great importance, Shah Zada Mahomed Saleh, one of the sons of Shah Zada Hashim, was sent on the part of Prince Taimur by the circuitous route of Gandab, with a detachment consisting of four hundred horse, twenty foot, ten swivels, and a party of jazaelchis from the corps of Lieutenant Dowson and Ensign Hillersdon, with orders to make the best of their way to Bajour and rejoin us on our advance to Jalalabad. The Shah Zada was also accompanied by the son of Mir Alam Khan of Bajour, Sayed Nizam Uddin, the elder son of Sayed Babajan of Kuner, who after the captivity of his father had taken refuge in the Bajour territory, and Gul Mahomed Khan, Mutti Khail, as well as some other Arbabs. The first three individuals were likewise requested to collect about one hundred foot and fifty horse each from their respective oolus, for which they were to be paid by the Shah Zada. This party was to proceed *viâ* Shabqadar, situated near the hills opposite the entrance of the Gandab Pass, to support Tura Baz Khan and Nawab Khan in the execution of the enterprise on which they had been despatched. Mir Alam Khan had already proved himself unworthy of reliance by withholding his assistance; but as he had excused himself for not doing his duty by ascribing his failure to the dilatory conduct of his oolus in assembling, a further trial of his fidelity was considered politic. Another letter was therefore addressed to him on the present occasion, intimating the approach of Shah Zada Mahomed Saleh, accompanied by his own son, and informing him of the strength of the party which he was required to maintain, and to support the prince either by his own presence or otherwise, as might be deemed expedient.

Mr. Carron, the British agent at Bajour, was also desired to join Shah Zada Saleh on his approach to the frontier of that territory, and was to co-operate with him in any way that might be essential to secure the success of this expedition, both by the advice which his knowledge of the affairs of that quarter would enable him to offer, and by the example of his personal energy and exertions in any military operations. Mr. Carron was also informed that his immediate duty on joining the camp would be to take charge of the two companies of infantry, which were to be soon after increased to two more; that he was also to superintend the Bazar, and to give the Shah Zada every information and assistance in his power.

With respect to the Naowaghi chief, the Shah Zada was instructed to require from him a restitution of the property seized from the envoys, as formerly stated, and a declaration of his allegiance to the Shah: at the same time a letter was written to Shah Zada Murid Ahmed of Sawat, who had already arrived at Bajour, to excite the people, desiring him to join Mahomed Saleh. This man proved himself very zealous in supporting the Shah's cause.

On the arrival of Mahomed Saleh at Shabqadar he was soon joined by Tura Baz Khan and Nawab Khan, Pindiali; also by Dilasa Khan of Machni; his brothers, Nawab Khan and Mahomed Sadiq Khan were at his request also permitted to join him, to prevent them, as he said, from joining the enemy and creating more disturbance; and to encourage them they were desired to collect two hundred men each from their tribe, for whom they were to be paid. They soon set about the business, while Mahomed Saleh engaged himself in completing other arrangements connected with the expedition.

It had been originally designed, as mentioned before, to have deputed Mr. Lord with the Shah Zada on this duty, and his presence at Bajour at the present time was considered highly desirable; but his health prevented him from proceeding. Every reliance, however, was put on the intelligence of Shah Zada Mahomed Saleh, and the personal exertions of Mr. Carron, to effect the object entrusted to them.

In these preparations we were occupied for

several days, during which a mutiny broke out in the Goorkha battalion, which, together with the Najibs, were now encamped with the Sikh Mahomedan contingent. They were very insolent to General Ventura, and left the camp, taking with them the two guns belonging to the Najibs.*

* "We had not been established many days at Koulsir when we received intimation that the Goorkhas, who now formed part of General Ventura's camp, had mutinied. It appeared that the general had been compelled to place their adjutant in confinement for misconduct; and as he was a favourite with the regiment, his imprisonment was regarded by the soldiers in anything but a favourable light. In the course of the day they unanimously resolved to release him by force; and to effect their purpose proceeded in a large body to the quarter-guard of the Najeeb battalion, where the prisoner was lodged, and demanded his enlargement. This was refused; and Ventura, happening to come to the spot at the time, determined to repel force by force, and ordered his Goorcherras and guards to load. The Goorkhas, perceiving him to be resolute in his intentions, abandoned their design, and returned to their tents, which they soon after struck, and, with colours flying and band playing, marched out of camp, taking along with them two guns that were attached to the Najeeb regiment. No attempt was made to molest them in this, nor were they prevented from moving to Peshawr, where they took up a position not far from the walls of the fort, and where

25th May.—We heard that Shah Shuja had sent his tents in advance of Candahar to the fort of Azim Khan, and that it was intended to establish a post at Kelat-i-Ghilzae, a commanding position on the Ghilzae and Durrani frontiers, between Ghazni and Candahar. It was supposed that the intended advance of the Persians against Herat had prevented the British army from advancing immediately on Kabul. Owing to these reports it was determined to await the receipt of further advices from the camp of the Shah, thinking it probable that the whole British force might not be able to move at once on Kabul; but a due regard for the support of our influence required that we should without delay improve, as far as our imperfect means would admit, the efficiency of the Shah Zada's own force, in order that he might be better prepared to act either offensively or defensively, as circum-

they were permitted to remain in a state of open mutiny, without any attempt being made to overawe them, whilst a report of their conduct was sent to the Maharaja at Lahore."—*Barr's Journal*, pp. 294, 295.

stances might demand. Colonel Wade, therefore, commenced raising another battalion of levies, the formation of which, from the scarcity of officers, he was obliged to commit to Captain Ferris, who, in addition to his numerous other duties, had been appointed Quarter-Master-General of our force. Lieutenant Mackeson and Mr. Lord, also, were directed to complete the levies of horse which they had raised to five hundred men each, besides two or three companies of jazaelchis. The increase of the levies was considered more advantageous than squandering away the public money on chiefs who could not yet separate themselves from Dost Mahomed Khan, whose power over them, in consequence of the long delay at Candahar, and of the Shah Zada at Peshawr, had not apparently been so much shaken as had been believed, by the capture of the former. Failing in his attempt to raise the people by preaching a religious war, he now began to announce to them the advance of the Persians and Russians against Herat, which kept his people still doubtful as to the course he intended to adopt. A few days after we had arrived at Koulsir a foraging party from the Sikh camp was attacked near the entrance of the pass by the Khaibaris, who carried off some of their camels and killed two or three grass-cutters; in consequence of which the Colonel sent for Wahab Malik, and desired him to occupy with his party the old deserted fort of Jumrud in front of Shadi Bagiar, the path by which the Khaibaris used to come out. Finding the outlet closed against them, they came down one night to attack the post: several men were killed on both sides; but Wahab, being reinforced by another friendly tribe, retained his position and did good service until we were prepared to advance. To keep the Khaibaris at a distance, the Durrani horse were directed to send a strong patrolling party along the hills every night, and pickets were thrown further out. On one occasion they came so near those of the Sikhs that they were mistaken for enemies; and before they had time to answer the challenge a volley was fired at them from the Sikh picket, which wounded some men and horses. To avoid the repetition of such accidents, the Sikh force moved to a position four or five miles off on the road to Choora.

About this time a letter, which had been addressed by Mahomed Akbar to a chief named Duria Khan, in the Peshawr territory, was intercepted by one of the Arbabs of Takal, named Amir Khan, and delivered to Sir Claude. The translation of it which follows will give an idea of the arts adopted by the enemy to excite the people. Duria Khan is a rebellious chief, and much harasses the Sikhs.

After compliments—

"I have received your letter, and am aware of your valour and your devotion to our religion. May the blessing of God be upon you! The affairs of Candahar, about which you ask, are as follows:—when the execrable tribe (the English) had reached Candahar, Haji Kakar, proving himself a Kafir, and forgetting all his former duty and services, deserted to the enemy, which has caused extreme dismay; and the Candahar Sirdars, having no alternative, were obliged to turn themselves towards Girishk and Nadir Ali (the ancient fortress of the Barakzae family), while they themselves with their followers have encamped on the banks of the Helmund river. The infidels have thus got possession of Candahar; but the servants of the Amir are now collecting forces from all quarters, and stirring up the people around them for their entire extermination. The men also of Turkistan and the Ghilzaes are preparing to fight for the faith. From the men of Iran and Roos (Persia and Russia) also, certain intelligence of their approach has come; and these Nazarenes (Christians) at Candahar are in a state of the greatest anxiety, and well nigh their wits' end, seeing they are about to be attacked from every quarter. At the same time Shah Zada Kamran has applied to this ill-omened tribe for aid to protect Herat against the Russians. When the Firangis at Candahar saw affairs taking this turn, they wrote off to their own country for reinforcements; but we trust in God that the heat will now prevent the arrival of any new troops, and that those who are here will be ruined and destroyed. With this object in view the Amir is now actively employed; and whenever Mahomed Shah (the King of Persia) approaches, he also will advance. The Firangis now intend to fortify themselves in Candahar. May God confound these enemies of his religion, and make their faces black! The people of Islam on all sides are up in arms, and from the Hotki and Tokhi tribes (between Candahar and Ghazni) fifty or sixty thousand men have already assembled and addressed the Amir to send his army. He has accordingly ordered off Mahomed Afzal Khan with three thousand horse and ten guns, that he may speedily raise the country about Kelati Ghilzae, and Makhoor, and extirpate the infidels, and enrich himself by their spoils. To-day I also, with my victory-gaining troops and lightning-darting artillery, am here encamped at Chardeh. If all is well, be sure of an early arrival in your quarter, for which be prepared, and send me intelligence of what is going on there, and of your own welfare."

I am not aware of any answer having been returned by Duria Khan; but such was the course which the ruling family of Kabul adopted after the fall of Candahar. However, the people were now too wide awake to be hoodwinked and deceived by the Amir or his sons; on the contrary, several overtures had been made to Lieut-Colonel Wade by the Durrani leaders with Mahomed Akbar to come over to the Shah Zada on receiving assurances that they would be employed by his father on the same terms on which they then served Dost Mahomed Khan; but the roads between our camp and them were so strictly guarded, that it was difficult to carry their wishes into effect, and only one or two of them came over. Towards the end of May the heat in camp had become very severe, and many fell sick; the thermometer in tents rose to 110°, and we all began to dig holes, and live in them like so many foxes.*

* A variety of expedients were adopted to mitigate the effects of the desperately hot weather; some of the officers excavating the earth beneath their marquees; others

On the 5th of June intelligence was received of Dost Mahomed's sending off his family on the road to Kholam. He delivered all his

having only one half of the area dug out, by which means a *change* of temperature was to be obtained; whilst a few constructed apartments under ground, at the depth of seven or eight feet. For myself, I preferred the simple canvas with a *tatter* (*khus-khus*, screen-wetted), although much warmer; but there was a dampness in the *Sard-khanas* (cool apartments) which in my opinion is not wholesome, and I also dislike the feeling of moisture that invariably clung to the dress after sitting in one for any length of time. F., whose tent was pitched opposite to mine, had built one of these "vaults for the living," on the most approved principles, and was sitting in it, on a certain sultry day, transacting the affairs of his company with his subahdar and havildar, when down came the whole fabric on the top of them, the beams, as they fell, fortunately taking such directions as completely saved them, if not from destruction, at least from broken limbs. I heard the crash, and immediately ran over to assist; but on reaching the spot, I became convulsed with laughter at the appearance of the gallant captain, who, being a stout man, had perspired freely, and dust from off the clay roof had stuck to his face and plastered it as if with a coating of mud: not a feature was to be distinguished; and beside him stood the subahdar, a poor, withered-looking old man, who seemed as if he was just issued from a baker's shop.

jewels and other valuables to the care of Mahomed Akbar Khan's mother, his favourite wife. They separated with feelings of great grief and sorrow. This circumstance convinced us that the Amir was positively determined on his flight, which proved to be true in the end.

From the present time to the 6th of August Sir Claude Wade was engaged in establishing his posts at the mouth of the pass in advance of the Sikh frontier, and in keeping Sadat Khan, who had entered the plains near Machni, in check, while Shah Zada Mahomed Saleh was advancing with his force by Naowagi towards Bajour, and the Sayeds of Tirah were desired to create a diversion in that quarter. As I remained in camp with the Shah Zada while these operations were carried on, I am not able to describe them from my own observation; and even had I been present I am sure that I could not do justice to them. I therefore hope that I shall be excused for supplying my own deficiency by inserting the description given of that important part of the expedition from the very interesting and excellent journal published by Lieutenant Barr, which has been sent to me from England by my friend Mohan Lal, and from which it will be observed that I have taken many notes to illustrate my own imperfect diary, which I hope that good gentleman will excuse.

CHAPTER XIV.

Preparations for advancing—Supply of Water stopped—Stockades erected—General Sickness—Death of Ranjeet Singh—Skirmishing near the Pass—Action with Sadat Khan—Sir C. Wade obliged to go to Koulsir—An Affray between the Mussulmans and Sikhs near Jamrud—Return of Sir C. Wade—His Force—Ill-feeling of the Sikhs to the British Power—Enemies to be encountered.

"PREPARATIONS were at length made that bore some indications of a speedy advance being contemplated. The levies under Lieutenant Dowson and Ensign Hillersdon were considered sufficiently *au fait* at their exercise to admit of their joining with the British troops, and taking part in the general duties of the camp. The artillery were busy in constructing ammunition-boxes, to be carried on the backs of mules, and in practising the mounting and dismounting of ordnance from the backs of elephants; and, above all, an advanced camp was formed beneath the walls of Fattehgarh;* and *sangas*, or rude breastworks of stones, were thrown up on the more commanding positions near the entrance of the pass. These rough pieces of fortification, so close to their own haunts, proved very offensive to the inimical

* "Considering that with reference to the probable date of the departure of the Shah from Candahar, and the declaration of the Khaibar chiefs that they would give hostages of their good faith when we appeared in the vicinity of Jamrud, and that it was desirable to endeavour to ascertain what the intentions of Mahomed Akbar Khan were, in the event of a demonstration to force the pass, it appeared to the Lieutenant-Colonel advisable that no further delay should take place in occupying the entrance to the pass in some strength. He proceeded therefore to the spot himself, and lost no time in erecting two stockades, supporting one another, commanding the principal entrance to the pass, and securing at the same time a communication with the Sikh garrison in Fattehgarh, where he formed an encampment of the troops which had been placed at his disposal by the Maharaja specially for service. On the following day he erected two other stockades, which gave complete possession of the entrance, and left Lieutenant Mackeson, with his levies added to the force already there, in charge of the post, visiting the ground occasionally himself."—*United Service Magazine* for 1842, p. 482.

Khaibaris, who soon evinced a disposition to get rid of them; and, on the 9th, came down in some force with an apparent intention of making an attack. Maule, however, having sent a few shells from a 5½ inch mortar, arrested their progress; but the fellows fired well and true, one of their bullets passing between him and Mackeson, and knocking the turban off the head of the latter's moonshee, who was standing close to them.

"On the 10th I relieved Maule at Jamrud, and took there a 6-pounder gun of the Alowalia Raja's, in case an opportunity should occur of getting a few long shots. Ferris accompanied me. There was no appearance of the enemy when we arrived; but as the evening advanced, first one head, and then another, and another, became visible on the heights in front; until, at length, a small body of jazaelchis from Ali Musjid had collected there. The dread of the shells, however, kept them at a distance; but they commenced firing at us with their long rifles, and one of their bullets passed over our heads without committing any damage. Shortly after, as night was closing in, and our foes had decamped, we returned to the fort of Fattehgarh, where we slept.

"Early on the following morning Colonel Wade rejoined us from Koulsir, where he had been for a couple of days; and, on his arrival, we rode to the mouth of the pass for the purpose of erecting another *sanga* on the right bank of the stream, or rather *bed* of the stream, as the Khaibaris had turned the water into another channel, because the Colonel had refused to pay some exorbitant tax they required for allowing it to flow. Ranjeet Singh is compelled to give 1200 rupees a month for the little of the 'pure element' that is required for the use of the garrison at Futtehgarh; and if the money is delayed beyond the stipulated day of settlement, the stream is instantly stopped, which no doubt proves a certain remedy for the cure of dilatory payment. At the new *sanga* we were occupied till past eleven o'clock, when the heat of the sun drove us to our camp.

"Our fortifications in front of the pass now consisted of four redoubts, three on the left bank and one on the right, the latter of which commanded the entrance, and also afforded a good cross-fire to the most advanced of those on the opposite side. The largest and most elevated in situation was in the centre, and was occupied by a strong body of friendly Khaibaris. The other *sangas* were occupied by picked men from Dowson's and Hillersdon's regiments, with a few of Lieutenant Mackeson's Multanis. Amongst the neighbouring hills we saw some deserted villages, or rather apologies for such, of the Khaibaris, consisting merely of caves dug in the earth, in the most rude manner, or as would be seen in the most savage countries. The site of the battle-ground where the gallant Harri Singh lost his life was pointed out to us, as well as the remains of the fort of Jamrud, near to which the encounter took place. Little, however, beyond a confused-looking mound is to be seen of the latter, it having been demolished soon after the fatal action, and the stronger and more substantial castle of Fattehgarh erected in its stead.

"We again slept within the walls of the fortress, our beds being ranged side by side on the roof of a building in its interior, to which we climbed by an indifferently constructed ladder. We were joined here by the 'Goroo,' or priest of the place, whose apartment was on a level with our quarters, and who, with the greatest coolness in the world, dragged his *char-paee*, or bedstead, close to ours, and stretching himself on the top of it, was soon in a snore. With nothing but the canopy of heaven for a curtain, we were as cool as it was possible to be at Jamrud, in the middle of summer, or, in other words, we found it unpleasantly warm; and to add to our grievances, the fatigues which the Colonel had gone through at the *sanga*, brought on fever, from which he suffered considerably during the night. The next morning I accompanied him to Koulsir, where he had a smart attack: but the terrible heat to which we were exposed was already telling upon most of our constitutions. Captain Farmer had been laid up at Peshawr, and was seriously ill for some days; Rattray followed, and was for weeks on the sick list. Corfield has been so extremely ill, that he is to return to the provinces with General Court, whenever that officer proceeds to Lahore with his brigade. Lord has suffered so much from fever and ague that he has been compelled to take up his quarters in General Avitabile's house at Peshawr, where he is not so much exposed to the weather. Lieutenant Cunningham, too, has had an attack of fever and been bled; and some out of the few that remain have also been complaining.

"On the 2nd of July, official information was received of the death of the Maharaja Ranjeet Singh, who, after a long struggle with life, quitted this world on the evening of the 27th ultimo, bequeathing his kingdom to his eldest son, Kharak Singh, and the famous diamond, the 'Kohinoor,' or 'hill of light,' to the temple of Juggernath, besides distributing above forty lacs of rupees in charity, a few days before his death.* As soon as he had ceased to breathe, the chief sultana took the hand of Dhian Singh, the vizier, and inserting it into that of Kharak Singh, the new sovereign, she placed them in that position on the breast of the corpse, and made them swear to be faithful to one another, and to the late Maharaja's wishes. I think it was on the day following his decease that the body was burned, and, melancholy to relate, no less than four of

* Ranjeet Singh being the only person in the Sikh nation who was well disposed towards his allies in the expedition, his death before that part of it was carried out which depended on their co-operation was a serious and embarrassing event, as it encouraged the hopes of the disaffected, both among Afghans and Sikhs, of our failure. Its first effect was to create a desire on the part of Nao Nihal Singh, and the Sirdars and troops with him, to hasten back to Lahore, where parties struggling for ascendancy were beginning to form their intrigues. They hesitated for a time between their inclination and duty, but the latter prevailed. No sooner, however, had the Shah Zada advanced than the whole of the reserve broke up their camp at Attok and marched in haste to Lahore; but the contingent, the command of which had now devolved on a Mahomedan officer, viz., Sheikh Bassowan, a colonel and brigadier in the French legion, remained faithful to its post.

his wives, and five or seven of his slave-girls, voluntarily sacrificed themselves on the same funeral pyre.

"A day or two subsequent to this, Wade and Ferris proceeded to the neighbourhood of the Kabul river, as our inveterate foe Sadat Khan had been busily engaged in inciting the population on its left bank to arm against us. On the 6th, I joined them with a small Sikh howitzer, escorted by a detachment of the Shah Zada Taimur's body guard; and as the Colonel intended to commence operations that day, and expected me at sunrise, I was obliged to leave Koulsir at 2 A.M. I arrived in the nick of time, as he had just assembled a number of horsemen who were to accompany us, and with whom we forthwith proceeded to occupy a height which overlooks the river, where it quits the Khaibar range, and enters the plain of Peshawr. This view was extremely pretty, the stream, which was far below us, being concealed every here and there by the jutting points of projecting mountains, with a few straggling villages on its left bank, fringed, in one or two places, with mulberry-trees; whilst in the middle of the channel a black rock or two upreared their heads, and broke the force of the current as it flowed swiftly by, causing the water to be lashed into a white foam, and which, as it receded from the obstructions, gradually resumed its unruffled appearance. The Momand country, a mere succession of barren and rocky hills, was to the north; and to the south, and to the east, the valley of Peshawr, over which were spread tracts of cultivation, and clumps of trees, bounded our view; the high range of the Khaibar mountains being to the west.

"The largest of the villages was pointed out by Colonel Wade as that which he wished to be shelled; but it appeared to me beyond the range of the small howitzer we had brought with us: however, I arranged matters to make a trial. Unwilling to commence hostilities, in the hope that the people might yet be induced to come in peaceably, the Colonel still deferred proceeding to extremities, notwithstanding some hours had passed by beyond that he had fixed as the limit of his forbearance. Presently appeared a couple of horsemen, who were hailed, and asked to join us. They replied only by hurling a torrent of abuse. Ball after ball was sent at them, and although I observed one or two plough up the ground in front of their horses' feet, they managed to escape unhurt; and I was glad of it, as they had displayed much coolness and daring. A party on foot now descended the hills on the opposite bank, and commenced blazing away at us; but without effect, as we were beyond the range of their matchlocks, though a few of our rifles reached one of the boldest of their set, who had crept to the water's edge, and who would have paid dearly for his temerity had he not been safely ensconced behind a huge rock, upon which the bullets told.

"This desultory mode of skirmishing continued for some time, and on its ceasing Wade ordered the remains of an old tower to be put into a state of defence, and lodged a guard there. He then proceeded with Ferris down a narrow cut, which brought them to the margin of the river, and opposite to a village, whose inhabitants he previously had warned (in order that the women and children might be sent out of the way) would be attacked unless they consented to acknowledge the Shah Zada. As this cut was no gun road, I was obliged to return by that we had come up, and which, being in many places rather steep, compelled us to have recourse to the drag-ropes, to pull the ordnance over them. Whilst occupied at one of these eminences, a few stray shots were fired at us from the heights above, but did no injury; and in half an hour I rejoined Colonel Wade. It was now necessary that the gun should be advanced with much precaution, to conceal it from a party of horsemen, located beneath a tree contiguous to the village; and this having been satisfactorily accomplished, the piece was laid and fired: the shell falling in front of them, and bounding onwards over their heads, exploded just beyond their position. 'Sauve qui peut!' was their cry, and away they scuttled to a place of safety as fast as their legs could carry them. Another shot, aimed at the largest house in the place, plumped into the midst of it, and raised a cloud of dust that took several minutes to settle. Our attention was then directed to a lofty tower, in which numbers of men had taken refuge; and whilst firing at this, a stray shell happening to descend into a corner of the village, turned out a number of individuals, who proceeded at full tilt across a hill at its back, and behind which another fell, and bursting, drove out a number of women who had taken shelter there, and who now, not knowing where to hide themselves from the deadly missiles, again sought refuge in their houses.

"The Colonel, unwilling to make an unnecessary sacrifice of life, but determined to show his threats were not to be disregarded with impunity, now ordered the firing to cease, and we moved along the banks of the river until we reached a small village, in front of which the stream makes a considerable bend, thus leaving an open space of ground, which formed an eligible situation for an outwork. A ditch and mound were forthwith dug and thrown up, but as there was nothing more for me to do, I returned to camp, which was pitched near a fortified enclosure, and which I reached at five in the evening, having been in the saddle, with scarcely any intermission, for fifteen hours. I was, as may be supposed, considerably well fagged, and, having had nothing to taste since the preceding night, tolerably nigh being famished, and glad to lay hold of a biscuit wherewith to stay the cravings of my appetite. At eight o'clock, Captain Ferris and Colonel Wade having waited until the position was entirely enclosed by a parapet and thick brushwood, by way of an abattis where such was required, came back, and told me that about an hour after I had left, some marksmen had got on to an island within range of their situation, from which they blazed away, and killed one man and wounded two others before they could be dislodged. A strong guard was left to defend the village and ground we had occupied.*

* From the raw levies and miscellaneous composition of the Shah Zada's force, it was the invariable practice of the

"A day or two afterwards, Ferris having constructed a very fair attempt at a battery in the enclosure, we rode there in the evening, taking with us the howitzer, and also a gun that had been sent from the camp at Koulsir on the Colonel's requisition. The left bank of the river was on this occasion crowded with the partizans of Sadat Khan, who was also said to be present; but they were wary, and kept almost beyond the range of shot. A few shells were sent at a building close to a garden, which we saw with a telescope was filled with men, who soon evacuated it; and a few shots from the six-pounder in the direction of Sadat Khan caused him and his train to fall back and take up a more distant and respectful position. Several marksmen again crossed over to the island, and a few of their bullets buried themselves in the parapet of

Colonel, in occupying a position, immediately to fortify it by a stockade, behind which the men might find a security the want of discipline could not supply. For that purpose a large party of *Bildars* or pioneers always accompanied every detachment, and the country being strewed with stones, these defences were easily and quickly erected.

the battery. Night put a stop to our practice, and we returned to our quarters. A trench had been sunk and a breastwork thrown up the previous day as a defence to the Shah Zada Jamhur's camp, situated a short distance behind the enclosure with the battery, and about a mile and a quarter in advance of our own position.

"Urgent business now requiring Wade's presence at Koulsir, he left Ferris and myself in charge of the camp near Machni, and as we had the use of his *khus khus* tent, we contrived to make ourselves tolerably comfortable in spite of the intense heat.*

"Of an evening we used to ride over to the Shah Zada Jamhur's camp, who was always glad to see us, and generally produced a collation of fruit, which he partook of with us. We then commonly adjourned to the banks of the

* The Sikhs had refused to despatch a reinforcement which had been requested; and it being the first occasion on which their disposition to support the Colonel's operations had been practically put to the test, it was essential that he should come to a definite understanding with Nao Nihal Singh on so important a point.

Kabul river, where, collecting a few fishermen, we made them cast their nets into the water, and in this manner caught numbers of fine fish, chiefly of a species of trout. As we were returning from these visits, we would often amuse ourselves by trying the mettle of our steeds against the speed of our escort, which consisted of some thirty or forty horsemen; and invariably the jemadar of the troop, who was mounted on a long gaunt racer, succeeded in heading us all.

"During our sojourn near Machni we heard of a serious affray that had occurred at Jamrud between the Mussulmans and Sikhs. How the quarrel commenced is not exactly known, but the latter shut the gates of their fort (Fatteh-garh), and set to firing briskly on their antagonists.* Mackeson, who, in addition to the difficult task of conciliating the Khaibar chiefs in its neighbourhood, had charge of our camp

* Some friendly Khaibaris in the neighbourhood had killed a bullock, a piece of which, it was supposed, had been brought into Lieutenant Mackeson's camp, which caused the outbreak.

there, on hearing the disturbance endeavoured to put a stop to it, and for this purpose was advancing to a wicket, when a *Chuprassie* was shot dead by his side, the Sikhs being heard by his cousin (who had joined him from Lahore a short time ago) to shout out, 'Shoot the Faringhi Sahib,' or 'English gentleman.' In spite of the danger to which he was exposed, Lieutenant Mackeson boldly insisted on being admitted within the fort, where he found the commandant, Boodh Singh, doing everything in his power to quell the tumult. A report of the circumstance was immediately forwarded to Prince Nao Nihal Singh, at Peshawr, who sent Sirdar Lehna Singh to inquire into the matter, and ordered the garrison to be relieved forthwith. Several individuals besides the *Chuprassie* lost their lives in this 'untoward event.'

"About the 15th Colonel Wade returned to us; and everything being now in readiness for an immediate advance on Afghanistan, we left Machni on the 18th, and rejoined our camp at Koulsir the same day. The 19th was a halt, as the Sikh contingent was not quite ready to move; but on the 20th of July the whole of the force at last quitted Koulsir and marched to Jamrud, where we encamped between the fort of Fattehgarh and our *sangas*; the latter being still tenanted by the friendly Khaibaris and levies from Dowson and Hillersdon's regiments. The heights, too, that the jazaelchis had occupied when firing upon us were now in our possession, and kept by a body of Ferris's irregulars under the personal command of that officer, who had struck across from Machni to Jamrud, instead of returning with us to Koulsir.

"The force now at the Colonel's disposal to effect the passage of the Khaibar amounted, at a rough estimate, to some nine or ten thousand men, six thousand of whom form the Sikh contingent, and are all Mussulmans. The co-operation to be expected from these allies is not of the most cordial description; for it is well known that the Sikhs, as a nation, are extremely jealous of the British power, and nothing would afford them greater pleasure than to see it meet with a reverse. Necessity alone compelled Ranjeet Singh to sign the tripartite treaty; but having *done* so, it is but justice to his memory to add, that as far as *he* was concerned, or when his health would allow him to attend to public business, the engagements entered into were observed. Strong, however, as the *Khalsas'* dislike is to us, I believe their hatred to the Khaibaris to be tenfold more bitter; and therefore we have at least the *passions* to work on our side, if we have not their *will.* Of the Afghan levies it is more difficult to speak. Some amongst them have no doubt been led to espouse the Shah Zada's side out of love to his cause; but the majority, it is to be feared, have done so purely from the desire of gain. Many also are secretly of Dost Mahomed's party, and these, in their quarrels with the Hindustanis, have, on more than one occasion, been *heard* to express their intentions of paying us off when once within the limits of the Khaibar Pass. Such individuals *can* only be willing to serve us so long as we continue paramount in power, and *they* are well paid; but were we once to meet with a reverse, it does not require much keen-sightedness to pronounce that their weapons would be turned against us. The British sepoys, the Hindustani irregulars, and a few of the Afghan levies, amounting all together to about two thousand men, are therefore the only troops that could be *implicitly* relied upon; but what is this small number to the host that can be brought against them! A whole brigade of our troops *ought* to have been sent with the Sikhs, and no doubt *would* have been, but for the jealousy of Ranjeet Singh. The Company's *ikbal** had hitherto been great in the eyes of our opponents, and it is now more necessary than ever that it should continue to be so.

"The foes we expect to encounter are the Khaibaris in general, and the Afredis in particular, the most bloodthirsty and the most numerous of the three tribes that inhabit the country around the Pass. When *united* (which fortunately is not always the case), it is com-

* Good fortune.

puted that these lawless marauders can bring from twenty to twenty-five thousand men into the field; but as some had joined the Shah Zada, and others, it is rumoured, are willing to be bought over, we cannot calculate upon meeting a third, or even a fourth of the number. These would, of course, be supported by Akbar Khan, who is encamped near the western extremity of the Pass, and can move up to their assistance whenever necessary. A portion of his men, it is also said, garrisons the fort of Ali Masjid. The possessions of the Afredis lie nearest to Peshawr; those of the Shinwaris being in the neighbourhood of Dhaka, extending from the entrance there to the vicinity of Ali Masjid. The Orakzaes live more in the interior.

Chapter XV.

March to Jubbagee—The Force is divided—View of Ali Masjid—Gallantry of Lieut. Mackeson—An Attack—Conduct of the Levies—Skirmishing—Ali Masjid captured—Illness of Lieut. Barr—Preparations for advancing—Dhaka—Order issued by Sir C. Wade.

"The commencement of active operations was hailed by us all with extreme satisfaction, for we were heartily tired of Peshawr and its vicinity, and longed to see what was at the other side of those hills on which we had been gazing for so many tedious months. On the 21st we marched in the afternoon, under a burning sun, to Kuddum, a mile and a half in advance, where we halted and slept. The next morning a strong party, consisting of artillery, cavalry, and infantry, assembled at day-break, preparatory to progressing up the Pass, and seizing on some of the heights in front. The Colonel, with Rattray and myself, joined this force, taking with us a small mortar, suspended upon men's shoulders, for the purpose of being carried up the steeps where necessary; the ammunition being conveyed in boxes slung over the backs of a couple of mules. Captain Ferris was, simultaneously, to keep moving with his regiment along the tops of the hills, and Mackeson to penetrate from Jamrud with his Multanis and part of the Sikh contingent, by a shorter and more confined pass, the Shadi Bagiar, only adapted for foot passengers and camels. At dawn of day our cortège was ready, and, as we mustered at the extremity of a lofty mountain, tinged by the grey of morning, with a rippling stream running at its base, the scene was one of extreme beauty and excitement, crowded as it was with a multitude of troops, and the tribes of the various districts in the neighbourhood who were friendly to our cause, and whose infinity of costumes added greatly to the picturesqueness of the display.

"After a short interval, everything being reported as ready, we commenced our march, having first sent forward a party of Lord's escort as an advanced guard, and who, dressed in long blue *chupkuns* with scarlet *cummerbunds* and trowsers, and the pointed kuzzilbash cap, looked extremely well as they appeared and disappeared from our sight round projecting rocks. We gradually ascended the Pass, and soon reached a spot so narrow, and confined on either side with cliffs so perpendicular, that a handful of resolute men might have stayed our progress for some time. Emerging from it, we presently came to Jubbagee, a Khaibari summer village, constructed on a low and somewhat level piece of ground, jutting from the hills on our right, and composed of rude huts thatched with leaves and branches of trees. It was deserted. On the opposite side was an opening in the mountains, from whence a small stream issued after passing through a very confined valley.*

"Here our party was divided: Lieutenant Rattray, with the guns and the Sikh contingent, continuing his route along the bed of the main stream, whilst the Colonel and myself, with an escort of horse and foot, and with the

* Formed by the Choora range.

mortar, ascended the hills on the right. As we climbed by degrees into loftier regions we felt the temperature becoming more agreeable and refreshing the higher we rose; but the sun was still exceedingly powerful, and produced a good deal of thirst, which we were glad to slake at a diminutive spring that we fell in with two-thirds of the way up. We rested a short time beneath the shade of some trees that had grown up in its vicinity whilst our followers partook of the grateful element; and then, dismounting from our horses to walk up a precipitous steep, we shortly afterwards gained the crest of the ridge, which must have been between two and three thousand feet in height.

"From this eminence we had a beautiful view of the Pass, with the long-desired fort of Ali Masjid in front of us, about four miles distant, and which, situated on a rocky and almost isolated hill, appeared an exceedingly strong place. It is considered the key to the defile, and our present operations are only preparatory to our endeavours to obtain possession of it. We looked around in vain for Ferris, who was nowhere to be seen; but in half an hour he joined us, the deep chasms in the hills having caused him to make several detours, which lengthened his journey considerably. Rattray, too, was descried winding along the bed of the stream, and a messenger was despatched with directions for him to halt and form the camp on a piece of level ground a little in advance, but far below where we stood. We could gain no tidings of Lieutenant Mackeson, and were wondering where he could be, when a man arrived and hastily requested that some assistance might be sent to him, as he had been driven back by a strong force of Khaibaris. This, from what we could learn, was consequent on the cowardice of a party of Nujeebs, who had accompanied his band of Multanis, and with whom he had at first succeeded in chasing the foe from one post to another, even to occupying a height on the opposite side of the Pass, when the Afredis, receiving reinforcements, made a bold sally, which struck such terror into the Sikh troops that they fled at once. Mackeson, however, retained his advantage as long as he possibly could with the Multanis alone, but increasing numbers having poured in, he had been compelled to fall back upon his present position, where, having thrown up a small breast-work of stones, which in some degree sheltered his men, he nobly maintained the unequal contest.

"Captain Ferris was forthwith despatched with his regiment of irregulars to the Lieutenant's assistance; and Rattray having been directed to secure the camp below, the Colonel and I proceeded along the heights by an execrable path that led us over some steep and rugged rocks, and eventually brought us to the summit of a hill, more level than usual, on which a *sanga* was immediately commenced, as it flanked the right side of our encampment. We had not been long here, when a note was received from Ferris, begging that the mortar might be at once sent forward, as the enemy's numbers had considerably increased, and our own men's ammunition was fast failing. Accordingly, accompanied by a small guard, I pushed onwards without delay, and, at the distance of a mile and a half, reached our position, a rising ground in front of a village surrounded by a quantity of brushwood as an abattis, and to which our troops could fall back if necessary. The intervening ground was considerably exposed, and shot after shot was sent at our party as we crossed it, but happily without doing any injury.

"The enemy, protected by some low stunted trees, were about 350 or 400 yards in advance of the rising ground on which Mackeson's embankment of stones had been thrown up, and also occupied the heights of a range of hills that nearly faced it; but, being a long distance off, *their* firing was not very destructive, though occasionally some of their balls told, whilst that from the former was most deadly. Another of their parties, and most probably some of the garrison from Ali Masjid, as they were dressed in a red uniform, lined the crest of a ridge below our left flank and from thence annoyed our people a good deal. A shell was sent at these fellows, and luckily pitched and exploded amongst them; the success being hailed by our party with a loud huzza, re-echoed again from the surrounding hills; but the enemy nevertheless stood fast and continued to blaze away at us, some of their bullets passing over our heads, and others falling short struck the ground and bounded onwards with a whizz like the twang of a bow-string. The next shell was not so happy, for it flew over the narrow ridge and burst harmless in the hollow on the other side; a huzza from the red coats in return being faintly borne to us on the wings of the breeze, as a testimony of their gratification for its innoxious qualities.

"This kind of warfare continued upwards of an hour, with more or less success, the balls from our foes in front every now and then passing through a small tree close to a hillock that partially sheltered us, and lopping off the more slender of its branches as clean as if cut with a knife. The heat had now become terrific, and the rays of the noon-day sun darted down with an intensity almost insupportable. Meanwhile, the dead and wounded were being carried from the breastwork to the village in the rear, and amongst the former I observed a particularly fine looking man, whose long black hair swept the ground as his corpse was being dragged away. The nature of the dependence we might place on our raw levies was manifested when their ammunition began again to fail, and who one by one, as the individual fired off his last cartridge, left the enclosure on the rising ground in spite of exhortations, encouragements, and threats to remain until Lieutenant Mackeson, who had gone for some, should return. All was in vain, and it was with the utmost difficulty that either Ferris or I could prevail upon a few to wait until the mortar was dismounted and packed. On this being done, a new difficulty arose as to who should carry it,—for with the exception of one, all the bearers had made off whilst we were too busily engaged to observe their movements,—and some delay arose ere we could persuade half-a-dozen of the irregulars to take it as far as the village. Had the Khaibaris at this time been aware of the straits to which we were reduced, and had made a bold dash, there is little doubt but they might easily have secured the piece of ordnance, with ourselves, and the small party that staid with us. They were deceived, however, by a few hardy spirits who still plied their matchlocks from the enclosure with unabated vigour, and whose bold front portended that other troops *must* be at hand ready to support them and take their places.

"These were at length called in, and our position was now of necessity being abandoned for want of ammunition. The cessation of our fire soon made our intentions known to the Khaibaris, who, preceded by a white banner, were rapidly advancing to occupy the ground we had quitted, when Mackeson happily arrived with reinforcements of men and material, and perceiving their object, gallantly rushed forward with an huzza, and succeeded in regaining the stockade before the Afredis, who returned to the clump of trees. As all the shells but one had been expended, it was not deemed expedient to unpack the mortar again, and as it was also thought hazardous to leave it at the village during the night, I was obliged to ride back to the Colonel's *sanga* for assistance to remove it to the camp. Having obtained an order from him for some *coolies*, and also received some fresh instructions for Mackeson, I once more retraced my steps to the scene of active operations, and on my way fortunately discovered a number of the deserters, who, in bands of twos and threes, had concealed themselves behind rocks and cliffs. By dint of persuasion, force, and no small proportion of coaxing, I succeeded in getting them to return with me, and having *seen* the mortar perched upon their shoulders, proceeded to give the Colonel's message to Lieutenant Mackeson.

"As I crossed the exposed piece of ground *alone*, it was easily perceived from my dress that I was a Faringi, and the shots in consequence flew around me rather thick. I, however, reached the stockade unhurt, where within I found Ferris and Mackeson comfortably reclining on the ground with their backs against the breastwork; and there I joined them, having first been cautioned to stoop when passing over the interior, as everything that appeared above the wall was immediately struck. Whilst seated here the balls occasionally rattled away at our backs, and yielded us the satisfaction of knowing the enemy was wasting his ammunition to no purpose. As it was getting late, I was not able to stay long, so after giving Lieutenant Mackeson his instructions, I took my leave, re-crossed the stockade, and received another salute of bullets as I returned over the exposed spot, one of which struck the ground not a quarter of an inch from my foot. On reaching camp I felt so exhausted from heat and fatigue, that I threw myself at once on my couch and was soon asleep.

"The next day was one of comparative rest to me, as my services were not required beyond the precincts of the camp. Colonel Wade, however, returned about a mile down the Pass to establish a post (which was not effected without opposition) near to where the Afredis, on the previous evening, had been doing considerable damage to our people, besides plundering the baggage and purloining sundry camels. It was much about the same spot, too, that Rattray's and Colonel Sheikh Bussowan's troops were fired on when ascending the Pass, by which they lost one man killed and two wounded. As soon as this encampment had been formed, a message was despatched to Captain Farmer, who, with the Shah Zada and the main column, immediately left Kuddum and marched to the new ground. A difficulty of furnishing provisions for the troops presented itself, and compelled Wade to order Ferris back to Peshawr to bring up fresh supplies.

"On the 24th the Colonel, accompanied by Lord (who had rejoined the camp at Kuddum with renovated health), Dowson, and myself, ascended the range of hills on the left, and gradually crowned the heights as we advanced. But little opposition was offered to our progress, for the enemy, who appeared in no great numbers, retreated as we neared, and at length fell back to a respectful distance. I obtained a few long shots at them with a six-pounder of the Sikh artillery, which had been brought to the summit of the ridge on an elephant, and a fire from it was kept up at intervals throughout the day. Mackeson, with Maule, had likewise been progressing on the opposite range, where they had some smart fighting, and the camp was moved forward to ground below the village of Lala Cheena, near to which our first day's operations took place. At night Lieutenant Dowson, with a party from his regiment, occupied the heights on the left, and Rattray, with a company of the 20th, those on the right. Mackeson secured his own position.

"*July* 25*th.*—As the storming of the heights in front of Ali Masjid was to form the chief occupation of the day, a company of the 21st under Farmer, and a large body of Sikh troops under Sheikh Bussowan, were added to the irregulars. We again ascended the heights on the left, Dowson's levies and Farmer's company, with the *Khalsas*, gallantly driving before them a party of Khaibaris, who retreated forthwith to the summit of a lofty and precipitous hill, on which they had erected a *sanga*, from whence they soon displayed a flag of defiance. Captain Farmer, with the Sikh troops, immediately took up a partially sheltered position directly below them, and commenced a rattling fire, which was returned with equal spirit by the Afredis. Colonel Wade, with Mr. Lord and myself, and one of the Maharaja's howitzers, occupied a hill behind them, and an order was despatched to camp for one of the British guns to be sent up the Pass as far as the foot of our situation, to be escorted by the grenadiers of the 20th and a hundred of Kharak Singh's ghorcheras. The firing between Farmer's troops and the Khaibaris was incessant, but every attempt to remove the latter from their impregnable stronghold proved unavailing. At last they became emboldened, and were descending somewhat to the left to take Captain Farmer in flank, when a shell from the howitzer had the effect of driving them back to their original station, where they were beyond the range of such missiles. The British howitzer having by this time arrived, I received Wade's instructions, and descending to the bed of the Pass, proceeded to put them into execution.

"At this spot the rocks and cliffs on either side were extremely precipitous, especially those on our right, which indeed were almost perpendicular, and surmounted by a tower seized upon in the morning by Lieutenant Mackeson, who had discovered and captured several Afredis concealed in its interior. The gorge formed by these crags closing upon each other bounded the limits of my advance, and from thence I was to fire on a cantonment of Dost Mahomed's soldiers, situated at the base of the hill on which Ali Masjid stands, but concealed from my view by a low intervening ridge sloping from the right. The ghorcheras were then to gallop forward, plunder the place, and retreat with the spoil behind our position. On emerging from the defile, preparatory to wheeling into action, we were received by a shower of bullets, fired fortunately from too great a distance to cause any serious injury, though sufficiently close to be unpleasant and disagreeable. One hit me on the bridle arm, impressing me for the moment with the notion that some one had struck me severely with a stick, and angrily turning round to chastise the supposed offender, I was as instantaneously enlightened as to the true cause of the contusion I had received. Soon after opening our fire, that of the enemy in front ceased, but a couple of jazaelchis, who had ensconced themselves in some hidden position overlooking our left flank, annoyed us a good deal; and as they were beyond the range of our grenadiers' muskets, I was obliged to send to Mackeson for a few of his riflemen to dislodge them. The half dozen that he ordered for the purpose were, however, unable to effect this desirable object, and in spite of their new opponents, the fellows still kept blazing at us.

"Nothing was now to be heard on all sides but the roar of musketry, momentarily drowned by the louder reports of a zumboor, a mortar, or a howitzer, the discharges from which were re-echoed from the narrow chasms of the Pass.

Meanwhile, I had explained Colonel Wade's commands to the ghorcheras' officers, who replied 'that it was the custom of their troops, when once they made an advance, never to retreat; that they were quite willing to seize upon the cantonments if it was the Colonel's wish, but they would also retain possession of it or fall to a man.' This intimation I conveyed in a pencilled note to Colonel Wade for his instruction, but he, either unwilling to risk so much when there was no actual necessity for it, or foreseeing no proportionate equivalent likely to result from the act, declined allowing them to proceed. After having expended several shells I ceased to fire, but to guard against contingencies, kept several in a state of readiness, to be used as occasions offered; and half an hour had scarcely elapsed, when some ten or twelve individuals were detected endeavouring to escape from their encampment by the left bank. A couple of rounds sent them back rather more precipitately than they had advanced, and subsequently others who attempted the same thing met with no better success. Affairs remained in this state till the evening, when the Colonel directed two guns of the Maharaja's horse artillery and two companies of his infantry, to relieve us, as we had been on duty the whole day; and on their arrival about half-past eight or nine o'clock, I sent the howitzer and British troops to camp; and then placing the Sikh auxiliaries in a proper position to guard against surprise, I returned to my tent, which I reached at ten P.M. The firing had ceased on both sides when darkness came on, and all was now as still and quiet as it had before been noisy and turbulent. Between eleven and twelve the Colonel came back, to whom I reported the arrangements that I had made with respect to the Sikhs, and who was pleased to express his approbation of them.

"Throughout the day, Captain Farmer and Colonel Sheikh Bussowan, with their troops, had been considerably exposed, the rugged height held by the Afredis almost entirely commanding their position, and thus enabling them to fire with tolerably accurate precision into our stockade. Many casualties ensued, one or two men having been killed at the former officer's side and several others wounded; but reinforcements having been pushed forward, Farmer was enabled to maintain his ground, notwithstanding the advantages possessed by his opponents. Mackeson and Maule, on the right, had been doing considerable execution, and one of the latter's shells was pitched with so true an aim, that it fell in the midst of a knot of Khaibaris, five of whom were either killed or wounded by the explosion.

"Being excessively tired and worn out with much exertion, I was soon in a deep sleep; but towards morning was roused by Colonel Wade, to tell me that Ali Masjid was in our possession, a party from Captain Farmer's position having silently pushed forward, and, to their surprise, found it vacated, the first individual to enter it being the adjutant to Ferris's irregulars, a mere lad, though a very gallant little fellow. Unfortunately for me, the very day on which we had entered the Khaibar, febrile symptoms manifested themselves; but unwilling to be absent from my duties at a time when every officer's services were most necessary, I had abstained from having recourse to those more violent remedies which most probably would have cured me at once. The subsequent day's exposure to a burning sun, when the fever was on me,—at times so severe as to compel me to recline on the ground, and in this posture give directions for the proper serving of the ordnance, or when the fire had slackened altogether, to throw myself beneath the leafless branches of a stunted tree, there to seek for the little relief its slight shade was calculated to afford,—did not, as may be supposed, tend to alleviate my sufferings. Fifty leeches were immediately ordered to my temples; but though the best that could be procured, they were very indifferent, and extracted but little blood. The consequence was, on the next morning I was obliged to be bled from the arm, as I was in a raging fever, greatly aggravated by the intense heat to which we were exposed; and on the third day it arose to such a height that I again suffered depletion to a great extent, and was also cupped on the temples. I slightly improved after this, but the fever returned daily as the temperature increased, and I then, on the slightest excuse, used to send every individual out of my tent, as I had got some absurd notion into my head, that could I only fall into a swoon for a quarter of an hour, and thus forget my sufferings, I should awake comparatively well. Every exertion, however, to effect this was in vain; for although I was so weak that a dozen or two of strides were sufficient to prostrate me, I was unable to produce a faint.

"In some such state as this I continued; during the week that our camp was pitched in the neighbourhood of Ali Masjid, whilst the Colonel was busy arranging affairs for keeping that part of the Khaibar open which we had just occupied, and in negotiating for a passage through the remainder, which is subject to the Shinwaris; tribes by no means so inimically disposed as the Afredis, and generally more peaceful in their habits. Meanwhile, Captain

Ferris had returned from Peshawr, with the grain for which he had been sent, his march back through the *Shadi Bagiar* pass having been disputed by the enemy, who fired on his party, and succeeded in carrying off a number of women belonging to the Nujeeb regiment, who, I believe, formed the rear of his escort, and who could not be induced to attempt the rescue of these poor creatures, their servants and concubines.* The result was, that the Khaibaris mounted these unfortunate demoiselles on their shoulders, and notwithstanding the scratching, kicking, and biting which they used in their defence, for want of better weapons, they bore them off in triumph, and carried them to their retreats.

"On the 1st of August, preparations were made for our advance, and Ferris, with the grenadiers of the 20th, and a host of irregulars, was ordered to garrison the fort of Ali Masjid, a by no means enviable situation, as the heat was so oppressive. A depôt for stores was

* The Nujeebs almost always move with their families, who cook for and attend them.

also formed in it, and all the spare tents and unnecessary baggage were sent there. On the morning of the 2nd we resumed our march; Hillersdon, who, poor fellow, had been dangerously ill with fever some days before we quitted Koulsir, and myself, being conveyed in *doolies;* and it was with no inconsiderable delight we found ourselves jostling in the narrow pass with camels, horses, donkeys, mules, bullocks, men, and women, bag and baggage, as all bespoke a removal from the dreadful hotbed into which we had been plunged so long. In a couple of hours we reached Sir-i-chusma, or the Fountain's-head, where our tents were pitched beneath the shade of a few straggling trees that afforded a slight relief from the sun. I at first felt better for the excitement, but as the afternoon drew on, I again suffered from fever. On the 3rd we moved to Lala-beg-gharri, a village of some size, situated in a more open part of the pass than we had yet seen, and indeed almost deserving the appellation of valley. Two tanks are in its neighbourhood, from whence the inhabitants obtain their chief supply of water; and the quantity required for our camp must have sadly diminished their store. Many other villages, invariably protected by a lofty tower, were to be seen from our position, and when within a mile of Lala-beg-gharri, we passed a Grecian tomb, or tope, erected on the summit of a high cliff, and similar in appearance to, though somewhat smaller than, that of Manikiala. A rude Khaibari tower surmounts it, and, from its elevated site, forms a most excellent watch-tower, which no doubt is constantly used. On the 4th we marched to Landi Khana, the road for some distance being very good; but after crossing the crest of the pass, terminating in a very precipitous and abrupt descent, cut for three miles on the side of a hill. The track here was villanously bad, and in some places nothing but the bare surface of a rock, down the centre of which a deep groove had been worn by the continued action of water, as age after age the superabundance of heavy showers had been carried off by this only channel of exit. To lower the guns down this rocky steep proved an arduous task, and when night closed in they were still a mile from camp; it was necessary therefore to halt the following day, to allow of their being rejoined to the force.* At Landi Khana are the remains of two forts, and tradition assigns them as the residences of two noble *ranies* or queens, who erected them at the extremity of their respective dominions, in order that they might enjoy each other's society; and, strange to say, the harmony continued until death separated them. On the 6th we left for Dhaka, passing midway a ruined castle on the summit of an isolated hill, in a more open part of the defile than usual, which again becomes enclosed between rocky and precipitous cliffs, before it terminates in the small and confined valley of the above name: two partially fortified villages are at one end of the latter. Having now got through the notorious Khaibar Pass, the following order was issued by Colonel Wade:—

* Dost Mahomed Khan used to pay the Khaibaris one hundred rupees a gun for carrying his artillery by manual force over this steep and rugged pass.

"'*August 6th.*—Camp Dhaka. The Mission with the Shah Zada having now effected the passage through Khaibar, and the fall of the fort of Ali Masjid having been the chief means of removing every opposition to its advance from that place, Lieutenant-Colonel Wade (although the heads of the Governments, whose officers and troops were engaged in the reduction of that fort, are the proper persons to appreciate the services performed by them on that occasion) cannot deny himself the personal gratification of expressing his own thanks and acknowledgments to every officer of the British Government for the able and zealous services rendered by them individually in the operations which led to the attainment of an object which, after a tedious detention at Peshawr, has mainly contributed to facilitate the progress of the Shah Zada to Kabul.

"'It fell to the lot of Captains Farmer and Ferris, and of Lieutenants Mackeson, Maule, and Barr, in following the directions of Lieutenant-Colonel Wade, to bear the most conspicuous part in the late military operations;

and the gallantry and perseverance with which these officers and the troops in general acquitted themselves of their respective duties claim the Lieutenant-Colonel's especial notice: but where 'every officer, whether immediately engaged in these operations, or in other duties which were allotted to them (of equal importance with those which devolved on others), vied with each other in a zealous discharge of them, Lieutenant-Colonel Wade is conscious that, while particularizing some, his obligations are alike due to all; and in his report to Government he has endeavoured to express his sense of the services of each.'"

Chapter XVI.

The Seven Wells—Shah Zada Jamhur rejoins the Mission —Sadat Khan refuses to submit—Lalpura is taken—Rewards to the Troops—Flight of Dost Mahomed and Akbar Khan—Arrangements for securing the Khaibar Pass—Official intelligence received of the capture of Ghazni.

I now resume my own journal. On the 6th August, after marching seven miles in a rather open valley, we cleared the Khaibar Pass and encamped at Dhaka, a small village on the right bank of the Kabul river, opposite to the town of Lalpura. The road strong all the way, but widens towards the end; no water the whole distance.

There are some dry wells midway, known by the name of Haft-chah, or the Seven Wells. It is a dangerous spot, as highway robbers generally lurk there, and fall unawares on poor travellers. I have since learnt that Captain Ferris has cleared one of these wells, but having to cut through rock, not without great labour and expense.

On reaching the encampment we were visited by several people of the Jalalabad territory who came forward to greet the Shah Zada and the British Mission. They brought abundance of fruit with them, and many *gosfands* (sheep) as presents. Among others, there were one of the younger sons of Sayed Baba Jan and Mahomed Zaman Khan, Barakzae, together with the Peshawr Arbabs who were in the late ruler's service. They had been waiting here for our arrival since the flight of Mahomed Akbar. After being assured of good treatment and proper consideration on the part of the Shah's Government, they were desired to remain in attendance on the Prince until his arrival at Kabul, when they would be introduced to his Majesty.

We were also joined here by the party of troops which had been detached, on our advance into the Pass, with Shah Zada Jamhur, by the Tatara route. He had met with no resistance during his passage from the

Momand people, to whom he had been opposed, but gave a long account of the great difficulty of the mountains over which they had to come, and considered himself fortunate in having joined us in safety. For the greater part of the way he said that he and his people were obliged to walk, leading their horses over the rocks and ledges by the reins. All the routes from the Peshawr territory, through the Khaibar and Momand hills to Kabul, meet at Dhaka, and that by Tatara is the most difficult. Travellers going to Peshawr generally drop down the river on *Jalas*, or rafts supported by inflated skins. Owing to the violence of the stream, which rolls through rugged mountains, no boat can be used.

Our first object on reaching Dhaka was to bring Sadat Khan, the Momand chief, to some terms, and to make him acknowledge the supremacy of his rightful sovereign, Shah Shuja. A letter was in consequence addressed to him, informing him of the arrival of the Shah Zada, and inviting him to wait on his Royal Highness, and that he would be generously pardoned for his late misconduct; but if he refused, Lalpura was threatened to be carried by force. Lieutenant Mackeson, who had proceeded a day in advance of us, had written to him to the same effect. We received no answer until next morning, when Sadat Khan declined to appear in person, but offered to depute his son. Another admonitory letter was addressed to him, requiring his submission to the terms prescribed; but two days passed in silence, without any settlement. At last Sadat Khan was told that if he still continued hostile and obstinate, he would be attacked the next morning; yet every persuasion failed to restore him to his senses. Colonel Wade proceeded accordingly with a party to assault Lalpura; and with that view, some rafts were prepared for the passage of the troops across the river; but just as the troops were about to embark, a report was brought of the flight of Sadat Khan to the hills, over which we saw them passing. The fort was therefore occupied and garrisoned by the Shah Zada's troops without any bloodshed, while the town of Lalpura was placed in charge of Tura Baz Khan, who was at the time absent on duty towards Bajour with Shah Zada Saleh, but arrived soon after the occupation of the place.

It afterwards came out that Sadat Khan, feeling afraid, as Lieutenant Barr truly observes, that "the unceasing enmity which he had evinced towards the Shah Zada since our arrival in Peshawr" had deprived him of every just claim to consideration; and judging of the policy and generosity of others by the secret treachery of his own countrymen, had no sooner heard of the flight of Dost Mahomed than he hastily despatched Nawab Khan of Pindiali, the half-brother of Tura Baz, whom it will be recollected that Sadat Khan had previously seduced, with letters to some of his friends, European and Native, about the court, full of expressions of loyalty and devotion, for which he had erroneously been receiving credit. These letters were accompanied by an earnest request for a *firman*, or royal mandate, addressed to himself, which he foolishly thought he had only to show the

Prince and Sir Claude Wade to be reinstated in his chiefship. Without hearing the other side of the story, as is too often the case with those who act with haste, and led by the advice of others, the Shah gave the messenger the mandates for which he had petitioned, who brought and delivered them; but the conduct of Sadat Khan to the last had shown how unworthy he was of the confidence which had been placed in him, and how heedlessly the authorities at Kabul had acted in listening to the one-sided statements of a persevering enemy.

It has been said that the late chief did not possess any legitimate claim to the Momand chiefship, and that he seized the place, and took the life of Nur Mahomed Khan, the father of Tura Baz and son of Moizullah Khan, who had been confirmed as chief by Taimur Shah, the father of Shah Shuja, had continued in it during the reign of his successors, Shah Zaman and Shah Shuja, and been deprived of it only during the supremacy of the Barakzais. It has been shown that Sadat Khan had pursued a system of open hostility which proved extremely embarrassing to the progress of the Shah Zada, as well as to the friendly disposition of his adherents; and even went the length of expressing himself contemptuously of him for his connexion with Firangis as infidels. All these circumstances showed Sadat Khan unfit for the enjoyment of his ill-gotten acquisition; besides, from the dependence of the passage by the Khaibar Pass on the Momand territory, it was thought essential for its safety that the chiefs at either end of the Pass should be completely in the interest of the Shah. With regard to the popularity of the two chiefs, it was stated, that on a late occasion, when Amir Khan, the chief of Naowaghi, found it necessary to seek the aid of Sadat Khan, the latter was not able to join him with more than sixty men of his tribe, nor did any inquiries among the peasantry of the country show that he possessed any hold on their affections; moreover the circumstance of several men who had deserted Lalpura in consequence of the oppressions exercised by the late chief having hastened to return to the place after an absence of several years, proved that his rule was not altogether popular.*

7th.—Camp, Dhaka. The force with the Shah Zada having now forced the Pass, Sir Claude Wade expressed his thanks and acknowledgments to every European and native officer commanding the Sikh as well as the Shah Zada's levies, and the detachment of the British troops, for the able and zealous services rendered by them individually in the operations which had led to the attainment of our object after a tedious detention at Peshawr. A donation of five thousand rupees, lately

* The measure and choice of Sir Claude Wade in dethroning one chief of suspicious character and elevating another, appeared judicious in the time of the disasters in 1841–2; for it was Tura Baz Khan who stood by the British when all the Afghan chiefs had deserted them. It was the new chief of Lalpura who became the medium of communication between our heroic garrison of Jalalabad and the Peshawr authorities; and, above all, it was he who escorted the supplies of ammunition, grain, and money to them when they were in great need. (Mohan Lal's *Life of Dost Mahomed Khan*, p. 272.) On the evacuation of Afghanistan he was abandoned to his fate.

made by Nao Nihal Singh on the part of the Sikh Government to the British troops and those of the Shah Zada, was ordered to be distributed; and on the same occasion a present of an equal sum was made to the Sikh troops by Colonel Wade in the name of the British Government.

A report was received to-day of the arrival of Shah Shuja with the British army at Kila Qazi, about five kos from Kabul, and that he would soon enter that city. It was further stated that Ghazni had been stormed and taken by the British army, when Gholam Haidar, the son of Dost Mahomed Khan, had been captured. We also heard, that on the capture of Ghazni the latter had deputed Nawab Jabbar Khan to make terms, if possible, for himself, and the release of his captive son; but the negociation not being so favourable as he wished the Amir had fled to Bamian, and from thence to Bokhara, leaving his guns and camp equipage behind; and that he was chased by a party of the Shah's troops, but was not overtaken. It was likewise stated that he would have boldly resisted the British army had he not been betrayed by his people. The very *Gholam Khana* of Kabul, in whom he had placed his chief reliance, refused to try the issue of a battle; and, on the contrary, had produced to him letters of assurance from the Shah, whose authority they declared their readiness to acknowledge: seeing which, the unfortunate Dost Mahomed had no other alternative than to seek safety in flight.

It was reported that Mahomed Akbar Khan, from the effects of sickness brought on by the fatigues endured by him in his retreat, had not been able to overtake his father; but it proved to be incorrect. After our arrival at Dhaka, we heard that Mahomed Akbar had proceeded as far as Lowaragi, within nine miles of Ali Masjid, in order to encourage the Khaibaris and the garrison to resist us, and that he was actually at the place on the day we arrived at Lala China, opposite that fort. It had, we found out, been agreed between Khan Bahadur Khan and Akbar Khan, that the former should ask the Mission a further delay of three days; but his application made when entering the Pass had prudently been rejected by the Colonel. His object in asking this time was to collect his whole *Oolus* in the interim; but he soon discovered that he could no longer play his tricks, which obliged Akbar Khan to leave the Pass and to return to Kabul precipitately. At that time some of the Maliks of the Kuki Khail tribe were the only Khaibaris in our favour.

9*th.*—Camp, Dhaka. Since our arrival here we had several proofs of the satisfaction of the people in the change of masters. The chiefs and the Maliks of the neighbouring country came from every quarter to declare their adherence to the Shah. Among others, those of Kama, Khosta, Beshbolak, Hazarnao, Basoul, &c., besides many officers of the late Government, who were immediately attached to Mahomed Akbar, joined our camp. The people of the country also resorted freely to it, and supplies became abundant.

It is worthy of remark, that only such of the Khaibar chiefs and Sadat Khan, who were connected with the Sikhs, should have been the foremost in declining our overtures and opposing the advance of the Prince; from which it might reasonably be supposed that they were secretly acting in concert with the Sikh officers, who were professing to correspond with them to forward our cause: but to counteract the mischievous effects of a double communication, Sir Claude Wade, some time before leaving Peshawr, had required the Sikh authorities to desist, a measure which the Maharaja confirmed.

To preserve the safety of our communication through the Khaibar Pass by some *permanent* system of control, was considered essential before we advanced farther. Arrangements were made, therefore, to leave a strong detachment near the western extremity of the Pass, besides the troops which had been left at Ali Masjid, and in different parts of Khaibar. Accordingly the following portion of the force then present with us was ordered to remain at Dhaka under Lieutenant Dowson, with outposts at Landi Khana, and the Haft-chah, and in a stockade on the top of the Pass, between the latter place and Lalabeg Gharee, viz.:

Dowson's levy; the two disciplined battalions of infantry, formed of Mahomedans from the *Campoo*, and commanded by Zorawar Singh; the whole of the Sikh artillery, with the exception of the howitzers and mortar belonging to General Court's corps, and the two six-pounders attached to the Najeeb battalions.

A party of Ghorcheras, with a company from the Prince's own personal guard, was left to form the garrison on the part of Shah Shuja in the fort of Lalpura, and a party of sappers and miners, or *Bildars*, was placed at the disposal of Mr. Mackeson,* to make the road of Landi Khana and Ali Masjid practicable for artillery, as it was by manual labour that our guns were brought over the former, and there was an obstructing rock below the fort of Ali Masjid which was ordered to be destroyed.

* A cousin of Major Mackeson, employed to assist him in his duties, and to take charge of the works in Khaibar.

Without establishing these posts it would have been impossible to overawe the Khaibaris or preserve a safe communication through the Pass, as afterwards proved to be the case. Engagements were at the same time entered into with the Shinwari people, by which they were to protect it within their precincts, reserving to the Shah, as in the time of the monarchy, the right of levying duties on the passing merchandise, which, during the late Government, was solely enjoyed by the Khaibaris.

Before leaving Dhaka, the troops which had been organised for Shah Zada Jamhur's expedition were discharged; and, though against his inclination, he was desired to return to Peshawr. A similar order was issued to Mirza Hasan Ali, the person who had been employed towards Tirah. Recruiting to supply vacancies was at the same time prohibited, a measure which caused some murmurs among the people who expected their services also would soon be dispensed with; but a strict regard to the interests of his Majesty predominated, and every superfluous expense was avoided.

The town and the fort of Lalpura stand in a commanding position on the left bank of the Kabul river, and present a fine and interesting view to the eyes of a traveller, after passing through the bare and burnt hills of Khaibar. The presence of a force on the other side of the river is considered rather a favourable situation to secure the safety of the route by it, and act as a salutary check on the Momand and other tribes in the hills across the stream.

Mr. Mackeson was directed to clear out the fort of Lalpura, and to erect some barracks inside, which rendered it both safe and comfortable for the troops.

On the 12th, official intelligence having been received of the capture of Ghazni, which we had only heard before as a report, and of the flight of Dost Mahomed Khan, a salute of twenty-one guns was fired from the different batteries in camp in honour of these important events to the British Government and its illustrious allies. There was a great profession of rejoicing at the end of our hostile operations. Congratulations upon congratulations were poured upon us by the Afghans, who, although they felt somewhat twisted in their hearts by the conquest of their country by those whom they had been calling Kafirs, yet now joined in every way in hurling curses on the heads of the disloyal family of the late ruler.

Chapter XVII.

Hazarnao—Order of March—Pillaging of the Sikh Troops—Jalalabad—Reception of the Prince there—Stores left behind by Akbar Khan—Intrigues of Raja Golab Singh—Chaharbagh—Tatang—Gandamak—Guns and Camp Equipage of Akbar Khan taken—Jagdalok—Rash Measures of the Shah's Government—Khurd Kabul—Troops paraded previous to entering Kabul.

We now grew exceedingly anxious to advance on Kabul, of which we had so long heard. Having completely established our authority in Khaibar and Dhaka, and being fully assured of the security of the Pass to travellers and merchants, as well as our own daks (post), on the morning of the 13th August we quitted Ḍhaka. The people who were left behind appeared rather disappointed that they were not to have the pleasure of seeing Kābūl; but they patiently submitted to the maxim, that "necessity has no law."

Encamped at Hazarnao, distant nine miles.

Close to the encampment commenced the Khurd or Little Khaibar Pass, being a mile and a-half in length over slate rock, and in one or two places narrow and awkward, and our progress was in consequence very slow; Lieutenant Mackeson with his own party and Hillersdon's levy formed the advanced guard, marching half an hour after daybreak. We now moved in the following order:—the detachment of British horse artillery and remaining companies of native infantry; the Shah Zada's personal guard, horse and foot; the four pieces of artillery in charge of Lieutenant Maule; Lord's Risala, the Colonel's escort from the Sikh Government, and the French battalions of Sikh infantry, with two guns, which accompanied the Prince to Kabul. The Najeebs and the detachment of Ghorcheras, with two guns, formed the rear-guard, and did not leave the ground until the baggage was cleared; every other precaution was taken to guard it, and a party of *Bildars* was ordered to accompany the artillery on the line of march to remove such obstacles to the progress of the guns as there might be on the road. Notwithstanding its narrowness, we met with no accident in this little pass, everything having safely reached the next camp, though our guns did not arrive till noon; those belonging to the Sikhs got sooner over the bad ground from their guns being lighter, and their horses, of a more hardy kind, were always accustomed to drag them over rough and hilly countries. Those who followed us could form no idea of this pass or of the Landi Khana, or the Shadi Bagiar, in the great one. We ourselves were surprised to see them six weeks afterwards, so much had they been levelled and improved by the officers left in Khaibar on our advance for that and other purposes.*

* "Our first march through the celebrated Khaibar Pass, which is in fact the northern gate of India. From our camp on the river bank we moved across a barren shingly plain for a couple of miles, when we entered the pass, two mountains rising on either side to a height of 2000 feet, leaving a space between their feet of about 100 yards in width. Beyond this the passage opens out to about a quarter of a mile, which continues with slight variation for about eight miles over a tolerably good road, and then begins the work. At this spot, where a strong

About mid-way to camp our notice was attracted by an extensive burying-ground. Each

piquet of ours is posted, you begin to ascend up the very steep side of the mountain, on a road cut out of the solid rock. This continues about twelve feet wide for three quarters of a mile, during which you ascend nearly 2000 feet. It is very much the same as one of the hill roads of the Himalayah, only worse from being all loose, and till lately was almost impracticable; but we have had 200 men at work on it for some weeks, and it is now comparatively perfect.

"After getting up this worst part, the road still continues much the same, though now not ascending, for another three quarters of a mile, in which are two short but very steep ascents, which bring one to another stockade and strong party of our irregulars, posted so as to defend this end of the pass. Beyond this we had about another mile of indifferent road, and three more tolerably good, which brought us to a small mountain valley and fort called Gurrhee Lala Beg; distance in all about thirteen miles. To say this pass is bad is far too mild a word. I never contemplated anything at all to be compared to its strength; and I can only say that, if a position is wanted to defend India on, this spot would be totally impregnable if properly defended by Europeans. From this we travelled seven miles along the pass over a tolerable road, except one or two bad spots, to Ali Masjid. This place, which commands the whole Khaibar, was the place at which the chiefs levied their passage-money on all travellers, for which its situation absolutely prevents their having a hope grave was marked by a piece of stone between three and four feet high erected at the head of it. These stones, placed close to each other, presented a curious sight, and verified the saying that every nation has its own manners and customs, as such graves are not found in India, and those we had seen on crossing the

of escape. It is very strongly situated on the top of a solitary mountain, rising direct from the mountain-stream below, which here runs through a passage of certainly not more than twelve feet wide. Though the place is in fact commanded by the heights around, so cragged and steep are they, that no hope of a gun being taken up them could be held out.

"Marched to Jamrud. Instead of keeping down the banks of the stream, as we ought to have done, we must needs go a short cut, and anything like the road or mountain footpath (for it was nothing else) I never saw. It was, for some three miles, at first up and down the rocky mountains, and then along a pathway on the side of one about three feet wide, which at length led down to a dry *Nala*, leading out into the plain of Peshawr, near the new fort of Jamrud; so that we have at last got into the plains, and away from those cursed mountains."—Fane's *Five Years in India*, pp. 211–215.

Captain Fane, who had entered Afghanistan with the army of the Indus by the Bolan Pass, returned with Sir Claude Wade's mission from Kabul.

Indus were rudely heaped together as of those who fell in battle.

Our encamping ground at Hazarnao was good and open, and water in abundance. In a small pool near the village, we observed numbers of tame fish. No one catches them; if any one do so, it is superstitiously believed that he is liable to be affected with leprosy. Good policy, and not fear of the supposed consequence, I dare say, prevented our camp-followers from preparing a palatable dish of these sacred fish.

Hazarnao is a small village containing about two hundred houses. Supplies were abundant and cheap. The proprietors of the place are respectable Afghans, and came out to meet the Shah Zada with baskets of fruits and vegetables as he approached. Mir Abul Hasan Khan and Mulla Shakur, the Shah Zada's officers who had been sent in advance to Jalalabad from Dhaka to conciliate the people on their way, had been cordially received, and made every arrangement for our reception.

15th.—Chahardeh, distant nine miles, the

place where Mahomed Akbar had formed his cantonment on our arrival at Peshawr, the road tolerable all the way, winding through a rocky ridge of hills about midway. Another road lies along the river Lundy, through Basoul, a large village, and is shorter but not so good, there being a marsh to pass; sufficient water on the way as well as in the camp. Across the river, on the steep face of a high hill, near the top, we saw several rows of caves inhabited by thieves and shepherds. There is a more direct route to Chahardeh through Batticot, but as that place is in the midst of a stony desert, water was very scarce. Small parties only can conveniently pass that way.

The Sikh troops, being in the habit, within their own territory, of destroying the cultivation and carrying away anything they like, commenced the same practice here, and pillaged some of the Bhoosa (fodder for cattle), and fuel belonging to the people of the village. The matter was brought to the notice of the Colonel, and officers commanding corps and detachments were reminded of the necessity of placing sentries to protect the crops wherever the camp was pitched, and strictly to caution their men against committing these depredations.

The village of Chahardeh is large, and situated on the right bank of the Lundy or Kabul river. The Khosta country on the other side, studded with green fields and orchards, looked very beautiful, and presented an interesting and refreshing scene after the barren and rocky country we had lately seen. It is inhabitated by the Momand people; the head of whom is Khalu Khan, then present in our camp. We, at least myself, had a high notion of the places we now saw, as they were much extolled by the Afghans; but on a near view of them we were disappointed, for they looked mere small villages, with tattered sheds and ugly mud huts. Mahomed Akbar, during our detention at Peshawr, amused himself in building a temporary residence for coolness on the banks of the river near Chahardeh. The climate of the country between Jalalabad and Peshawr is exceedingly hot. What the late

Captain Burnes mentions of the pestilential wind in the Batticot desert and its fatal effect is too true; we heard of one or two instances during our sojourn at Takal; but I will not mention any fact traced by that or any other distinguished traveller, unless I find any difference between their observations and mine.

Our ground of encampment was on either side of a small *Nala*, a mile west of the village, covered with reeds; until the tents were pitched most of us took shelter from the sun under some trees in a *Faqir's* shrine close to the village. Marching in a hostile country is very inconvenient; we could not send our tents ahead, and they were obliged to be struck and moved in the morning at once.

16*th*.—Alibaghan, twelve miles. The road was in some parts over strong ground, and no water met with till within half a mile of the camp, which was on an open plain close to the river. Passed through a defile called Soorkh Diwar, a dreary-looking place, where Sir Alexander Burnes seems to have been falsely alarmed by his Persian guide, although the spot is a famous haunt for banditti.

On arriving at our encampment some of the citizens of Jalalabad came out to greet the prince. Some of them brought a quantity of fine water-melons and plenty of grapes, which supplied us with delicious refreshment after a long march. They were well received and kindly treated, and then believed their change of masters a propitious event, as they expected it would lead to a prosperous and settled reign. Near the camp we passed a *Kahrez*, or the subterraneous canals used in Persia and parts of Afghanistan for supplying water to irrigate their fields. The Shah's authority was introduced and readily admitted in every district as we passed along, on the assurance of a recognition of their rights by the Shah, before whom they were desired to present themselves.

17*th.*—Jalalabad, six miles; road good all the way, though much intersected by cuts and canals; spacious ground for encampment outside the gateway, west of the town, but soil very sandy; a watercourse supplied the camp with water.

The population of the town seemed much more numerous than is mentioned by Captain Burnes in his travels, but still the place looked in a ruinous state. It is enclosed by a high mud wall pierced with loopholes, which had fallen down in some parts, particularly towards the river where the ground was very rugged and broken. On the southern or opposite face of the fort was the residence of the Governor with a small garden of limes and cypresses, a part of which had been used by Mahomed Akbar as a magazine, and where we found cannon balls, &c. strewed about. Near the western gate is the tomb of a Mahomedan saint, and at one of the angles to the south a shady grove of trees occupied by a Hindoo *Faqir*, who is allowed to follow his religion without hindrance in the midst of the Afghans. There are many Hindoo shopkeepers in the town, by whom their Hindoo shrine is supported.

It was very gratifying to see the manner in

which the Prince was greeted on his approach to Jalalabad by the inhabitants of the city, who assembled in crowds to receive him. We remained there three days, during which the Maliks and the leading men of the country came to profess their allegiance to the new government with alacrity. From the representations of the people, it would appear that Akbar Khan, in his endeavours to support an army disproportionate in extent to the territory subject to his rule, was obliged to make exactions and to levy contributions on them, which had rendered his rule oppressive, and made them hail with satisfaction the prospect of amelioration which the new order of things seemed to promise.

The only chief who yet remained openly rebellious was Sayed Hashim, the new ruler of Kunar. A conciliatory letter was addressed to him and also to the Ghilzae chief, Mahomed Shah Khan, who, on the flight of his son-in-law Mahomed Akbar, had retired to his own place, desiring them to make their appearance, when their case would be taken into consideration.

The former sent his cousin, and the latter his brother named Dost Mahomed; and from the reports we heard of their intentions, they would most likely have come and waited on the Shah but the precipitous measures taken at Kabul for the restoration of Sayed Bahauddin to Kunar (forgetting that great projects are often ruined by precipitation), as will soon appear, alarmed that chief and others, and prevented them from trusting in the sincerity of our overtures.

Had the Shah's government consulted those who were then on the spot and acquainted with the subject, and avoided haste, the lives and property which were subsequently lost in the recovery of Kunar, and asserting his power in that quarter, might have been saved.

The royal authority was established throughout the Jalalabad territory, and Mir Abul Hasan Khan, the *Sandukbardar*, or keeper of the King's wardrobe, was appointed the governor of it, pending the orders of his Majesty. A quantity of powder and about five hundred rounds of ball which had been left by the young Sirdar, together with some unwrought materials for making gun-carriages and saddles for swivels, were found and handed over to the Shah's officers. People were also sent in different directions to recover other property of which we had heard belonging to the late ruler. Such is the frail nature of mankind, that the very same men to whom they had bowed and obeyed most humbly the other day were now detested and treated as an enemy.

The climate of Jalalabad is highly admired by the natives as producing extreme cold and heat within twelve kos.* The Safeid Koh, or Snowy Mountain, is visible, and presents an imposing view. The Kajja district, which is well known for its fine pomegranates sent to India, is also situated towards the hills within this province. The town of Jalalabad is of

* "Afghanistan generally presents more changes in scenery and climate than any country in the world; and a striking instance of both occurs at this place: in the first, in the immediate change from the barren and stony track we have so lately been travelling through, to the rich valley of Jalalabad; and again from the extreme cold of the highlands of Kabul to the heat of the country around us."—*Fane's Five Years in India*, pp. 207, 208.

itself very hot, and subject to high winds in the summer weather.

While we were here repeated reports were received from Peshawr that the Sikhs, although precluded by the tripartite treaty from holding any intercourse of a political nature with the Afghan states beyond their own frontier, yet finding us out of their way, were attempting to establish an influence of their own with the tribes in Khaibar. They also employed the agency of Sirdar Pir Mahomed Khan to incline the people of Sawat and Buner to acknowledge their government, and attempted at the same time, through his elder brother, Sultan Mahomed Khan, to extend their influence in other directions beyond Kohat. A correspondence was also said to have been carried on between Raja Golab Singh and the Malikdin Khail and the Kuki Khail people. These attempts, which were premature in some instances and altogether unwarranted in others, were encouraged by the new *darbar*, and confirmed the report we had previously heard of the intrigues between the Sikhs and the Afghans on their frontier. One of the Raja's objects was to exact from Sultan Mahomed the cessation of the trade in salt carried on through Kohat and the territory of the Sayeds in Tirah. The Raja was said to have even gone so far as to station his own people in that quarter with the view of working out his design and embarrassing the government of Shah Shuja. Experience of the character and policy of the Sikhs, and especially of the deep and artful ways of Golab Singh, assured us of the truth of these reports. They looked with great jealousy on the success which the British arms had lately met with in Afghanistan, and were ready, as has been seen from the beginning, to create obstacles; and a strict watch on their actions was constantly necessary to keep them within their proper bounds. Having now no fear of the presence of Colonel Wade nor his Mission near Peshawr, they returned to their old machinations, and were, it is believed, in a great measure, the cause of the commotions which broke out in Khaibar while we were in Kabul. A letter was addressed to Kour Nao Nihal Singh, drawing his attention to the proclamation which had been issued on the reduction of Ali Masjid, indicating the leading persons in Khaibar, who, by their late conduct, had proved themselves hostile to the interests of the Shah, and requesting that the Kour would require his officers to desist from carrying on the communications in which they were engaged, without a due regard either to the obligations of their duty to the British Government or to that of his Majesty. At the same time Shah Zada Taimur was advised to address letters in the name of his father to all the chiefs of the places not inserted in the tripartite treaty as belonging to the Sikh Government, informing them of the restoration of the Shah to the throne of Kabul, and claiming their allegiance to him as their rightful Sovereign. The object of these letters was to put the people on their guard against the deceptive plan of the Sikhs; but the disaffected had hesitated not to yield a ready ear to their proposals, as the course of events and the subsequent outbreak, not only in Khaibar, but the Ghilzae country, led us partly to believe.

It being considered necessary to leave a part of the troops at Jalalabad, Hillersdon's levy, the Najeeb battalion under Captain Jacob, one hundred Sowars, together with that portion of Mackeson's levies still with him, were ordered to remain stationed here until further orders. The two guns attached to the Najeeb battalion, the howitzer and mortar received from General Court, and the piece of artillery and ten swivels attached to the Shah Zada's guard, were likewise left with the force above detailed. A company of the 21st regiment N. I., of the British detachment, was also ordered to remain at the place, under the command of a Subehdar, there being no European officer present with it.

Lieut. Mackeson was also to remain for the purpose of aiding the officers of the King in establishing his authority, and likewise for the protection of his Majesty's interests, in that important district, and the safety of the road between Peshawr and Kabul. He was also invested with the general control, both political and military, of the force left behind. In consequence of the number of the sick in hospital, they were also left at Jalalabad.*

Having arranged affairs there, we quitted that place on the 21st inst., and moved to Chaharbagh; distance, four and a half miles; road sandy, and rather heavy. Encamping ground to the left of the stream, with a water-course running through it

Owing to the force left at Jalalabad, there was a change in the order of march. The

* "At noon the thermometer never stood lower than 102°, and a hot wind blew all the day; but at night it became so cold that counterpanes and blankets were absolutely necessary to defend us from its influence. In addition to one-third of the several regiments and detachments being on the sick report, numbers were daily swelling the list, and amongst others the surgeon, who about this time was laid up with fever, brought on by exposure and attention to his arduous duties. Amongst the levies deaths were frequent; and to such a height did the sickness at last attain that it became necessary to make arrangements for the reception of the invalids at Jalalabad, as there was no carriage to convey them further."—*Barr's Journal*, pp. 359, 360.

advanced guard was formed by the Rissala of the Prince's personal guard; while the British detachment was paraded in front. Mr. Lord having received permission to proceed to Kabul in advance of the Mission, the Rissala raised by him was ordered to escort him to that place. He was also accompanied by Mulla Shakur, the Shah's minister, who proceeded in advance to give a detail of the expedition in person.

Chaharbagh is a royal garden, but since the fall of the monarchy it has been much neglected. It has a dilapidated summer-house, and is amply watered by artificial canals, cut from the Soorkhab river not very far off.

22*nd*.—Marched at daybreak, and encamped at Balabagh, eight miles distant; road over strong ground, and heavy the whole way. Encamped a mile from the village of Balabagh, on a broken and confined spot; a water-course close by, of good water.

Balabagh is a small village, situated near an old garden of the same name on the banks of the Soorhkab, and off the main road. Fatiabad is the more direct course, which we were obliged to leave through the mistake of our guide.

During this day's march, I rambled into the country to the right of the road; and passing the villages of Sultanpur *paen* and Sultanpur *bala** to Balabagh, saw them to great advantage. I was delighted to see the artificial canals, and the waterfalls and gardens, along their course. Nature seemed to take pains in adding to the verdure of the scene; and the sight was highly refreshed by the display of various thriving trees. The land appeared very rich and productive, and the climate most agreeable. We had been gradually ascending since we left Jalalabad. On the right was the Kabul river, with a high rocky range running parallel to it; on the other side of which is the valley of Lughman, and on our left was an extensive plain stretching to the foot of the Raja and Hissarak ridges. The fort of Tatang, which belongs to Nawab Jabbar Khan,

* *Paen* means the lower; *bala*, the upper.

and is much extolled for its fine healthy situation, is about a mile from Sultanpurbala, below the range to the right, and is a very retired and enchanting place. The Nawab himself is the founder of the village, and has laid out two gardens, which have not yet reached to maturity. It is the winter retreat of the Nawab and his family, and contains a convenient mansion for their accommodation. Notwithstanding its beauty, the place looked very gloomy from the want of tenants, and the absence of its master. The subjects of the Nawab, both Hindoo and Mussulmans, who remain, have much respect for him. He is not a prejudiced man or a bigot, but regards alike with benevolence the infidel and the faithful. A Hindoo shrine, which he has built at Tatang besides a mosjed, is sufficient proof of his impartiality. It was not without grievous disappointment that we saw this place abandoned by the self-exile of its good master, and wished him an immediate return to it with the enjoyment of the work of his own hands. After the above was written, I learned that the Nawab returned to Kabul with the family of Dost Mahomed Khan. He is the friend of every one, and the first and best the English ever had in Afghanistan.*

23rd.—Gandamak; distance, thirteen miles. Road over strong ground, gradual ascents and descent, formed by hills of loose sandstone, till a place called Nimla is reached, famous for its beautiful garden, which abounds with flowers and trees of great size; but it is now in a very neglected condition. Nimla is also known as the place where Shah Shuja was defeated, and lost his throne. A turn to the right leads to a steep and stony ascent half a mile in length;

* "Instead of keeping along the line of march, we turned off towards the river and passed through some very fine country to the house and estate of Jabbar Khan, an elder brother of Dost Mahomed, whom neglect has driven away, although he has always been notoriously our best friend in Afghanistan. He was much respected in the country, and never interfered in any way in its political squabbles. His house was a very extensive one, situated in the midst of splendid cultivation, and his people had prepared a breakfast of a lamb stuffed with nuts for our benefit. His departure is universally regretted, both by Europeans and natives."—*Fane's Five Years in India*, pp. 205, 206.

after which the road runs along the ridges of the hills, with a very gradual ascent for two and a half miles, till another long descent shows the plain. Two more miles of good road brings to the bridge of Gandamak, which being in ruins, we had to cross the stream, the left bank being rather steep and stony though short. On approaching the bridge is observed a large piece of white stone, which is celebrated for its beneficial quality in strengthening or curing defects of sight: native travellers who pass break off a piece from it for that purpose. I found, however, on trial, that it is merely a popular prejudice, and the stone is quite destitute of the quality which is ascribed to it. Close to the bridge is a spring under a willow tree: the water of it is very pure, transparent, and cold; people generally stop here to drink.

Leaving the bridge we soon after came to another stream of the same description, from which the road continued good to camp. Encamping ground on a fine open plain near the garden, and water-courses on all sides.

Gandamak is a small village, with a garden

a short distance off. It is peopled by the Mama Khail people, the head of whom is Mir Afzal Khan, the son of the Amin-ul-mulk, the person who lately distinguished himself in supporting the cause of the Shah, and harassing Mahomed Akbar by raising disturbances to cut off his communications between Jalalabad and Kabul. As already mentioned, he joined us when we entered Khaibar, and had been in friendly correspondence with us all along. He brought us plenty of fresh grapes from his garden, and abundantly supplied the camp with everything requisite. Gandamak is in a beautiful valley, where we had a good view of the Safeid Koh. Some of the party returned with Mir Afzal to visit his castle, and returned much pleased with their visit. He was very anxious to give us every proof in his power of his hospitality and devotion. We found the climate of Gandamak very cool and refreshing.

The road as above stated being very difficult and rough, the guns did not reach the camp till very late, and some pieces arrived the next morning. We were in consequence obliged to halt on the 24th inst. It also appeared that a party of *Bildars* which were to have come with us had by mistake been left at Dhaka, and the nature of the road in advance was stated to be equally bad. Some were therefore hired from the villages with such tools as are used by them, and sent ahead in charge of a non-commissioned officer, and some of Mir Afzal's people, with instructions to remove such obstacles as might impede the progress of the guns. I must not forget to mention that, during Mahomed Akbar's retreat, it appeared that he had been compelled to abandon the whole of his artillery and baggage, and that after leaving Gandamak, so hard pressed had he been, that he had with difficulty effected his escape with only a few followers. Seventeen of his swivels with ammunition and equipments, which had been left at Khosta, were, on the requisition of the Colonel, made over to us before we quitted Jalalabad. A large brass gun called the Qazee had been abandoned by the young Sirdar on the road near Balabagh,* and on his arrival at Gandamak, where it appears he first received the news of the fall of Ghazni, he determined to abandon the remainder of his guns, consisting of twelve very good pieces of artillery, two of which had been captured from Shah Shuja on his defeat at Candahar in 1833, and two from the Sikhs in the battle of Jamrud in 1837. Most of these were traced out and taken possession of by people who were sent ahead to secure them. From the latter a salute was fired in honour of the Shah's restoration, and they were all ordered to Jalalabad to be disposed of according to the Shah's orders.†

* This gun was afterwards one of the trophies of General Pollock's army, which he wished to convey to India; but it was burst and abandoned in Khaibar, in consequence of the rapidity of our retirement from Kabul.

† "Notwithstanding I had suffered from an attack of ague in the morning, I was able to *walk* (my first essay for a long time) a short distance to inspect some ordnance that had been abandoned by Mahomed Akbar Khan during his flight from the Khaibar, and which fell into our hands here. It consisted of ten or twelve brass cannons, mostly of small calibre; and I omitted to mention that between Jalalabad and Chaharbagh we passed a very large brass

Some parts of Akbar Khan's camp equipage, a few horses, draft bullocks, and jazails, constituted the other property which fell into our hands on the occasion, but we did not claim them as prize.*

26*th*.—Marched from Gandamak at daybreak, and encamped on the bank of the Soorkhab, of the stream so called from the red colour of its water. Road up and down hills the whole way, over stony and uneven ground. Some of the ascents and descents rather long and steep; crossed the stream by a dilapidated stone bridge built by Ali Mardan Khan. This stream, of which I have already spoken, forms the natural boundary between the Jalalabad and Kabul territories. The Afghans say that the hot climate ceases on this side of the bridge, and the cold begins to be felt on the other;

gun, mounted on a most rudely-constructed carriage, the naves of the wheels being about two feet and a half in diameter, and the felloes thick in proportion, which he had also been unable to carry away in his retreat."—*Barr's Journal*, pp. 362–3.

* The Sikhs afterwards claimed their guns, and they were restored to them.

but no such exact difference was experienced by us. As we proceeded farther on towards Kabul the climate became much cooler and more agreeable.

From Soorkhab commences the Ghilzae country, and Jhoke, the capital of their territory, is situated about ten kos off to the left hand. Aziz Khan is the principal chief of these Ghilzaes, and Mahomed Shah Khan of those in Lughman. The land is said to be fertile, but very little cultivation is to be seen. The people are given to predatory habits. Our ground of encampment was very limited, and the tents were crowded together; supplies are scarce. The guns not having again reached the camp till very late, the order for the march was countermanded, and on the 27th we halted; but an officer with the advanced guard proceeded at daybreak for the purpose of improving the roads, and making it as practicable as time would admit. Our guns had now to be dragged almost the whole way by main force.

28*th.*—Jagdalok, twelve miles. A grove of

mulberry trees denotes this place. Formerly there was a fort, and the Afghan monarchs on their way from and to Kabul used to encamp here. It is also the place where Shah Zaman, one of them, was blinded, by his eyes being pierced with a needle by order of Shah Mahmud, his half brother. Close to the last ground is a steep and difficult ascent, then a gentle slope along the side of a hill, then in the bed of a stream for a long distance, then another long and steep ascent, on the top of which is an old ruined fort, where in the time of the Moguls a strong garrison was posted to keep the road. They did not trust as we did to the neighbouring tribes for that important measure, but their own military force; down a stream for three miles, and then into camp. A most tedious march for the artillery; stony ground the whole way, very bad encamping ground except for a few tents amongst the trees: a part of the camp was pitched under them, and a part opposite the grove of trees.

There is no village on the roadside but one at some distance to the left of it. On reaching the ground, the Malik of the place brought a small quantity of grapes which were very acceptable, and received with many thanks from people whose profession is to live only by robbing others.

29*th*.—Barikab, ten miles distant.

The road passed down a stream for about three miles, narrow in many places, with high and steep rocks on both sides, up a steep ascent, over ridges of hills with further descents and ascents then to the bed of a stream to camp. The road covered with round stones and rough the whole way, without a vestige of cultivation. Barikab, or the "Thin Water," so called from being a very narrow stream, is the site of an old fortification by the side of the streamlet. It was likewise originally built for the protection of the road. No encamping-ground but for a small party just about the bed of the stream: the camp was scattered over its bed and on the adjoining ridges. Supplies and forage very scarce; water abundant. The guns had to go round by the Peridarra, or Faiery's Pass, following the course of a stream to the right. In the narrowest part of it the precipices on each side almost meet, leaving barely room for the carriage to pass. It is a wild and picturesque spot, with a spring trickling from the rocks.

A letter was received from the Secretary to the Government of India in reply to the report made by Sir Claude Wade of the operations which led to the capture of the fort of Ali Masjid, and the following extract of it was published by him in his orderly-book for the information of the officers serving with his Mission.

1. "I am directed to acknowledge the receipt of your despatches under date of the 27th and 29th ultimo, reporting the fall of Ali Masjid, and in reply to state the Governor-General has much satisfaction in acknowledging the energy and determination evinced by officers and men in the approach to the fort and the previous operations.

2. "It is particularly creditable, I am desired to remark, to troops so raised and constituted as those with the Shah Zada, that they

remained for several hours exposed to the fire of the enemy without evincing impatience or hesitation.

3. "The conduct of the Maharaja's Mussulman contingent is also highly creditable; and it is the intention of the Governor-General to request that Colonel Sheikh Bussowan may be permitted to accept a sword from him in testimony of his high satisfaction.

4. "You will not fail to apprise Captain Farmer, Lieutenants Mackeson and Maule, Mr. Lord, and the other officers with you, of his Lordship's gratification at their zeal, promptitude, and gallantry."

30*th.*—Teizeen, distant eight miles.* Close to the last ground a short but steep ascent, then along the sides of the hills by a succession of gradual ascents and descents up a stream, over the most rough and stony ground that we had ever seen, for three or four miles, till we came to the mud wall of another Mogul

* There is a shorter road between Gandamak and Teizeen, across the mountains called *Karkatcha.* It comes out at Seh Baba, in the Teizeen valley.

fortification. Turned off the bed of the stream by a path to the left, and then reached the camp, which was on good ground, but not capacious. Supplies abundant; water from the stream. On the road we met numbers of wandering people, with their families and property, going down to the warm regions of Jalalabad and Peshawr to pass the winter. Several flocks of sheep were also seen being driven by the Ghilzaes in the same direction. They remain absent from their cold mountains during the winter, and as soon as summer returns they also return to their own haunts. Such a free and rural life is very agreeable to these independent people. A good quantity of fruits was received from my friend Mohan Lal, as well as some other of our acquaintances at Kabul. Several persons also came out to meet the Shah Zada. Among others was Ghous Mahomed Khan, with some of his relatives and friends, the chiefs of the Logar tribe. As already mentioned, these people were the first to throw off the authority of Dost Mahomed; to excite disturbances, and to distract the enemy, confiding in our assurances that they would be approved and rewarded for their conduct, and Logar being nearer on the road to the Shah than the route by which his son Taimur was advancing, by our advice they joined his Majesty before his entrance into Kabul; but their services were not appreciated. They had not been performed before himself nor any of the British officers with him; and being no longer thought of any use, the men retired to their homes disgusted.

We were also informed of another rash and questionable measure of the Shah's Government, which caused a general suspicion of his designs. Haji Khan, Kakar, the first to desert from the enemy and join the King near Candahar, who had been sent with some European officers and a party of cavalry to pursue Dost Mahomed, was, on a charge of conniving at the escape of the Amir, put in confinement along with Aminulla Khan Logari, one of the principal chiefs of that tribe.* This sudden

* The man who incited the insurrection in Nov. 1841, by proclaiming the intention of the British Government

act of the English, however pleasing to some, naturally alarmed the Afghan nobles; and those who had come to Kabul to offer their homage instantly fled, from a dread of sharing the same fate, which prevented others also from coming to court. Among the fugitives were Aziz Khan and some other Ghilzae chiefs who had adhered to the late ruler to the last: and yet at the time we entered his territory he was

"to banish every suspected Afghan to London." Read Lieutenant Eyre and Mohan Lal. The former says, "The two great leaders of the rebellion were Aminulla Khan, the chief of Logar, and Abdulla Khan Achakzae, a chief of great influence, and possessing a large portion of the Pisheen valley. Aminulla Khan had hitherto been considered one of the staunchest friends of the existing government, and such was the confidence placed in him by the Vazir that he had selected him to take charge of Himza Khan, the lately superseded governor of the Ghilzaes, as a prisoner to Ghazni. This man now distinguished himself as one of our most inveterate enemies. The immediate cause of the outbreak in the capital was a seditious letter addressed by Abdulla Khan to several chiefs of influence at Kabul, stating that it was the design of the Envoy to seize and send them all to London!"—Eyre's *Journal of the Disasters in Afghanistan*, pp. 15-17.

working hard to endanger the road; for on our arrival at Teizeen we heard that it was beginning to be infested by the Ghilzaes, in consequence of which the Colonel took the necessary precautions to guard against surprise or accident. The Afghans now appeared to lose their confidence in the new Government. Had the Shah and his advisers acted with prudence, and not at once have put Haji Khan in arrest, the commotions which followed would not probably have occurred. Every one now began to be fearful of appearing at court, and every assurance failed to dispel their alarm.*

* When the ministers and a good many followers of the Amir returned from Turkistan, they told us that he, the Amir, instead of having the slightest hope or thought of the good offices of Haji Khan in delaying the march of the English, not only threw loads of abuse on his head whenever his name was mentioned, but concluded that he would do all to facilitate the means of his being overtaken. Whatever the faults of Haji Khan Kakar were, it was very impolitic to punish him. He was three months ago nominated Nasir-ul-daulah, with a considerable salary; and now we made him a prisoner, and banished him to India. We gained no good by this, but rather shook the confidence of many other chiefs. Immediately his fate was known in the capital of Afghanistan, Aziz Khan, the

31*st.*—Khurd Kabul, thirteen miles. A tedious march. Close to the last encampment another steep ascent; then up a stream for three miles in a narrow defile called the Tung-i-Tarikee to the Haft Kotal, or "Seven Heights," a steep pass, the first part over stony, the latter over good ground; then two miles of good road to Qabar-i-Jabbar. Here also, to the left of the road, a ruined fort is to be seen. It was built by some of the Mogul governors

principal chief of the eastern Ghilzaes, fled from Kabul, fearing that he might be forced to share the fate of Haji Khan; and Yar Mahomed Khan, the Vazir of Herat (as it will be observed by the official extracts), called us the "faithless dogs" in the presence of Major Todd, the British Envoy, alluding to the case of Haji Khan. Sir Claude Wade was in the meantime directed to conciliate Aziz Khan, the Ghilzae chief, and endeavour to restore confidence enough to induce him to wait upon the Shah and the Envoy. He had great difficulty to efface from his mind the suspicion and fear which had been already implanted in his heart by the example of our treatment of Haji Khan; yet at length he succeeded in persuading him to meet the expectations of the Kabul Government. He gave him letters of recommendation, pledging his word for honourable treatment, in addition to the reward he was promised; but very little attention was paid by us to his stipulations.

of Kabul, and now only serves as a haunt for highway robbers. Jabbar, whose remains lie beneath the above tomb, is said to have been one of the principal men of the Ghilzae tribe, and his memory is held by them in great reverence. The Ghilzae robbers generally hide themselves in the tomb, and if they succeed in their predatory excursion, make an offering to their departed forefather for assisting them in their success. Thus this great robber has still high command over the minds of his posterity.

The rest of the road was good. Encamping ground just off the stream; water abundant, but few supplies. Sayed Bahauddin, the ejected chief of Kanar, arrived in camp on his way to Jalalabad. It will be remembered that he had been sent to Kabul, and there confined; but on the flight of the Amir he obtained his liberty. He told us that Shah Shuja had issued a letter patent to him to resume the territory then held by Sayed Hashim, and a mandate was also precipitately issued by his Majesty to the latter to evacuate it, without awaiting, as has been said, the result of the negotiations in which we were engaged for the recovery of the territory, and the submission of its actual possessor. Such a strange measure surprised every one much, and the disastrous consequences which issued from them were easily foretold. The Sayed, without any assistance in men or money, now proceeded to procure the evacuation of his territory, believing that he could effect it by the mere aid of the royal mandate, which was very absurd, and he afterwards learned to repent his folly.

1*st Sept.*—Butkhak, nine miles. Road enters another narrow defile, called the pass of Khurd Kabul, with high perpendicular sides; a stream flows down it, which is crossed many times, for four or five miles. The road then turns off to the left over a good level piece of ground, and opens into a very fine extensive valley, at the extremity of which the city of Kabul is situated. We heard that the road was infested by the Ghilzaes after we had passed it, and that two or three travellers, going to Jalalabad, had a very narrow escape, and we saw these robbers in passing, perched on the tops of the hills, with their matchlocks in hand; but our party, owing to good care and vigilance, came through without meeting with any accident.*

Butkhak, so named by Mahmoud of Ghazni, having buried the idols of Somnath at this place, is a small village surrounded by a high wall. After passing through bare hills, and a rocky

* "On the 1st of September we moved to Butkhak, our road for the first five miles being confined to the Khoord Kabul pass, a narrow defile bounded on either side by precipitous and lofty mountains, whose frowning summits darkened the chasm, as in the early morning we crossed and recrossed a small rivulet that rapidly sped down its shingly bed. We then entered on an open valley, bounded on the west by a low range of hills, which concealed the long-desired city of Kabul from our sight, and in half an hour arrived at our encampment. Some stragglers having lagged in the pass, were attacked by the Ghilzaes, who killed one or two, and wounded the remainder before they could effect their escape. In the evening we were rejoined by the guns that last night had remained near the Haft Kotal, the men having with the greatest difficulty succeeded in dragging them up the stupendous ascent of the pass under the superintendence of Maule, who has had charge of them ever since leaving Gundamuk, and to whom, therefore, much credit is due."—*Barr's Journal*, p. 367.

and most dreary looking country, our eyes were refreshed by seeing some verdure here and there about the village. With the assistance of a telescope, we had a fine view of the scattered camps of the Indus army, pitched on the slopes and summits of low hills; and had also a partial glimpse of the town. The encamping ground spacious, and water and supplies abundant. As the Prince was to be received in state by his father at Kabul, the troops forming his personal escort, or otherwise attached to the Mission, which were now reduced to about one thousand men, were ordered to clean their arms and accoutrements, and prepare for the ceremony. We consequently halted on the 2nd instant against our inclination, as every one was anxious to see Kabul. In the evening of that day, the troops in camp were paraded and inspected minutely by the Colonel, who also explained to the officers the intended order of march.

Chapter XVIII.

The Shah Zada arrives at Kabul—The City—State of the Country—Murder of Colonel Herring—Misconduct of the Shah—Order of Merit—An Execution—Sir Claude Wade takes leave of the Shah and of the Prince.

On the 3rd of September the Prince proceeded towards Kabul, distant nine miles. All the officers and troops appeared in full dress, and the cavalcade moved in grand style; the detachments of cavalry consisting of one hundred picked Ghorcheras in their gorgeous dresses of shawls and silks; a troop of Lancers from the French Legion, and the Rissala of his Highness's personal guard; formed lines on the left and right of the road, and attended him in that order with a band playing before them. About two miles from the encampment of Lord Keane's army, the Shah Zada was met by the British detachments of artillery and infantry, with us his two companies of irregular infantry, the two pieces of the Sikh artillery, and the French auxiliary battalion, together with two companies of Colonel Wade's own escort, who had, agreeably to instructions, gone in advance to await the arrival of the Prince and received him here in two lines forming a street.* The approach to Lord Keane's camp was very imposing; numerous lines of tents were scattered about the heights, and the people crowded on all sides to see the sight, and recognise their friends in our party. As the Prince passed by the camp he was received with an honorary salute from the British artillery, and a distinction becoming his rank by a deputation from his Majesty and the Envoy and

* "At length the day arrived on which we were to reach the long-desired goal, and as my health had considerably improved, I resolved, with the doctor's permission, to take part in the procession. Accordingly, on the morning of the 3rd of September, I stepped into my litter, and having been carried half way, mounted my charger, and drew up my detachment on the right of the road. On the Shah Zada's appearing in sight, we saluted him with twenty-one guns, also a signal for the troops at Kabul to get under arms; and as he neared us we wheeled into column, and headed the procession."—*Barr's Journal*, pp. 367–8.

Minister at his court, and by his Excellency the Commander-in-Chief of the grand army in person. The procession was now much increased in numbers, but no confusion occurred, everything went on as at first. As we entered the seat of empire the crowd increased more and more; the balconies and terraces of the houses were filled with women wrapped in *barqas* or long veils to see their Prince. A man on the part of the Shah preceded him and cleared the way, which was necessary, as the streets were very narrow, and we advanced very slowly. The bustle was great; the spectators stood admiring the procession; they observed that his Majesty himself even did not make his entry in such majestic style. At length we entered the Bala Hissar and the palace, where his Royal Highness was received by the King his father, who welcomed him on his arrival, and seated him by his side among the other princes. After a while the Mission retired to the camp, which was pitched to the north-east of the city, close to the walls of the fort in a meadow with a small garden in the rear. The Prince now no longer formed a part of our camp; he withdrew to the residence assigned to him within the fort by his Majesty.

The road was good all the way; about half-way came to a stone bridge made by Dost Mahomed Khan through a marsh formed by the Logar river. The city did not present any striking view from without, nor has it any conspicuous building to distinguish it at a distance.

The first object on our arrival at the place was to see the city, which I did the same day in the company of my friend Mohan Lal. The bazars were so crowded that we did not pass through them easily. Kabul is certainly a very busy and noisy place, and was made more so at present by the presence of our armies in its vicinity. Numbers of the camp followers, European soldiers and Indians, were seen mixed with the natives making their respective bargains, or satisfying their curiosity. The shops appeared to be well supplied with everything; the fruit in particular was arranged with great taste, and presented a fine sight; the shops of the bakers, confectioners, drapers,

&c., also looked very well, decorated with the different articles which they professed to sell. "If you want to purchase victual for any ordinary number of guests, you can get them ready prepared in one shop; or if you want to organize an army of ten thousand men you can procure everything to equip it in one day." These are the remarks which a Kabúli would make in favour of his native place, and they certainly do not partake of much exaggeration. Of all the bazars of Kabul the Chaharchata is the best and finest I have ever seen. It was commenced by the celebrated Ali Mardan Khan, but not finished by him. A part of it was said to have been repaired by the late ruler. The roof, which is vaulted, appears to be much damaged, and has many large cracks. The people expected that Shah Shuja would take early notice of the tottering state of this noble building.* The city does not contain any good houses, which are mostly made of sun-dried bricks, two stories high. It seemed,

* It was destroyed by the army on our return to Kabul in 1842.

however, to be well-peopled, and its bazars always crowded from early morning till evening. It is supposed that if well managed, and with proper attention to commerce, the prosperity of Kabul is capable of being doubly or trebly increased within a few years.

The common people and the merchants seemed much delighted at the change of government; trade has been greatly promoted, and every one is said to have made a good fortune during the short stay of the army. Almost all the people, Europeans and Indians, purchased something, and no doubt were highly charged for every thing by the natives. The approaching return of the army made the purchasers very brisk, as every one wished to take some presents from Afghanistan for his family or friends in India; but soon afterwards an order arrived from Government, which prevented the whole of the troops from returning, to the great regret of the Kabulis, as it partly stopped the sale of their goods; however, they had filled their purses with their exorbitant profits. It was said that since Ahmed

Shah's time,* they had never made so much money.

The nobility of the country did not, however, consider themselves as well off as the lower classes of the people. By the late ruler they were treated very attentively, almost on equal terms, and enjoyed much influence, while now they were obliged to undergo many hard ceremonies. In the first place, they found it very difficult to obtain an admittance to the royal presence; and those who by flattering the darbars or ushers could do so, were made for hours to stand at a respectful distance before his Majesty with their hands folded in a most humble manner, and often compelled to retire from the darbar without being allowed to say a word to the King. Exclusive of this degradation of their dignity, they were deprived of the many benefits which they enjoyed during the late Government, and saw that they had now no voice in its councils.†

* The first Durrani king of the Afghans, and the grandfather of Shah Shuja.

† "The more we found the people quiet, the more steps

All these circumstances offended the Durrani and Kasalbash nobility to a high degree, and they appeared quite disgusted with the Shah and his allies even at the time of our arrival at Kabul, when he had not been a month there. They often remarked that they had believed that the Shah would enjoy the same absolute power that he possessed before his dethronement, but that they were altogether deceived, and now found him merely a puppet in the hands of the English. I heard some of them often scolding each other for favouring the Shah's cause and deserting Dost Mahomed, who they said was like one of their own brethren. They also used to say that if they had but resisted his Majesty's advance with the British army, they would have been vic-

we took in shaking off their confidence. We neither took the reins of government in our own hands, nor did we give them in full powers into the hands of the Shah. Inwardly or secretly we interfered in all transactions, contrary to the terms of our own engagement with the Shah; and outwardly we wore the mask of neutrality. In this manner we gave annoyance to the King on the one hand, and disappointment to the people on the other."—Mohan Lal's *Life of Dost Mahomed Khan*, p. 313.

torious; for they now saw that the British troops were only looking formidable from having a horde of camels and numberless tents which they carried with them, that they were not so in reality or in numerical strength.*

Such were at that time the opinions and sentiments of the nobles of Kabul; and to these circumstances, as well as to two or three other rash measures to which I have alluded, may be ascribed the origin of the disaffection which

* "The Amir Dost Mahomed would have certainly given us one or two battles before his flight to Bamian, had he had to oppose us only on one side. We, however, threatened him at once in three different directions: besides that, we had to a considerable degree caused him to mistrust the chiefs and people around him. From the south, the army of the Indus, after obtaining possession of Candahar, and taking the fortress of Ghazni, had reached within a few marches of his capital; and on the north, or in Kohdamam, it was only about twenty miles from the city, we had succeeded in inducing his own subjects, the Kohistanis, to stand up against him; and from the east side we had sent the Shah Zada Taimur, the eldest son of the king, with about 10,000 foot and horse, through the Panjab, to divert the attention of the Amir towards Jalalabad and Khaibar; and we thus prevented his son Mahomed Akbar from joining his father in Kabul."—Mohan Lal's *Life of Dost Mahomed Khan*, pp. 248, 249.

destroyed the merit of the policy of restoring Shah Shuja to that country.

During our stay in Kabul I often received invitations, especially from the Kazalbash people, with whom I became acquainted through my friend Mohan Lal, and had many opportunities of examining and observing their habits and manners. They are a very social and familiar race of people, very fond of good living and good clothing, and every other luxury within their reach; and really they seem to live from hand to mouth, and have nothing to spare. Their parties are very pleasant and agreeable, and on the whole I was highly delighted with their society. They appear much more polished in their manners than their neighbours, the Afghans, who are considered by them a very headstrong race. It is proverbial when they happen to make any mistake or to go wrong, to say that it was "*Afghani*," or like an Afghan. When they sit down in a *mahfil*, or assembly of guests, they will make you laugh excessively by telling their tales and anecdotes in a mimic way.

Among others, I was often very much amused by the gay Naeb Mahomed Sharif, who is certainly a very odd and ingenious man.

The head of the Jawan Sher people, one of the branches of the Kazalbashes, is Khan Shirin Khan. He is a very fine, courteous-looking person, and possesses great influence in his tribe. During the late Government he was considered a chief of great weight: the Shah has also employed him in his service with six thousand Sowars of his own tribe, and treats him more kindly than any other of his race.*

Notwithstanding these favours Shirin Khan also appeared to be disaffected, and did not like his situation; saying that he was not so respectfully treated as before the restoration. He also added, that on the approach of his Majesty to Kabul, when he went out to greet him, as he passed, the Hindustani people on the way called out to him, "That is a *Nawak-haram*, or disloyal;" and uttered some other

* He used to correspond with the Shah in his exile at Lodianah.

terms of abuse; and that this was the taunting manner in which they were all regarded by the conquerors. In fact, these slight circumstances tended to increase the dislike of his people to the Shah, even among his old friends. Great dissatisfaction began generally to prevail, and some satiric couplets also were in circulation among them, which they took a pleasure in repeating. Such beginnings were a sign of a bad ending.

The country was already in a disturbed state; the communication between Jalalabad and Kabul became daily more difficult, the Dawk runners were being plundered and molested by the Ghilzaes. Lieutenant Conolly and an envoy on the part of Shah Shuja, going to Lahore with some horses, as a present for Kharak Singh, and to escort Lady Macnaghten to Kabul, were stopped even so close by as the pass of Khurd Kabul; and although they were escorted by a large party of horse and foot, were only able to effect their passage with great difficulty. The Kohistan of Kabul was likewise in rebellion; to quell which

Gholam Khan, the Popalzae chief, who had before been employed in inciting them against Dost Mahomed, was hastily despatched.* In the opposite direction Lieut.-Colonel Herring, who was coming with his regiment from Candahar, had been murdered between Ghazni and Kabul; and a force was sent to trace out and punish his murderers. The country towards Bamian was likewise reported to be disaffected; a detachment, along with Mr. Lord, was despatched to that quarter to preserve tranquillity, and watch the movements of Dost Mahomed Khan and his son Akbar. The communication through Khaibar was still kept open, but only by the presence of the numerous troops we had left there and at Dhaka and Jalalabad; as in consequence of

* It is strange that Mir Masjidee, who is mentioned by Lieutenant Eyre as "putting himself at the head of a powerful and well organised party in 1840, with the avowed intention of expelling the Feringees and overturning the existing government," so soon after should be also of the number of those who was the foremost to fight for the Shah, and to receive for that purpose a Shah Zada in disguise in their country!

the chiefs, who came with the Shah Zada to Kabul (to be presented to the King for the purpose of having their respective claims and relations to the new government settled), being treated ill, the chiefs were disgusted. If they went to the Shah they were referred to the Envoy, and so from the one to the other; and the result was that nothing was done for them by either during the month we remained at Kabul.

A few days after our arrival General Wiltshire quitted with his division, to return to Bombay, and punish Mehrab Khan, Birohi, the chief of Belochistan; in which they succeeded. Such was the state of affairs in the country which, instead of reducing, required the active employment of the whole army.

Shah Shuja seemed to take very little notice of what was passing. He did not act like a person who was responsible for the consequences, but submitted in everything to his supporters. He only cared about holding his darbar, and in speaking in a very haughty way to the people. The Durranis, who had joined Prince Taimur on his expedition, were received as coldly as the other chiefs. Although they had been recommended very strongly for their loyalty by both the Shah Zada and Colonel Wade, they complained that no consideration was shown to them, and many of them, wearied out and tired of waiting, returned in disgust to their homes. Europeans and natives even then observed the change, which clearly foreboded some misfortune, yet it did not appear to make any serious impression on those in authority.*

I am sorry to say, that owing to the unsettled state of the country, we had not an opportunity of making any distant excursions, and seeing the celebrated gardens of Astalif, in the kohdaman, or skirts of the hills, which are spoken of in high terms of praise by the natives. Kabul mostly depends for its supplies of fruit on these gardens. I had, however, the satisfaction of making some rambles into the gardens to the north-west of the city. They

* The account of every writer on the subject has sadly confirmed the truth of these early observations.

appeared well laid out, and watered by the canals cut from the Kabul stream. The fruit was ripe, and we had the pleasure of pulling them off with our own hands, and eating them fresh. The grapes and *sarda** are produced in profusion here; but the Kabul bazars are supplied with them only from Astalif. There were such quantities of grapes sent to us as presents that we used to make our horses feed on them. The natives do not eat them in this month; they consider them yet in a raw state, but they enjoy them in the winter season. I think this was the chief cause of the illness of the Indians. They certainly ate too much fruit, and became ill with dysentery, but it was seldom attended with any fatal effects.

We also visited the tomb of the Emperor Baber, which is in a perfect state of ruin, and were sorry to find the remains of that noble emperor lying so neglected. If Shah Shuja would restore the tomb to its former splendour, it might be done without much expense, as

* The delicious melon of Kabul.

the slabs of marble which formed it are lying scattered here and there; and such a work would redound to his good name and popularity. The garden in which the tomb stands lately served as a stabling to Dost Mahomed Khan's horses, which were tied under its fine grove of trees. The pickets of the horses were still visible. It was said that the late ruler had little or no regard for tombs or such like places.

From the summit of the hill behind Baber's tomb we had a magnificent view of the valley of Kabul, which is extremely rich and beautiful on that side of the city. Seating ourselves on a dilapidated *baradari*, built there by Shah Zaman, we observed the interesting valley to great advantage. The face of nature appeared fully animated, and perfect verdure refreshed the sight in every direction within a circumference of twelve miles.

Passing a barren and hilly country from Peshawr to Butkhak, I had considered it quite unworthy of conquest by the British arms; but on seeing the valley of Kabul, I thought its labours were well compensated.

The climate of Kabul is very delightful and healthy, but the cold predominates. In the month of September, at night, we could not sleep in tents without quilts or blankets, but the days were not so cool. At noon the sun did not feel agreeable. The winter of Kabul is said to be very severe; but it is a time of great enjoyment to the rich, who collect sufficient supplies for the consumption of their families during that season, and never step out of their houses when it snows. It is then called the *Gandabahar*, or the dirty weather, and the communication becomes very scarce and difficult throughout the country. The poorer classes of the people generally go to pass the winter in warmer climates, and business almost remains at a stand in the city.

Two or three days after our arrival, the Sikh officers who had accompanied the Prince were introduced to his Majesty, on which occasion they were presented with *khilats*. Their troops were likewise inspected by the Shah, who was joined on that occasion by the Commander-in-Chief and the Envoy and minister at his court. The party seemed well pleased with the discipline and exercise of the Sikhs, and his Majesty made a present of 5000 rupees to be distributed among the sepoys. The Afghans seemed much surprised at the able manner in which the Sikh troops acquitted themselves.

When we had been encamped a few days, the thieves began to annoy us. Scarcely a night passed that they did not attack stragglers from the British encampment, and cut to pieces those they caught. Sheikh Bussowan, the Sikh Sikhs, commander, reported the occurrence to Sir Claude, and proposed that he should place a picket of his men in ambuscade on the road from Beymaroo by the Siah Sang heights which were in the rear of our camp, stating that, in their warfare with the Afghans, the Sikhs had found this the only way of dealing with them. The Colonel gave his consent; and the following night, these villains, who were bold enough to come in a party of eight or ten, were intercepted by a volley from our picket which killed and wounded four or five of them, who proved to be notorious thieves; and such was the effect it produced, that not only our own camp, but those in our neighbourhood for many days, were quite free from molestation. No one had dared to fire a shot into our camp until we came to Kabul.

On the 17th of September, the European officers who were attached to the Mission attended the court of the Shah for the purpose of being present on the occasion of his Majesty conferring on the principal officers of the British Government an order of merit which he had newly instituted. Lieutenant-Colonel Wade, Major Mackeson, and Mr. Lord were among those who had accompanied the Shah Zada on whom his Majesty conferred the order; and they felt highly gratified by these marks of his royal distinction: but they were not justly bestowed on some, and withheld from others who deserved them. Captain Farmer, the officer who to his command of the British detachment had added the general control of Dowson's and Hillersdon's levies, amounting to 1500 men, well merited the same consideration for his gallant and worthy conduct in the late operations; but that officer was neglected, and so was our excellent Sikh commander, Colonel Sheikh Bussowan. The latter, considering his rank and that he was in the service of an old ally of the British Government, fully deserved to be distinguished by the Shah, along with the European British officers of equal rank with him.*

We heard that his Majesty contemplated also conferring a medal on the whole of the officers and troops, whether of the British Government, or his own commanded by British officers, present at Ghazni; but no similar mark of distinction was thought of for the Sikh troops, &c. employed towards Peshawr, and in the reduction of Ali Masjid. This measure was supposed by the people to have proceeded from the unjust partiality of the Shah and his advisers to the British troops under his own eye. Every one who has seen or is likely

* However great their deeds of gallantry or devotion, the natives of India are seldom named or thought of on these occasions.

to see the Khaibar Pass will easily conceive the difficulties which the troops with the Shah Zada must have undergone in forcing it, well protected and defended as it is by a race of independent men who had hitherto never yielded to the arms of any nation; and at the same time judge whether these troops did not deserve to be honoured equally with their brother officers of Ghazni.*

During our stay, a man was executed. He was a native of Kabul, and hanged for murdering his own wife, on the plea of her being a loose woman, and having prostituted her chastity to a stranger. The murderer was seized and tried by the officers of the Shah, and sentenced to be hanged.

On the evening of his execution, a mob, as usual on such occasions, assembled in prodigious numbers, filling the whole plain in front of the palace, adjoining the western face

* "The small fort of Ali Masjid has from its situation long held the Sikhs in check; and it is not upon record that the celebrated Khaibar Pass has ever previously been forced."—*Extract from Lord Auckland's Letter to the Secret Committee, Simla, Aug.* 29, 1839.

of the Bala Hisar, where the execution took place. As the miserable creature was being conducted by a party of the troops from the jail to the scaffold, the people generally expressed their displeasure at the sentence. They remarked that the prisoner, according to the usages of the country, was quite right in taking the life of his wife, who, they said, justly deserved death for her conduct; and that the present measure would only encourage the women to prostitution with impunity; which some of the bystanders disputed by contrary arguments, and spoke of the oppressions to which the female sex were subjected by their cruel husbands. However, the majority were of the former opinion, and the people loudly cried out against the injustice of the Government. The prisoner did not appear to feel any compunction or remorse, but seemed quite resigned to his fate. The mob which had surrounded the gallows was dispersed by the military, and on another order having been received from the Shah (who was then passing the place to take the air) to carry the sentence into effect, the hangman hastened to throw the halter round the prisoner's neck, and he was instantaneously launched into eternity. He soon died, and the body, which remained hanging for some time, was afterwards removed and buried. Although the justice of the sentence may not be doubted, yet it was very impolitic in the actual state of affairs. The Kabul women are notorious for their intrigues, and the punishment inflicted on the man gave them full liberty to act as they pleased; and hence the indignation of the people, a result which was considered very detrimental to the interests of the Government in its infancy.*

The time of our short sojourn at Kabul was chiefly employed by the Mission in communication with the Envoy and minister at the court,—in settling such matters as required immediate attention, the principal of which was the final disposal of the levies and establishments which were entertained in the service of

* *Vide* Mohan Lal's *Life of Dost Mahomed Khan* for the causes which led to the insurrection in Kabul.

the Shah Zada, and of the officers who accompanied the Mission; besides the consideration of the most eligible plan for the settlement of the Khaibaris, and the permanent security of the passage through their territory, which was an object of the first importance: yet we had been nearly a month at Kabul without anything being asked on the subject; and the chiefs, in despair, had, in the meantime, returned to Khaibar without giving any one notice of their intention.

These points having been arranged, and the Shah having promised to provide the necessary *parwanas* or orders to reassure the Khaibaris and confirm them in their rights and privileges, Sir Claude Wade prepared to return with the Sikh auxiliary troops to India. The British detachment was made over to the Commander-in-Chief, as well as such of the British officers as were not transferred to the Shah. Lieutenants Maule and Rattray were among the latter. The former of these officers was appointed to raise a corps of Kohistanis for service in that quarter. His departure was regretted by every one, more especially by the officers and men of the Shah Zada's household and personal guard, with whom he had become a favourite by his mildness of temper, and for kind manners towards them. Lieutenant Rattray was nominated an assistant in the political department, to accompany Mr. Lord to Bamian.* Lieutenant Cunningham was

* Of these three excellent men not one survives. The fate of Mr. Lord has already been given; that of Lieutenants Maule and Rattray is subjoined:—" On this day (3rd Nov. 1841) Lieutenant Richard Maule, commanding the Kohistanee regiment, which on its return from Zoormut had been stationed at Kahdarra in Kohistan, about twenty miles north-west of Kabul, with the object of keeping down disaffection in that quarter, being deserted by his men, was, together with local Lieutenant Wheeler, his adjutant, barbarously murdered by a band of rebels. They defended themselves resolutely for several minutes, but at length fell under the fire of some jazails. Lieutenant Maule had been previously informed of his danger by a friendly native, but chose rather to run the risk of being sacrificed than desert the post assigned him. Thus fell a noble-hearted soldier and a devout Christian. The following is an outline of what had taken place in Kohistan from the commencement of the insurrection up to the present date. * * * * *
In the course of the forenoon of the 3rd of November

the only one who still remained in our camp; but we were afterwards joined by Lieutenant J. Anderson as an acting assistant. At first it was intended that Sir Claude should conduct the return of the returning portion of the army through the Panjab; but an order having arrived from Government countermanding the departure of the whole army from Afghanistan, it was determined that the Mission should retire, leaving Lieutenant Mackeson, who had come to Kabul, to conduct Sir John Keane with his escort as far as Peshawr, where he was to make over his charge to another officer, who would be appointed to relieve him.

On the 4th of October, Colonel Wade, with the remaining members of the Mission, went to

Major Pottinger had an interview with a number of the more influential chiefs in his house or fort, and about noon went into the garden to receive those of inferior rank, accompanied by his visitors; here they were joined by Lieutenant Charles Rattray, Major Pottinger's assistant (the Major had succeeded Mr. Lord). While thus engaged, this most promising and brave young officer apparently became aware of intended foul play, and turned to leave the place, when he was immediately shot down."—*Eyre's Journal*, pp. 38, 68, and 70.

court to take leave of the Shah, who was sitting in private on a chair in his palace. It was a large and extensive square, open, with a garden in the centre, and surrounded by buildings made of beautifully carved wood, but it had fallen into decay and required much repair. It was built by some of the Mogul emperors.

Shah Shuja expressed his regret to part with us so soon, and especially with the Colonel, whom he had known, and been so long intimately associated with at Lodianah. He made a long speech; and amongst other topics spoke of the scantiness of his resources, and many wants, observing that he was very economical in his expenditure, and tried to keep it within his income, which was said, no doubt, to reach the ear of the Governor-General. He added that, besides his army and other public expenses, he had a large family to provide for; that the number of the Shah Zadas alone amounted to upwards of a hundred persons; and that each of them required a handsome allowance. He was complimented on his desire to economise, and every wish was offered for the prosperity of his government. His Majesty next desired the Colonel to endeavour to reconcile the parties on the side of Jalalabad and Peshawr, who had fled from Kabul, and alienated themselves, as *he* said, from him; requesting that every exertion might be made to reclaim them; and repeating his intention of addressing letters on his own part to each of the rebellious chiefs, directing them to negotiate their terms of allegiance through that officer.* The Shah then desired Sir Claude Wade to convey his acknowledgments to his Lordship the Governor-General, and dismissed the Mission without any honorary marks of favour. We were all surprised at the omission, as it was contrary to the custom of every court on similar occasions. He afterwards, however, sent a sword, with a few pieces of cloth, and a horse, to the Colonel, but nothing to any one else.

After leaving the Shah, we went to take

* These letters, though promised next day, were never sent.

leave of Prince Taimur, who was living in a confined place in the outer court of the palace. As we had long been together, the parting scene with him was very painful; both parties could not suppress a deep sigh as they separated, and heartily wished well to each other. The Shah Zada is a very good man, and popular; but he is thought to be too good and inexperienced in the ways of the world to make a statesman. Spectator as he is of the passing events, it is hoped that his mind may improve.*

* "The prince is kind in the extreme, and has on several occasions sent me lumps of hardened snow to apply to my temples when throbbing with pain. His attentions to Maule, for whom he has taken a fancy, are unbounded, and day after day large trays of fruit and ice are brought to him with the prince's salaam. It is a pity he is so deficient in energy, as his whole nature is replete with the milk of human kindness; and without it he will never be able to control the tumultuous passions of the turbulent Afghans, should it ever be his lot to rule over them. Consequent on the events that have lately occurred in Afghanistan, the prince is again a pensioner of the British Government in India."—*Barr's Journal*, pp. 358–59.

Having been constantly kept within his father's haram from his childhood to the present time, it is not surprising that he should know so little of the world.

Chapter XIX.

Departure from Kabul—Correspondence with the Ghilzae Chiefs—Adventures of Shah Zada Mahomed Saleh—Murder of Sirdar Cheit Singh—Communication with Sadat Khan—Ill-health of the Troops at Ali Masjid—Colonel Wade takes leave of the Sikh Troops—Outbreak of the Khaibaris.

Early on the morning of the 5th inst. we quitted Kabul on our return to Lodianah, and the separation from our Afghan and Kabul friends was one mingled with joy as well as sorrow; the former because we were glad to find that we were again proceeding to our native land and our friends and relatives; and the latter, because we were sorry to leave Kabul without seeing its winter and spring.*

* The feeling of delight that pervaded the army when, after so many hardships, it once more turned its face towards Hindostan, was universal; and I may say, the regret that filled the breasts of those who were destined to remain in Afghanistan was as unanimous. Many appointments in the Shah's service had been offered to officers,

For the sake of protection several parties, both European and Native, availed themselves of our escort to return to India. Among the former were Colonel Sandwith of the Bombay cavalry, and Captain Fane whom we had known at Lahore during the visit of Sir Henry Fane to celebrate the marriage of Kour Nao Nihal Singh in 1837.

The weather was now getting cold; so much so that on re-entering the pass of Khurd Kabul our fingers were almost benumbed, and we could hardly keep hold of the reins of our

and declined by them; and even soldiers who could have got salaries of 100 or 200 rupees per mensem, in lieu of their comparatively trifling pay, refused to remain behind on even these (to them) splendid terms. The paradise that all expected to see in the beauties of Afghanistan had faded as we advanced, and a dreary spectacle of barren mountains and swampy valleys occupied its place. True it is, a few bright gleams of scenery do occasionally meet the eye, but they are scarce, and travellers in their hasty journeys have allowed their thoughts to dwell on these lovely spots, rendered more beautiful by the contrast of the surrounding country; and in their descriptions have forgotten to mention the more marked features of the province, which consist of desolation and barrenness."—*Barr's Journal*, pp. 380–81.

horses. A sharp wind blew in our faces, and the water on the sides of the *Nala* which flowed down the pass was completely frozen.* There is a footpath over the hills to the left, which people generally prefer in winter.

The Ghilzaes, observing how things were going on at Kabul, had now become very bold. At night, while encamped at Khurd Kabul, we could hardly sleep, the thieves being very troublesome in their excursions. The 3rd Ca-

* "On the 17th we moved to Khurd Kabul, the ascent of the narrow defile leading to it being accomplished in a cold wind that cut us to the skin, whilst the splashings from the water, as we crossed the stream, froze before it could drop from the skirts of our cloaks or the tips of our steel scabbards. The next day we marched to Tezeen, and as we neared the summit of the lofty *Haft-Kotal*, we passed the dead body of a native who had evidently died from the severity of the weather, and who with outstretched arms was lying flat on his face, apparently having fallen in that position while making a last struggle to gain the top. He had been stripped of every rag. Not far distant the corpse of another was seen in the cleft of a ravine, which the poor fellow had entered with the vain hope of screening himself from the keen blast that hurried up the pass, and where, instead of the repose of sleep, he had found a more lasting rest in death!"—*Barr's Journal*, pp. 383, 384.

valry with a quantity of treasure was encamped here on its way to Kabul, and the thieves were probably encouraged to annoy us in consequence of the tempting prize before them.

On our way to Jalalabad Sir Claude Wade opened a communication with Aziz Khan and the Ghilzae chiefs, by inviting them to join him, with a view to effecting a reconciliation between the Shah and themselves. At first, such was their alarm from the arrests which had taken place at Kabul, that they hesitated to come. Some of them, as already stated, were amongst those who had joined the Shah Zada in our way to that city, but had retired to their homes from the same cause. At length, on our arrival at Soorkhab, after some negotiation, and many assurances of good faith and protection, Aziz Khan promised to come; but when the time came he still showed a distrust of our intentions, proposing that the Colonel should visit him first in his own fort, attended by a few followers, which Sir Claude declined; but offered instead to send a *Reesh Safeid* and confidential agent of his own, as well as a Sayed, who was a highly respectable native of Loodiana, named Bheka Shah, to inspire his confidence; which had the intended effect. Aziz Khan agreed to hold a conference with the Colonel in the garden of Nimla, on encamping near which the next day, Sir Claude went himself to the place, and ordered it to be prepared for the reception of the Ghilzae chief, whom we soon afterwards saw approaching from the hills with about a thousand of his armed retainers, with drums beating and colours flying. After they had alighted, the Colonel sent some supplies of fruit and forage to them, with a friendly message, that agreeably to appointment, he would now be happy to visit the Khan whenever he liked. His reply was very gratifying. He said he would, if allowed, come himself to the Colonel's tent, where he arrived, accompanied by Khodabaksh Khan, Sadatmand Khan, Mirza Khan, and Himmat Khan, the Ghilzae chiefs, without a single armed follower! They said that their hesitation in coming arose chiefly from their dread of the machinations of their enemies at

Kabul. They frankly observed that they had no other desire than that of proving their allegiance to the Shah, and performing his service, as they had done that of Dost Mahomed while he was in power; that their principle was to acknowledge the supremacy, and to serve the Government of the reigning chief; and that though allied by marriage with the late Ruler of the country, they had no interests in common with him; that Aziz Khan himself, it was well known, seldom attended his court, and that his only anxiety was to preserve his honour. On the strength of the Shah's request, they were assured of his favour and consideration if they would appear in his presence. They expressed their readiness to do so on the arrival of his Majesty at Jalalabad, where he was soon expected to pass the winter. A letter of introduction was accordingly delivered to them for the Envoy and Minister, explaining the interview which had taken place with these chiefs, and the principal object of their solicitude; after which they took their leave, with mutual pledges of satisfaction.*

Mahomed Shah Khan, another great Ghilzae chief, did not make his appearance; but he proposed to depute, and actually did, his brother, who had joined the Shah Zada on our advance to Kabul, but quitted us before we arrived there, in consequence of the arrests at that place. A letter of introduction and assurance was also sent to him, and he was desired to wait on the Shah, or send his brother to make terms for him.

On our return to Jalalabad we found Shah Zada Mahomed Saleh and his party, together with Mr. Carron and Sayed Bahauddin, encamped there. Since I took leave of him at Peshawr, I recollect that I have made no allusion to him. I shall therefore give a brief account of his adventures. It appears that

* The manner in which these pledges and assurances were treated by the authorities at Kabul has been already stated in a preceding note from Mohan Lal's 'Life of Dost Mahomed Khan.'

on receiving authentic intelligence of the fall of Ali Masjid, Mahomed Saleh with his party advanced to Pindiali, then occupied by Sadat Khan's people, which he captured without much resistance, at the period of our arrival at Dhaka, on our way to Kabul. Further operations in that quarter being considered useless, a letter had been written to him from that place to disband his newly levied troops, to send the Durrani Sowars to camp, and to return himself to Peshawr, and there to wait the orders of his Majesty, who in fact did not wish to be at the expense of retaining him, although one of his own family. The proposal did not please the young Prince, who unfortunately determined not to lay down his arms without trying to signalize himself by the performance of some important military action. Instead of obeying the order which he had received, he proceeded to punish Nawab Khan of Naowaghi, and besieged his fort. Mahomed Saleh had now been joined by Mr. Carron from Bajour, the chief of which territory still avoided acting in concert with him. In his new companion the Prince found one as warlike as himself. Soon after an engagement took place between the parties, and the battle was well sustained by both for some time. At last the besiegers were repulsed, and obliged to retreat, partly on account of the misconduct of their people, and partly owing to the scarcity of supplies, for which they were much straitened. Their loss was, however, not beyond a few lives, among whom was Khan Mahomed Khan, a Popalzae chief, who had joined us at Lahore, and one of the best of the *Khawanin*. He was of a very respectable family, a gallant soldier, and is said bravely to have led the assault against the enemy: his fall chiefly occasioned the disaster. The most surprising part of the story is, that a few days before his death the Khan came to our camp when at Dhaka on some private business; and when leaving us told me in a very grave manner that he took leave of me for ever, as he was sure that he would never return alive, if, as he expected, Mahomed Saleh attacked Naowaghi: and ultimately his prediction was literally verified, as if he had seen his death before his eyes. His loss was much felt and lamented in our camp. The defeated party afterwards thought of no other plan than of advancing across the hills to Jalalàbad, where they hoped to be comforted in their distress. Just as it was on its way, Sayed Babujan or Bahauddin, accredited by the royal mandate to recover his lost territory, was proceeding towards Kuner. On coming in contact with the above party, he induced its commander to support his cause, assuring him of being provided by himself with the means of maintaining his levies. Notwithstanding that the young Prince had been repeatedly and strictly enjoined to desist from hostilities, he accepted the Sayed's offer, thinking it gave a hope of retrieving his character.

The combined troops then proceeded against Kuner by the Nurgal route, where they met with a shameful defeat from Sayed Hashim, and were compelled to retire to Jalalabad, after enduring many hardships and privations on the way. I should mention that they had arrived there before we quitted Kabul. Sayed Bahauddin now entirely threw himself on the support and favour of his Majesty for the recovery of his territory, urging that he had suffered for his ill-timed declaration in his favour, as has already been mentioned, and for giving shelter to Mr. Carron, the British news writer, who had been left in Kabul by Sir Alexander Burnes on the failure of his negotiations; that he had now neither credit nor money to effect his object; and that, all his own exertions having failed, he relied now only for assistance on the Shah's troops, and offered to pay for them rather than employ the peasantry of the country, on whom he could not depend. The Sayed's application was, it appears, granted; but a conciliatory course was recommended to be tried in the first instance, and Sir Claude Wade was authorised by the Shah to open a communication with the rival chief in actual possession of Kuner.

On our arrival at Jalalabad, a letter was accordingly addressed to Sayed Hashim, and forwarded to him by a person in the confidence of both parties. The Sayed, in reply, offered to accept any reasonable terms; and by the advice of the Shah's officers at Jalalabad, it was settled that each party should be limited to the territory possessed by him before the expulsion of Sayed Babujan, a proposal with the justice of which every one was satisfied and contented, excepting the foolish Babujan, who, still relying on his influence at court, expressed some hesitation to it on his part, wishing to have the whole of a territory, which, in consequence of their former disputes, had been divided between him and his rival. The Colonel would not, however, admit his objection, and entrusted the settlement of the case, on the proposed terms, to Aghajan, the Government renter of Jalalabad, and a clever man, who was well acquainted with the local affairs from having been for some time its governor in the late reign. But I do not know how the matter ended, further than that the plan was not executed, and that after the arrival of the Shah at Jalalabad, Sayed Bahauddin succeeded in procuring the services of a part of the British army to enforce his own claim, which led to the siege of Pashut, from which the troops were driven back, but during the night Sayed Hashim quitted the place, and became a fugitive; he and Sadat Khan joining each other in disturbing the peace of the country. After a time we heard that they had both been persuaded to pay their respects to the Shah, when it was found politic to restore Sayed Hashim to his share of Kuner; but Sadat Khan was not so easily gained over, and continued refractory to the end.

Had the course proposed by Colonel Wade been followed with the Kuner Sayeds, as well as the other disaffected chiefs in the Jalalabad territory, much bloodshed and disorder, it is the general belief, might have been avoided. We afterwards heard with extreme grief that in presenting themselves, as they had been directed, to the Shah at Jalalabad, the chiefs whom he had conciliated a second time were not well treated, which entirely destroyed their faith in our words and promises.*

On leaving Jalalabad, our fighting friend Mahomed Saleh was desired to disband his party with the exception of the Durrani horse, who were to join the *Khawanin* at Kabul, and to return to Peshawr; but he was permitted to

* "Whatever we might boast of our diplomatic successes during the campaign of Afghanistan, we were certainly very wrong in not keeping up our adherence, even for a short time, to those engagements and promises which we had so solemnly and faithfully made to the various chiefs, in return for their taking up our cause and abandoning their long-known and established masters. Our letters, pledging our honour and Government to reward and appreciate their services for our good, were in their hands; and as soon as we found that the chiefs of Candahar were fled, and there was no necessity for wearing longer the airy garb of political civilities and promises, we commenced to fail in fulfilling them. There are, in fact, such numerous instances of violating our engagements and deceiving the people in our political proceedings, within what I am acquainted with, that it would be hard to assemble them in one series. I shall, however, mention them in their proper places, and the time in which they were made, in order to show how soon they were forgotten, through our vain pride of power, and of our tact shown in the temporary and speedy gaining of the people."—*Mohan Lal's Life of Dost Mahomed Khan*, pp. 208, 209.

await the arrival of his Majesty at Jalalabad, for the purpose of being presented to him. Here we took leave of the Shah Zada and his party. Mr. Carron was placed at the disposal of the Envoy and Minister at the court of Shah Shuja, but did not long survive, having died of fever, brought on by the hardships which he had encountered in Kuner and Bajour.

We received a report from Lahore on our way to Dhaka of the horrible murder of Sirdar Cheit Singh, the favourite of Kharak Singh, then Maharaja of Lahore. It was stated that he was assassinated in the palace on the 8th of October, by Raja Dhian Singh and Kour Nao Nihal Singh, accompanied by their wicked associates. They had demanded the removal of Cheit Singh, which his master having boldly refused, they were determined to carry their point, and having formed a conspiracy to take his life, the Kour proceeded on the morning of that day to the palace, on pretence of paying his duty to his father, preparatory to his pretended departure to bathe in the holy pool of Amritsir. The door of the palace was at once opened to him without suspicion, and the Kour and the Rajas, viz., Golab Singh and Dhian Singh, with others of their party, approached his Highness, and by the assistance of candles (for it was before daybreak) sought out and seized Cheit Singh; one of them, Atr Singh, Sindhanwalia, laid hold of the Maharaja by the hair and dragged him outside the palace, lest he should have recourse to some violence on observing the murder of his favourite; when those who were inside barbarously fell on their victim and put him to death in a very cruel manner. His body was chopped in pieces; three or four other persons shared the same fate. The remains of the favourite were buried inside the palace, and the Maharaja was said to be in a state of stupidity, brought on by fear, from which he did not recover for some days. We now saw the motive of Nao Nihal Singh in wishing to leave us when he heard of the death of his grandfather. The object of his ambition was to usurp the throne of his father, and in the Rajas of Jammoo and their partisans he found ready means to assist him. Some days before this event took place, a mission had been dispatched by the Kour and his party, *as if from Kharak Singh*, to the Governor-General in return for one which it appeared had just left Lahore from his Lordship; the presence of which, at that particular time when each was intriguing against the other, is believed to have encouraged Raja Dhian Singh, Bhae Ram Singh, and others, to carry out their project.

In the opinion of impartial people it was certainly thought the Mission of the Governor-General had been sent too soon; that he should have waited a little longer to see the course of events, as the Sikhs were labouring in great suspense, since the death of Ranjeet Singh, and might at that time have been made to do anything agreeable to the wishes of the British Government to confirm the succession, as it had been desired and left by the Maharaja, who had for many years been the faithful friend and ally of the English, and on whose good advice and guidance his son Kharak Singh had depended.

On our return to Dhaka a letter was received from Sadat Khan, expressive of his willingness to meet Lieutenant-Colonel Wade; and we heard that he arrived at Goshta after we had passed that place. He was recommended to wait there the expected arrival of the Shah, who he was told would no doubt take his case into consideration. A communication was also held with Khalid Khan, Khosta, who again waited on us at Chahardeh to renew his pledges of loyalty. A letter of introduction was delivered to him for the King and Sir W. Macnaghten, of similar import to those which had been given to others, with which he was likewise desired to wait on his Majesty on his arrival at Jalalabad, when a permanent arrangement respecting his jaghir would be made with him. On our way a settlement was also effected with the Maliks of Basoul and Hazarnao, confirming to them their villages on the terms on which they had enjoyed them before; but they were prevented from levying duties on passing merchandise, the right of which the sovereign of the country was only entitled to exercise. Among other negotiations for the same object, our friend Tura Baz Khan, as present ruler of the Momand tribe, agreed to take the rents of seven and a half villages which had formerly belonged to his family, instead of the collections made by him on the transit trade.

Reports of these interviews and their results were transmitted *as they occurred* to the authorities at Kabul; but we neither heard anything further about them nor of the promised *parwanas* from the Shah for the Khaibaris, though urged to be sent, as they were known to be in a restless state when we left the court.

We were not therefore surprised to learn on our arrival at Dhaka that Khan Bahadar Khan and his son Abdul Rahman, the chiefs of the Malikdin Khail, were collecting their men in the vicinity of Ali Masjid. Abdul Rahman was one of those who had attended us to Kabul, in the hope of settling his business with the Shah; but it appeared that he had been sadly disappointed in the manner of his reception at Kabul after the assurances which he had received from the Shah Zada and Colonel Wade, and the whole tribe having lost their confidence, were resolved to show their independence. The Sikhs were also reported to have encouraged them to attack that fort; but failing in their endeavours to obtain support from the other chiefs in Khaibar, those of the Malikdin Khail had, *for the time*, abandoned their design. To prevent however any surprise, the troops at Dhaka and Jalalabad were ordered by the Colonel to concentrate immediately in the valley of Lala Beg, near Ali Masjid; and further measures were taken at the same time to occupy the pass with other troops.

Besides these causes of disaffection, the Khaibarees saw the critical condition to which the troops at Ali Masjid, Dhaka, and Jalalabad had been reduced by sickness and mortality from the pestilential climate of those places. The reports we received exhibited an extraordinary number of deaths among the troops, generally, but especially at Ali Masjid. A company of the 20th Native Infantry, consisting of sixty men, had lost no less than twenty-three since the month of September; while the rest were in too sickly a state to perform any duty; Captain Ferris himself being also a severe sufferer. In fact, on our arrival at Ali Masjid we found almost every sepoy in a wretched state, and reduced to a mere skeleton. We could not but sympathise with them, but they were enjoined to continue at their post until the arrival of Lieutenant Mackeson with the portion of the army returning to India, when they would be relieved. Captain Ferris was also informed of the precautions which had been taken to reinforce his garrison and the outposts in Khaibar, and the necessity of relieving them every month from the new cantonment at Lala Beg.

I ought to mention that on our way from Kabul letters were repeatedly sent to all the Khaibar chiefs, informing them of the day on which Sir Claude Wade would be at Ali Masjid, and inviting them to meet him there, which they failed to do, although we waited for them a day beyond the appointed time, which convinced us that the treatment they had experienced from the Court had filled them with rage and distrust; yet, that everything might be done to reassure and encourage them to return, a proclamation was issued by the Colonel to the whole of them, not to be disheartened; that Lieutenant Mackeson would be there in a few days with full powers on the part of the Shah's Government to attend to their claims and see them rightfully settled.

We halted a day also at Peshawr, which was employed in settling the accounts of the Mission with General Avitabile, and in taking leave of the disciplined battalions of Sikh infantry and the *Ghorcheras*, forming the Mahomedan contingent which had returned with us. The ceremony was a melancholy one. They paraded and formed a square, to receive Sir Claude, who made a speech to them, acknowledging the bravery and perseverance with which they had performed their duty. While we were engaged in encouraging the Sikh troops to remain at their post, the Darbar was urgently requesting their withdrawal altogether from Afghanistan; and although no troops had been raised to supply their place, yet, in the absence of the Colonel from Lahore, it will be seen that Raja Dhian Singh and the Kour either took, or were very improperly allowed to have, their own way in this as well as in other matters, without regard to the probable consequences.

The Najib and Aligol battalions had been left at Ali Masjid and Jalalabad; that belonging to the French legion being the only portion of the troops which accompanied us to Lahore. I have mentioned in former parts of my journal the delays and difficulties we had to contend with before the Mahomedan contingent was formed. The occasion now seemed to have arrived for deciding whether the Sikhs were to maintain it. By the tripartite treaty they were required always to have such a force in readiness at Peshawr; and it is much to be regretted that instead of being made to observe this important article of the treaty, they should at once have been permitted to urge the return of their force. Referring to the state of Khaibar before we left Peshawr, the attention of General Avitabile was seriously drawn to the necessity, notwithstanding the orders of his court, of detaining the contingent. A report of the circumstance was at the same time made to Lahore, and the Sikh Darbar reminded of their obligation; but the troops hearing that their Government wished them to be withdrawn, marched off; and we heard that on the outbreak in Khaibar, which afterwards occurred, when ordered by General Avitabile to halt and return, they would not obey him, although they had not then re-crossed the Indus. Such was the change which the death of Ranjeet Singh had produced!

On the 24th of October we quitted Peshawr and hastened on our return to India. We had scarcely passed the Tope of Manakiala, when we received intelligence of an outbreak in Khaibar. It was reported that on the night of our departure from Peshawr, the Khaibaris, headed by Khan Bahadar Khan, &c., had attacked the troops in Ali Masjid, but were repulsed; that they repeated their attack on the following night also without any success, having previously attacked the positions occupied by the Najibs on the heights of Lala China, who were so much reduced by death and sickness that they do not appear to have resisted the attack. The Khaibaris rushed sword in hand into their stockade or *sanga*, and compelled them to fly, with the loss of many killed and wounded, including those who were too sick and helpless to move. During the prevailing sickness in September they had lost their old commandant, Praem Singh, who had joined Ranjeet Singh from Holkar's service after the battle of Mahedpore in 1819 with his corps, and been in command of these men for fifty years; which likewise dispirited them and destroyed their discipline.

The chief instigator of these disturbances was Khan Bahadar Khan. We were happy, however, to learn that the troops which had been ordered into the Pass from Dhaka and Jalalabad on our arrival at the former of these places, had opportunely arrived at Ali Masjid, and prevented any serious injury being done to the garrison; but the defeat of the Najibs emboldened the Khaibaris to renew their attacks, and harass the portion of the army which was returning with Sir John Keane; and they were not put down without much bloodshed.

CHAPTER XX.

The Khaibaris attack Lala China—Imminent peril of Captain Ferris—Supplies to Ali Masjid—The Sikhs attacked by the Afridis—Further operations against the Khaibaris—Little confidence to be placed in the Sikh troops—Skirmishing near Lala China—Baggage abandoned—Departure from Peshawr.

FOR a description of the military operations which ensued, I must again refer the reader to the journal of Lieutenant Barr, who was then returning with Lord Keane. It was, I think, a great mistake to withdraw any of the British or Sikh troops from the country, as it had not been conquered, although they had marched to Kabul.*

* In speaking of the causes of the triumph of the British army in Afghanistan, on the entrance of the Shah in the first instance, and of the subsequent discontent of the people, Mohan Lal, in his *Life of Dost Mahomed Khan*, says: "Undoubtedly we held possession of Kabul; but its late ruler was not in our hands, and there was therefore sufficient reason for apprehension that as long as he or any of his sons were at liberty and fugitives on our

"From Ferris I received the particulars of the late assaults of the Khaibaris, who commenced them by attacking a post at Lala China, garrisoned by 500 Najeeb soldiers, the majority of whom they succeeded in slaughtering: the rest with difficulty made their escape to Jamrud. Having committed this terrible massacre, they proceeded to attack Ferris's position, at the fort of Ali Masjid, but were repulsed with some loss; and night drawing on, compelled them to desist. The next day, F. went to Lala China, and interred no less than 300 bodies of the Najeebs; and when it is considered that many of those who reached Jumrood must have been severely wounded, it is very probable no more than 150 survived

northern frontiers, there would be no difficulty for the people of Kabul to invite him whenever we gave them any annoyance. Yet notwithstanding these points of grave concern, we sent a large portion of the army back with Lord Keane to India, and interfered in the administration of the country, and introduced such reforms just on our arrival as, even in India, the quietest part of the world, Lords Clive and Wellesley had hesitated to do but slowly, and to extend over many years."

that terrible onset. Another attack on the part of the Khaibaris was expected, and, as the sequel proved, was not long in being made. F. had, however, prepared a warm reception for them, and he described the appearance of the pass, as they advanced, to be nothing but a sea of heads. Onwards they came till within thirty or forty yards of a low wall, behind which a party of picked men had been reclining with their matchlocks in readiness, and who, starting up at the word of command, poured a deadly and unexpected volley into the midst of the foe, which caused them to send forth an unearthly and terrific yell, heightened by the shrieks and groans of the wounded. Ferris then, at the head of a party of horsemen, at hand for the purpose, boldly galloped forward, and was in the act of turning round to give a shout of encouragement to his followers, preparatory to charging, when he discovered he was, with one exception, *alone*; the cowardly sowars having hung back. He was, by this time, close to, and partly intermixed with, the Khaibaris, who could have killed him in an instant; and how they allowed him to escape he knows not to this day. They, however, had suffered enough, and only thought of making off with their dead and wounded; and thus affairs remained when the returning army reached Ali Masjid. As F. had only irregulars to depend on for the defence of the Khaibar, he applied to Sir John Keane for two companies of infantry, which were granted to him; and those of the 27th Native Infantry, under Lieutenant Laing, that had escorted the treasure to Kabul, were ordered on the duty.

"On the 6th we moved to Kuddum, a few stray shots having been fired at the guards in charge of the baggage; and on the 7th we halted at Koulsir, close to the ground so long occupied by the Mission, and which was now covered with fields of grain. The next morning we marched to Peshawr, and encamped on the eastern side of the city, where we were only to have remained a couple of days; but a longer sojourn was rendered necessary, *as the Sikh troops could not be prevailed upon to con-*

vey grain to the garrison at Ali Masjid, who had but a day or two's provisions left. To effect this desirable object, it therefore became necessary, on the 10th, to send two companies of the 21st Native Infantry under Farmer, and one of the Sappers and Miners under Lieutenant Macleod, of the Engineers, on that duty, accompanied by 500 Sikh soldiers, and escorted by a squadron of cavalry and two guns to the entrance of the Pass. They succeeded in making over their charge in safety; but on their return were opposed by the Khaibaris in force, who boldly attacked them as they were threading the hills. The Najibs, without attempting resistance, immediately took to flight, hamstringing such camels as obstructed their progress: and, at last, our own sepoys, having expended all their ammunition, were obliged to follow the example thus set them of showing a quick pair of heels. The Afrídis, perceiving the dismay they had created, threw down their matchlocks, and advanced to close quarters, with their deadly knives; and the ferocity with which they used these murderous weapons was spoken of as being quite fiendish. A large booty and a vast number of camels fell into the enemy's hands, and were forthwith transferred to their strongholds. The conduct of the Sikh troops on this occasion gave so much offence to General Avitabile, that he, in his capacity of Governor, denied them admittance into the town of Peshawr, and ordered any of them that should be seen in it to be severely beaten with a slipper, the most derogatory punishment that can be inflicted on a native.*

"After this defeat, it was necessary for the returning army to remain at Peshawr until Colonel Wheeler, who, with the 48th Native Infantry, had been sent for from Jalalabad,

* The Sikhs, whose dread of the Khaibaris was always great, were terrified at the slaughter of the Najibs; no less than 10,000 of the regular Sikh troops were employed to occupy the heights between Ali Masjid and Jamrud, a distance of only five miles, to keep open the Pass during the advance of Sir G. Pollock, in 1842. The Najibs were principally Hindoos, and both they and the Sikhs wanted the fitness of the Mahomedan contingent, which, as had been anticipated, was not now forthcoming for such service.

should arrive to the succour of the garrison of Ali Masjid, as that fort was now sure of being attacked by the Khaibaris. Meanwhile balled ammunition was being made up in our camp as fast as possible, and all the available infantry, including the drafts for the 2nd European regiment, were sent to Jamrud on the 14th, to proceed from thence to the assistance of our troops in the Pass, whenever such a step might be necessary. At twelve o'clock the same night, I was ordered off with a couple of 6-pounders and a Risallah (troop) of Local Cavalry, to escort a quantity of ammunition to the troops at Jamrud, who were to take it on to Ali Masjid. We reached the camp at Jamrud at nine A.M., and immediately on arrival made the ammunition over to Captain Prole, 37th Native Infantry, who commanded.

"My tent was once more pitched amidst scenery with which I was familiar; but the landscape, though the same, had been changed in some of its accompaniments. It is true, the *Sangas* still existed, and were even occupied by the friendly Khaibaris, who, to show their zeal for our service, had kept up an incessant fire (whether necessary or not is unknown) during the previous night; but the immediate camp was altered, and in lieu of Durrani horsemen and raw Afghan levies, it was filled with British sepoys and European soldiers.

"It was at noon, the day after I joined Prole's camp, that the political agent (Mackeson), having received no tidings from Dowson (who commanded at Ali Masjid, consequent on Ferris's departure for Peshawr, again very ill), and being anxious about his safety, ordered us to move forward; but a letter from D., in which he stated that he thought he could yet hold out without assistance, having reached us after we had advanced about a mile and a half, we returned to our old position. *Mackeson had on this occasion directed the Sikh troops to enter the Pass by the main route, to create a diversion; but in spite of his arguments, and those of Colonel Courtlandt, an officer in the Maharaja's service, who was to have gone with them, they refused to do so,* shielding themselves under the excuse, that their orders were to *accompany* the British troops, and that, therefore, whichever way *they* went, the Khalsas would follow.

"Negotiations were now set on foot with the Khaibaris, and it was hoped some amicable arrangement would have been entered into, when a communication from Dowson informed us that they had appeared in considerable numbers, and had hoisted a black flag close to the tower above the gorge near Lala China. Mackeson, fearing that Colonel Wheeler had, at his requisition, taken a more circuitous route by Choora, and would not therefore be in time to succour Dowson, ordered an advance to take place the following morning. Accordingly, at daybreak we commenced our march, my own duty being merely to accompany the troops to the entrance of the Pass (the Shadee Bagiar, where there is no gun road), as it was thought a small *sanga* which commanded the gorge might be in the Khaibaris' possession; and if so, they were to have been dislodged by a few shrapnels. Before reaching this defile, a sort of council was held to consider whether it would be most advisable to trust the baggage to the care of the *Sikh* regiments, or to a small party of peasants who lived in the neighbourhood of Peshawr, as the British troops were only sufficient to guard the long line of camels that carried the ammunition. *So meanly was the courage of the former thought of, that it was unanimously resolved to commit it to the charge of the villagers*; and this disposition having been completed, the column again moved on. As we neared the entrance, it became evident that the *sanga* was unoccupied, and a party under Farmer having been pushed forward to secure it, I wished them all a successful expedition, and, agreeably to instructions, commenced my return march to Peshawr, accompanied by the Risallah of Local Cavalry.

"At 4 P.M. I rejoined the camp at Peshawr, and in the course of a day or two we received accounts of Prole's detachment, who had safely convoyed the ammunition to Ali Masjid. For the first three quarters of the distance our troops were allowed to pursue their way unmolested, but on approaching the heights near Lala China (a favourite spot of the Khaibaris) they were fired on, and met with considerable opposition. The majority of the officers being in blue surtouts, were very conspicuous amongst the soldiers, and the Afridis took good care to select them for their marks, and with such true aim, that Prole and Macmullen fell almost at the same moment, both severely wounded in the thigh. A party of sappers, under M'Leod, immediately rushed up the hills, and gallantly drove the enemy from their position; and the convoy eventually arrived at its destination, with the loss of several men killed and wounded. Colonel Wheeler, with the 48th, having been obliged to abandon the Choora route, on account of the road being impracticable for guns, reached Ali Masjid the next morning, and the following day, after having strengthened the garrison, marched from Jamrud by the main Pass. Negotiations of an amicable nature having been made with the chiefs, it was thought there would be no opposition. Still, the crowds of Khaibaris that occupied the heights, and the known treachery of the tribes, rendered it necessary to move with caution. The Colonel had not advanced very far, when the true intentions of the Khaibaris were manifest, for they made a desperate attack on the baggage, and such camels as could not be carried off they hamstrung, by which means the loads eventually came into their hands.* Colonel

* The fidelity of the Khaibaris and the safety of the Pass itself were attainable only while they could *see* that we really possessed the power of punishing them for any breach of the former, and of securing the latter by the presence of our own or the Shah's troops, on the system which had been adopted in the time of the Mogul emperors. They were *never* to be restrained by the *mere* force of engagements; Lieutenant Mackeson's presence only led to a partial truce, as the promised *parwanas* had not even yet been issued; and it was not until nearly a month afterwards, when Sir W. MacNaghten himself came through the Pass and saw its formidable difficulties, that *any* settlement of terms was made with them, which they broke no less than three times afterwards: in the first place on account of some dispute among themselves regarding a fair distribution of the allowance settled on them; secondly, from some complaint of a real or imaginary grievance in our conduct to them; and lastly, after the insurrection in November, 1841—thus showing that they were not to be bound by any obligations of good faith beyond the scope of their convenience.

Wheeler immediately moved up his force, and drove the enemy from their plunder; but, in consequence of so many camels being mutilated, he was compelled to abandon a large quantity, as there was no conveyance to remove it, and several officers thus lost all they possessed. The 37th and 48th regiments, and the sappers, behaved most gallantly.

"Colonel Wheeler's arrival having obviated the necessity of a longer detention at Peshawr, the Commander-in-chief, with the first column, broke ground on the 23rd, and on the 24th the second column encamped at Pubbee."

Chapter XXI.

Our arrival at Lahore—Miserable condition of the Maharaja Kharak Singh—He attempts to fly to the British frontier, but is overtaken and forced to return—Intrigues at the Court of Lahore—Tomb of Ranjeet Singh—The Sikh escort dismissed—Order issued by the Governor-General relative to the Operations of the Mission—Conclusion.

On the 10th of November we reached Lahore, where the Mission was received by Raja Dhian Singh and Bhae Ram Singh, deputed for that purpose by Nao Nihal Singh, who took care, after the bloody tragedy and artful intrigues in which he had been engaged since his return to Lahore, to keep out of Sir Claude Wade's way, well knowing that he could not approve of his conduct. He took the Maharaja along with him to prevent any interview between him and the Colonel, for which Kharak Singh was very anxious: but he had *impru-*

grievances to that officer, whom he considered in the light of a brother, and who was a sincere friend of his late father; which put his son on his guard, and they were determined that he should have no opportunity of communicating with him in person. He was now strictly watched and kept in a state of arrest, being merely a puppet in the hands of his son, and surrounded by his creatures, his own old and confidential servants being removed from about him.

The Maharaja was said to have been bewildered by the savage and cruel treatment of his son. We learnt from good authority that he used sometimes to burst into tears, and was heard to say that he would never be satisfied until he had fully revenged the death of his favourite. He also expressed his surprise that the British Government should have received the Mission of his son without inquiry, and encouraged these outrages by its silence.

The Maharaja once attempted to fly from his persecutors to the British frontier, but was overtaken and carried back to his house, or more properly to his dungeon. It was indeed highly mortifying to every friend of both Governments to see the successor of so celebrated a ruler as Ranjeet Singh so miserably treated; and that the British Government, which had made so many pledges of friendship and professed such a sincere and lasting regard for the government of his father, should have remained a passive spectator of the bloody deeds of his grandson to destroy the rightful authority of his own son. What is the world to think of such a policy?*

Every dread of the displeasure of the British Government or its officers being removed, the Court of Lahore now became a scene of in-

* The motive was *non-interference*; but its undoubted effect was anarchy and confusion, brought about by a succession of personal struggles for power, which, having caused the extermination, by the assassination of each other of the principal actors, destroyed the vital principle of the State, and led to an assumption of its authority by a mutinous soldiery, productive of a state of disorganization in its affairs, on which we have *ultimately* justified a military *interference* in them, which a timely exercise of our political influence would have averted.

trigues which I leave others to describe, as there are subjects connected with it which I am afraid would not be agreeable to some of the parties concerned, and perhaps neither safe nor becoming in me to disclose.* Such was the state of affairs at Lahore on our arrival. The town looked dull and melancholy, as if its prosperity had died with Ranjeet Singh. The ashes of that renowned chief have been deposited within the walls near the Saman Burj, where we took leave of him on our departure for Peshawr. A magnificent tomb was being built over him, the plan of which was presented to Lieutenant-Colonel Wade.

We halted there one day; and on the evening of the 11th of November, 1839, the Colonel proceeded by *Dak*, or express, to wait on Lord Auckland, by his desire, at Karnal, and our Sikh escort was dismissed, while the rest of the Mission proceeded to Lodianah, which we reached on the 19th, and were glad to find

* An account of the progress of these intrigues, as given by the author, is left out.

ourselves at the end of our journey after an absence of exactly one year. On the same date an order was published by the Governor-General relating to the operations of the army across the Indus, of which the following is a paragraph :—

"His Lordship has also much satisfaction in adding that the best acknowledgments of the Government are due to Lieutenant-Colonel Wade, who was employed on the Peshawr frontier, and who, gallantly supported by the officers and men of all ranks under him, and seconded by the cordial* aid of the Sikh government, an aid the more honourable because rendered at a painful crisis of its affairs, opened the Khaibar Pass, and overthrew the authority of the enemy in that quarter, at the moment

* Inasmuch as Ranjeet Singh himself *personally* represented the Sikh government, the term is quite applicable, but no further, as has been shown in the narrative of the expedition; and to show how long their co-operation lasted, their *Mahomedan* contingent, which would have proved of the greatest aid to meet those sudden exigencies which occurred, was never efficiently maintained after the Mission returned to Lodiana.

when the advance of the forces of Shah Zada Taimur could most conduce to the success of the general operations."

Here my journal ends; and in bringing it to a conclusion, it may be expected that I should make some observations on the course of policy which led to the events I have related, and their disastrous result; but in so humble an individual as myself, anything that might be said on that subject can be of little importance. I cannot however refrain from observing that the failure of the scheme was not a necessary consequence of its adoption.

If the intrigues and designs of Russia were such as to demand a decisive interference on the part of the British Government in the affairs of Afghanistan, it is remarkable that the means of counteracting them, by the restoration of Shah Shuja, should not only have been pointed out to the Governor-General by every authority on the spot, including Sir Alexander Burnes and the gentlemen of his mission, but that it should have occurred, without concert, at the same time to the authorities in England; a coincidence which marks a weight of testimony in favour of the decision of Lord Auckland, and a concurrence of opinion as to the expediency of the measure, to which future historians will, I am confident, do full justice, when the prejudice of parties has subsided; and which was borne out in an extraordinary degree, as my readers will have perceived, in the almost unanimous consent with which the Afghans hailed the return of their lawful sovereign, and deserted Dost Mahomed Khan and his brothers. It was not until they were deceived in the promises which had been held out to them, and they found that the Shah was made a puppet in the hands of his supporters, that they began to distrust the intentions of the English, and set the authority of both the one and the other at defiance. Even then the Afghans could not but observe, that in the determined resolution and bravery with which Sir William Nott at Candahar and Sir Robert Sale in Jalalabad defended and maintained their isolated positions, they had to deal with a power over which they would never have been able to acquire the fatal ascendancy they did at Kabul, if affairs had been managed there with equal skill and determination.

THE END.